233. du program

children
in
danger

JAMES GARBARINO

NANCY DUBROW

KATHLEEN KOSTELNY

CAROLE PARDO

children IN danger

COPING WITH THE

CONSEQUENCES OF

COMMUNITY

VIOLENCE

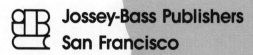
Jossey-Bass Publishers
San Francisco

Portions of Chapter Two are based upon material that originally appeared in Garbarino, J., Kostelny, K., and Dubrow, N. *No Place to Be a Child: Growing Up in a War Zone.* Lexington, Mass.: Lexington Books, 1991. Reprinted with permission of the publisher.

For sales outside the United States contact Maxwell Macmillan International Publishing Group, 866 Third Avenue, New York, New York 10022

Printed on acid-free paper and manufactured in the United States of America

---

Library of Congress Cataloging-in-Publication Data

Children in danger : coping with the consequences of community
    violence / James Garbarino . . . [et al.].
        p.   cm. — (A joint publication in the Jossey-Bass social and
    behavioral science series and the Jossey-Bass education series)
        Includes bibliographical references and index.
        ISBN 1-55542-416-3
        1. Children and violence—United States.   2. Children—United
    States—Crimes against.   3. Violent crimes—United States—
    Psychological aspects.   4. Children of minorities—United States—
    Psychology.   5. Inner cities—United States—Psychological aspects.
    I. Garbarino, James.   II. Series: Jossey-Bass social and behavioral
    science series.   III. Series: Jossey-Bass education series.
    HQ784.V55045   1992
    305.23—dc20   91-42319
                                                                                    CIP

FIRST EDITION
HB Printing   10 9 8 7 6 5 4 3 2 1   *Code 9239*

A JOINT PUBLICATION IN

The Jossey-Bass
Social and Behavioral Science Series

AND

The Jossey-Bass
Education Series

CONTENTS

PREFACE

Thousands of young children in America's cities are growing up amidst a worsening problem of community violence: shootings and stabbings on the street, domestic violence that spills out of households into public view, widespread awareness of murders and serious assaults within a community, evident gang activity. In Chicago, for example, the rate of "serious assault" increased 400 percent from 1974 to 1991. Most of this violence takes place in poor, inner-city neighborhoods and public housing projects. During the 1980s, Chicago's largest public housing project—Robert Taylor Homes—had a rate of murder and aggravated assault twenty times that of the city as a whole. More than half the murders and aggravated assaults in the city take place in a few high-crime "war zones"—neighborhoods that are poor, socially isolated, and often dominated by gangs.

Young children are enmeshed in this problem of community violence in many ways. They are witnesses to it: by age five, most children have had first-hand encounters with shootings. By adolescence, most have witnessed stabbings and shootings, and one-third have witnessed a homicide (Bell, 1991). Many of these children are also witnesses to or victims of domestic violence: rates of child abuse are substantially higher in these poor, inner-city communities than in other areas. And most of these children know, and in many cases depend upon, the perpetrators of community violence: gang members are also their brothers, their cousins and uncles, their fathers, or their mothers' boyfriends. "Them" is "us" for many inner-city children. These youngsters are in and of the community; the "problem" of community violence is the fabric of their lives. Victimization and loss are rampant. Homicide is the leading cause of death for young males in these communities.

> Robert is four years old. He lives in a public housing project in Chicago. His ten-year-old sister was raped last month by a teenager in the building. His fifteen-year-old cousin was killed in a gang shoot-out last year. His mother's current boyfriend used to beat him and his sister when they misbehaved, until his sixteen-year-old brother and his gang threatened to kill him if he continued hitting the younger children. Recently, Robert's brother was arrested on charges that included drug dealing and assault with a deadly weapon. Now he can no longer help out financially or offer his protection. Such is Robert's complex connection with "community violence."
>
> Among Robert's classmates at school, Anna saw her brother shot on the street. José's arm was broken by his stepfather. Anita was trapped on the playground when a gang shoot-out started. Manuel's brother is a leader in his gang and brings him presents and his mother rent money. Shawna's brother is a drug dealer and drove a fancy car before he was arrested.

How can their teachers and other caregivers help Robert and his classmates cope with their complex feelings about violence in the community—feelings that include fear and terror but also admiration and excitement? What can these professionals do and say to aid the children as they wrestle with their feelings and their ideas about growing up? This task is complicated by the fact that inner-city teachers and child-care professionals often have feelings and ideas about community violence that overlap with the children's. They themselves are often victims of violence, or at least they confront the threat every day. They too must live with the power of the gangs and the limits of the police to protect them.

This book is written for these professionals—the inner-city teachers, social workers, psychologists, and community workers—and for anyone who wants to understand what it is like to live in an urban war zone.

We finished this book in the fall of 1991. As the year was coming to an end, our home city of Chicago seemed hell-bent to break its own record for the number of homicides, a record that had stood since 1974. It was no contest. By early October, the 1974 record had been reached and exceeded. What made these mortality rates all the more ominous was that—what with improvements in medical trauma technology—many of the victims of violence who would have died in 1974 were now living.

At the time we were finishing our book, another book was climbing the best-seller list. *There Are No Children Here*, by our friend Alex Kotlowitz, offered a biography of two boys growing up amidst the violence and poverty of one of Chicago's war zones, a high-crime public housing project. The high level of interest in Alex's book told us that Americans, perhaps, were finally ready to take a hard look at what had become of the hundreds of thousands of our nation's children who had been abandoned to their fate by public policies that give priority to military spending and improving the life-style of affluent families.

This is the context for our book. We have set out to help professionals do something about the children who live with chronic community violence in America. We wrote the book as part of our work with the Erikson Institute for Advanced Study in Child Development, a graduate school and research center focusing on issues of child development and early childhood education. The book serves as a companion to our 1991 book *No Place to Be a Child: Growing Up in a War Zone*, in which we explored the experience of children in war zones around the world: Mozambique, Nicaragua, Cambodia, the Middle East, and inner-city Chicago.

We appreciate the financial support we have received to complete this task: from the Smith-Richardson Foundation, the Spunk Fund, the Harris Foundation, the Johnson Foundation, the NYNEX Foundation, the Chicago Community Trust, and the William T. Grant Foundation. We also appreciate the interest and advice of our colleagues who read and critiqued early versions of our manuscript: Jane Grady, Robert Halpern, Fran Stott, Lorraine Wallach, Abe and Lois Wandesman, and several anonymous reviewers.

We also thank the professionals in the field who shared their experiences with us. These Head Start teachers and directors, child-care providers, and social workers provided us with an opportunity to enter into a dialogue that enriched our writing and thinking. In particular, we would like to acknowledge the generous assistance and insightful contributions of the following individuals and organizations in the preparation of the material presented in Chapters Seven and Nine: Lutheran Social Services of Illinois Children's Day Care Program staff; Judith Bertacchi, director, Virginia Frank Child Development Center of Jewish Family and Community Services of Chicago; and Daniel P. Toomey, former coordinator of the "New Mourning" program, Evanston Hospital, Evanston, Illinois.

Finally, we offer our special thanks to Norma Richman for her assistance in preparing the manuscript.

Chicago   James Garbarino
March 1992   Nancy Dubrow
                                                  Kathleen Kostelny
                                                  Carole Pardo

THE AUTHORS

James Garbarino is president of the Erikson Institute for Advanced Study in Child Development and author of thirteen other books, including *What Children Can Tell Us, The Psychologically Battered Child, Children and Families in the Social Environment, Understanding Abusive Families,* and *No Place to Be a Child: Growing Up in a War Zone.* In 1989, he received the American Psychological Association's Award for Distinguished Professional Contributions to Public Service. In 1988, he received the Vincent De Francis Award from the American Humane Association for his work on behalf of abused and neglected children. In March 1991, as part of a UNICEF mission to Kuwait, he conducted the first assessment of the psychological impact of the occupation and war on children in Kuwait.

Nancy Dubrow is a consultant to international organizations, including UNICEF and the World Health Organization in Eastern Europe, Africa, and the Middle East. She represents the World Federation for Mental Health at UNICEF and chairs the working group on Children in Especially Difficult Circumstances. Formerly a research associate at the Erikson Institute, child development administrator for Chicago Commons Association, and a fellow of the Chicago Community Trust, she is currently affiliated with the Chicago School for Professional Psychology and is a coauthor of *No Place to Be a Child.*

Kathleen Kostelny is a research associate at the Erikson Institute. Before joining the institute, she worked at the National Committee for Prevention of Child Abuse as a research analyst and as a counselor for emotionally disturbed children at the Orthogenic School of the University of Chicago. She has served as a member of the executive committee of the Division of Children, Youth and Family Services of the American Psychological Association and is a coauthor of *No Place to Be a Child.*

Carole Pardo is a research associate at the Erikson Institute. Before joining the institute, she served as executive director and education director of the Children's Day Care Program at Lutheran Social Services of Illinois, supervising Head Start, Title XX day-care, and school-age programs for disadvantaged children in five Chicago inner-city neighborhoods. Formerly a child life specialist at Wyler's Children's Hospital, she is currently serving as consultant on the development of the child-care program at Argonne National Laboratory.

children
IN
danger

1

The Meaning of Danger
in the Lives of Children

Community violence puts young children in jeopardy. It threatens the very core of what they need to make a go of their lives. We start with this fundamental concern, with the essence of childhood. It provides the foundation for our subsequent efforts to wrestle with the concept of danger, in developmental and ecological perspective.

What is the essence of childhood? In Western culture, childhood is regarded as a period of special protection and rights. Our concept of childhood hinges on safety. Initially, the child inside its mother's womb is safe from the elements. Once born, the child is kept safe, fed, sheltered, and nurtured so that it can grow and develop, fulfilling its potential. In the first year of life, children become attached to parents, and the safety of these attachments permits children to explore the environment with confidence, knowing that they can always return to a safe haven. As children pass through the first decade of life, they should be able to broaden this "safe haven" to include the home, the neighborhood, and the school. When children feel safe at home, they are ready to grow. When safe in the neighborhood, children are ready to play and explore and form relationships with other children. When they feel safe at school, they are ready to learn and to become confident and competent adults.

But what happens when danger replaces safety as a condition of life for a child? What does living in chronic danger do to the child's experience of exploration, growth, and development? These are not idle questions. Many children live in environments characterized by day-to-day danger. This danger may come from living with abusive or neglectful parents—and thus takes the form of familial assault or unmet basic needs. It may come from living in an environment fraught with danger linked to physical hazards—such as unregulated vehicular traffic or toxic wastes. And it may come from living in a war zone—an inner-city neighborhood dominated by gangs, in which crime, exploitation, abuse, neglect, and assault are rampant. This is the situation facing growing numbers of inner-city children. They live in a world in which chronic danger resulting from community violence displaces the fundamental safety that children need. For young children already at risk because of personal or family problems, community violence may be the last straw.

The Last Straw: A Cumulative Model of Childhood Risk Factors

Life is not fair. Some children are blessed with positive, well-functioning families *and* strong, healthy constitutions *and* quick minds *and* supportive communities that provide financial, social, physical, and spiritual resources. Other children contend with troubled families *and* hostile communities *and* weakened, impaired minds and bodies.

Few children escape risk completely, however (just as most children have *something* going for them). Most children must contend with risk: a parent dies; the family experiences divorce, unemployment, or poverty; a parent is mentally or physically incapacitated; the child incurs a physical disability. An emergent model of risk, presented by Sameroff, Siefer, Barocas, Zax, and Greenspan (1987, p. 347), tells us that most children can cope with low levels of risk—one or two risk factors. It is the *accumulation* of such risks that jeopardizes development—particularly where no compensatory forces are at work. In such instances, as illustrated in Figure 1, mental retardation is a likely result when there are more than two major risk factors in the child's life.

Figure 1. Effects of Multiple Risks on Preschool Intelligence.

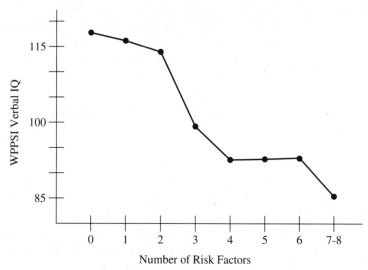

Number of Risk Factors

Note: WPPSI Verbal IQ is an individually administered test of the child's intelligence.

Source: Sameroff, Siefer, Barocas, Zax, and Greenspan, 1987, p. 347.

Sameroff and his colleagues studied such factors as chronicity of maternal mental illness, poverty, lack of social support, large family size, parental rigidity, early negative interaction with parents, high parental anxiety, low level of maternal education, and single parenthood. They found that the average intelligence scores of the children remained good until the third and fourth risk factors were added. Then the scores dropped into the problematic range. We assume that we can generalize this model to other domains of development. It highlights the challenge to policy makers and practitioners: prevent the accumulation of risk factors. Children who are poor are already in the danger zone, where preventing the further accumulation of risk becomes imperative.

We must rise to the challenge of protecting the children of urban war zones from danger. They are already poor, and perhaps already face parental problems related to poverty—

both as cause and as effect. Untreated trauma related to community violence may well be the last straw for them. Professionals and volunteers who work with young children in urban war zones must commit themselves to understanding and intervening in the social and psychological dynamics of danger.

Objective and Subjective Meanings of Danger

At the outset, we must recognize two senses of the term *danger*. The first refers to an objective accounting of the likelihood that an individual will suffer injury in a particular situation. For example, the odds of a person's being killed by lightning are 1 in 1.9 million, the odds of being attacked by a shark are 1 in 100 million, and the odds of being killed by a shark attack are 1 in 300 million (Christrup, 1991). Of course, any general statement about the odds of objective danger depends on the context in which an individual lives. If one never swims in the ocean, one's risk of shark attack is zero. If one never leaves an affluent suburb to enter an inner-city neighborhood, one's risk of being killed in a gang shoot-out is minimal.

The second meaning of danger is subjective: *the feeling of impending harm.* For some people, riding in an airplane creates a vivid sense of being in danger; others feel safe and secure. Some suburbanites are terrified of the city; many tough inner-city kids are terrified of being out in the woods.

Objective and subjective danger may be weakly correlated. Some people feel much more threatened by swimming in the ocean (sharks) than they do by walking around in a storm (lightning). Some people feel terrified walking the streets of downtown Chicago, even in the daytime. Others are nonchalant. Some people seem unaware of the objective dangers around them—that is, they feel safe when the odds of harm "ought" to make them afraid. Others feel endangered when, in point of objective fact, they are at negligible risk of harm—that is, they feel endangered when the odds heavily favor safety.

Children who live with community violence may be susceptible to both senses of danger. They are exposed to objective danger, and they are plagued with feelings of being in jeopardy. Adults, with their broader base of experience, generally can distinguish between what is dangerous and what is safe and can use abstract reasoning to make sense of the world. People are more prone to misperceive danger when the threat seems mysterious and is a low-probability event.

Young children are more vulnerable. Their physical immaturity places them at risk for injury from trauma that would not hurt adults because they are larger and more powerful. Their psychic immaturity means they are more easily shocked by the awful things that adults have grown accustomed to knowing about. Also, young children tend to believe in the reality of threats from what most adults would define as the "fantasy" world: monsters under the bed, wolves in the basement, and invisible creatures that lurk in the dark corners of bedrooms. Inner-city children who contend with the horrors of community violence may tie these real horrors with the horrors of the fantasy world: Godzilla joins the gangbangers. (*Gangbangers* has come to means gang members or gang fighters in many urban neighborhoods.)

On the other hand, young children may perceive resources and reassurance in this same fantasy dimension. One young boy living in a dangerous neighborhood in Boston took solace from an empty deodorant bottle that he kept by the side of his bed, a bottle that was labeled "guaranteed 100 percent safe" (Fish-Murray, 1990). Although many adults seek similar reassurance in religious icons and good-luck pieces, few adults have this capacity to rely on totems with such confidence. What is more, young children can find reassurance in their belief that the adults who care for them are powerful enough to protect them from any danger. (Of course, that is one reason why they may be more traumatized when hurt than adolescents or adults, who have fewer "illusions" and thus lower expectations regarding adult power to protect.)

Community Standards for Assessing Danger

In our efforts to understand danger, perhaps our best course is to approach it along the lines developed for the study of child maltreatment, where we face a similar need to reconcile and integrate objective and subjective criteria (Garbarino, Guttmann, and Seeley, 1986). Thus, child maltreatment constitutes a social judgment that a specific treatment is inappropriate and will jeopardize the child's growth and development. This judgment is based partly on objective fact and partly on the opinions of one's society and culture.

In this same sense, there is a social meaning of risk, and a cultural and social *authorization* for emotional and moral response. Subjective danger is a phenomenological construction, the "recognition" of liability to injury or evil consequences. Objective danger is an empirical determination regarding the probability that liability will be translated into injury. Both elements are necessary for a complete understanding of danger, particularly if we are to understand the dynamics of danger in young children.

Those whose sensibility falls very much below the social standard (that is, those who feel imperiled by what is socially defined as mundane, benign, or improbable) may be judged "neurotic," "phobic," or perhaps just "fearful." For example, unless there has been some specific sighting of a shark, someone who would refuse to swim in the Atlantic Ocean for fear of a shark attack would be judged to be violating the community standard of what constitutes danger. Those whose sensibility to risk is not activated until threats are (by common social standards) extreme, imminent, and terrifying we classify as "reckless," "numbed," or "pathologically brave." For example, someone who insisted on going swimming in the ocean moments after a shark had been sighted would be labeled reckless.

Of course, we want to identify and understand the forces that push individual people (particularly children) away from the norms (in either direction). How do parental child-rearing styles enhance bravery or fearfulness? How do internal dynamics lead to recklessness or timidity? How do traumatic experiences affect the victim's perception of danger? We also want to understand the forces that change those norms. For example, children in the 1950s never wore seat belts in the family car. Now, in the United States, there is an expectation (one that is met in a slim majority of cases) that children and youth (and their parents) will "buckle up," and parents who fail to insist that their children use seat belts are subject to a charge of "child neglect" (Garbarino, 1988). Well-socialized children and youth now feel "endangered" if asked to travel without being buckled up, even if for a brief time. In such instances, objective danger decreases (seat belts reduce injuries by 60 percent and deaths by 90 percent, but subjective danger may well increase. Safety, like danger, has costs associated with it—costs that go beyond the financial and physical to include the psychological and philosophical (Garbarino, 1988). For children living with community violence, these costs include the energy drain of hypervigilance and, in some cases, risk avoidance so extreme that it leads to a diminished sense of achievement and mastery.

The greater our awareness of the risks around us, the more we feel impelled to act safely, *and* the more guilty we may feel if harm befalls us or those whom we are responsible for protecting—for example, parents who thought they had taken every step to protect their children from harm only to have harm intrude. This phenomenon seemed to figure prominently in the Laurie Dann case, in which a crazed young woman entered the Hubbard Woods School (in Winnetka, Illinois) in May 1988, and began shooting children. In the wake of the shooting (in which one child was killed and several others seriously injured), many parents in this affluent suburban community were plagued with feelings of bewilderment, outrage, and violation that the absolute peace and safety of their community could be "infected" with the criminal violence they thought lay outside the bounds of their world. A year later, many still felt betrayed and in jeopardy (Egginton, 1991).

A Developmental Perspective

In the broadest sense, child development is the process of becoming fully human. A child's experiences combine with a child's biological givens, and from this mixture emerges a complete person, ready for the challenges of day-to-day life— as a student, a worker, a friend, a family member, and a citizen (Garbarino and Associates, 1992). To succeed in these roles, children must acquire the basic skills of modern life: social competence, a secure and positive sense of one's own identity, proficiency in thinking and speaking clearly, an understanding of the many ways in which people communicate with one another. The foundation of all these skills is the child's emergent *capacity to know*, in the broadest sense of the word, for everything else is tied to this competence.

How well do children understand possible matches between situations and self? Do they see how social realities are organized? Are they able to reshape or redirect these realities to achieve their own goals? If they are to enhance their competencies and minimize their weaknesses (Sternberg, 1985), they must not be subjected to an accumulation of risk factors, and they must have opportunities to enter social systems that offer material and psychic rewards and resources. The threats to their development are early deprivation that suppresses intelligence, repressive environments that stultify creativity and foster rigid thinking, and dead-end settings that are cut off from a society's principal resources. All three threats are disturbingly common for children who live in situations of chronic violence in inner-city war zones.

But the problem for such children is not solely one of basic competence. Beyond the demands of everyday social existence, children need a sense of wonder to sustain their development. They need to appreciate the wonder of being alive. We want them to do more than just learn to read. We want them to experience the joy of literature and the pleasure of reading. We want them to do more than just cope with human relationships. We want them to know love and friendship.

How is all this to happen when the child is exposed to chronic community violence, which compromises the child's ability to meet the challenges of childhood: forming attachments, learning to trust, developing confidence about self and social reality (Erikson, 1950)? The child's capacity to experience "trust" depends on the ability to recognize continuity and regularity in care and caregivers. To *feel* that the world is a regular and safe place, the child must *know* the difference between safety and danger. To become autonomous, the child must *know* who she or he is. To become confident about fantasy and reality, the child must *know* the difference between them. To take on the role of student, the child must *know* the basic behaviors required for mastery. The processes of knowing are inextricably bound to the processes of feeling.

An Ecological View of Development

Approaching children developmentally means that we recognize the child's capacity for change (Garbarino and Associates, 1992). It also means that we recognize the social environment's power to produce change. The child's life is not fixed in some unalterable genetic code that predetermines what and who he or she will be. Each child contains the potential to be many different children, and caring adults can help to determine which of those children will come to life.

The social ecology of the community creates the context for these possibilities. For example, when genetically identical twins are raised together or in very similar communities, they grow up to be very similar, even to the extent of having very similar IQ scores. However, when genetically identical twins grow up in very different environments, their IQ scores are likely to be much less similar. One study reported a correlation of .86 for identical twins reared separately but in similar communities, and only .26 for identical twins reared separately in dissimilar communities (Bronfenbrenner, 1986). Although genetic heritage can (and usually does) make an important contribution to cognitive development, other biological influences—such as nutrition, which affects brain growth—also can be powerful. What is more, the social environment a community provides will substantially determine whether biological potential will bloom or wither, whether the biological underpinnings of cognitive development will be fulfilled or denied by experience (Bronfenbrenner, Moen, and Garbarino, 1984). Early trauma, socially induced, can produce neurological damage (biological injury), which in turn can impair later social competence (van der Kolk, 1987).

In the developmental process, the child forms a picture or draws a map of the world and his or her place in it. As children draw these maps, they move forward on the paths they believe exist. If a child's map of the world depicts people and places as hostile, and the child as an insignificant speck relegated to one small corner, we must expect troubled development of one sort or another: a life of suspicion, low self-esteem, self-denigration, and perhaps violence and rage. We can also expect a diminution of cognitive development and impediments to academic achievement and in-school behavior.

Threats to a child's physical health can jeopardize mental and emotional development. Trauma can stunt intellectual development and impose stress that undermines social development. Instability in a child's caregivers can threaten the child's sense of security and continuity. Living amidst community violence can produce such caregiver problems, and thus compound the direct effects of trauma on the child. Here is the destructive accumulation of risk factors noted earlier.

What about the role of community adults and parents in compensating for risk factors in the child's social environment? Community violence suppresses and diverts this important developmental function in adults. They are often too angry, frightened, traumatized, or preoccupied to be psychologically available to the child.

Development as a Social Process

Piaget's (1936) view of development is based on the idea that children form concepts representing reality. As their brains mature and they experience the world, they either fit these experiences into existing concepts (assimilation) or they adjust or change the schemes to make sense of new or incongruous ideas (accommodation). Thus, for example, the child develops the concept "dog" to cover four-legged furry creatures and is able to accept the fact that German shepherds, collies, and dachshunds are all dogs. The child then must alter this concept of "dog" to acknowledge the fact that some four-legged furry creatures are not dogs but, rather, are horses, cows, cats, or llamas.

But there is more to development than maturation and individual experience. Development is a social process, for it is through relationships with people that the child learns about the world and how it works (Vygotsky, 1986). Who points out that this particular four-legged furry creature is a cat rather than a dog? Who reassures the child when he or she is frightened? Who affirms the child's need to play and daydream and interprets the meaning of those experiences? Who guides and helps the child in learning society's rules and beliefs? Who encourages the child to think creatively?

Child development proceeds through and because of social relationships. The earliest and most important of these are the social relationships between infant and parents (and others who care for the child). These attachment relationships are the training ground and the foundation for subsequent social relationships. Problems in early attachments tend to translate into general social problems, cognitive deficiencies, and emotional difficulties. Depriving the child of crucial social relationships is a threat, a major risk factor for impaired development.

What the child needs are responses that are *emotionally validating and developmentally challenging* (Garbarino, Guttmann, and Seeley, 1986). Such responses move development forward. When the child says, "Car go," she needs the person who responds with a smile, "Yes, honey. That's right, the car is going. And where do you think the car is going?" The child needs people to teach him how to be patient, how to follow through, how to behave responsibly, as well as how to tell a dog from a cat, an *A* from a *B*, and a 1 from a 2. A child needs people who care for *that* child, know *that* child, and validate *that* child emotionally.

It is not so much our capacity for learning that distinguishes humans from other species but, rather, our capacity to teach. All animals can learn. But humans consciously set out to teach as a way of facilitating development. Human beings construct elaborate and sophisticated cultures and teach them to children. It is because we teach that we do not need to invent the wheel or discover fire over and over again. Children learn from adults in many ways, some of which are inadvertent on the adult's part. Deliberate teaching, however, plays a special role in this learning process.

Vygotsky (1986) went beyond Piaget's concept of development to emphasize the role of the adult as a teacher in the child's development. The good teacher understands the difference between what the child can accomplish alone and what the child can do when helped by an adult or a more competent peer. This "zone of proximal development" is the critical territory for interventions that seek to stimulate and support the child's development. When a child's parents and other family members do not provide such stimulation and support, outside intervention is needed. The key is to shape the behavior of adults in the child's life—a special challenge when those adults themselves are traumatized as a result of their own experience with community violence.

Implications for Children Exposed to Community Violence

What does all this mean for understanding child development under conditions of danger linked to community violence? It means that adult mediation of community violence is central to our concern for the development of young children. Fantasy and play (particularly "pretend play") are vital to a child's development. Through them, children have a chance to explore the meaning of the world around *and inside* them. In this sense, play is the child's vocation. It serves both the need to work through unconscious forces and the need to practice basic life skills (Paley, 1988). Unconscious forces play an important role in the child's life, and adult mediation must extend to these processes as well. Unconscious processes are at work when the toddler suddenly resists going to sleep, acquires imaginary playmates, has nightmares, and invents monsters, ghosts, witches, and bogeymen.

How does the experience of chronic danger affect the child's emerging social maps and the development of competence? We can concern ourselves with several paths of influence. The first is simply that the experience of chronic danger may suppress the development process itself. The creation of healthy and effective social maps depends in part on the child's ability to see the world clearly and intelligently. Living with danger can suppress exploration, immobilize the child, and thereby impair the development of competence. Second, the experience of danger may stretch the child's schemas to the breaking point and beyond. Indeed, one definition of "trauma" in the psychological domain focuses on stressful events that are "beyond the normal range of human experience" (American Psychiatric Association, 1987, p. 250). Such events are likely to produce psychiatric consequences (as we shall see in Chapter Four, where we discuss post-traumatic stress disorders—PTSD).

For children, this focus on the limits of an individual's experience is doubly important. Because children have a narrow range of concepts with which to work, safety is especially important to them. We must protect them from experiences beyond their understanding. The traumatic stress resulting from chronic exposure to community violence is just such an experience. Researchers report that traumatic events experienced prior to age eleven are three times more likely to result in PTSD than such events experienced after age twelve (Davidson and Smith, 1990).

But what about desensitization (in the sense of becoming acclimated to danger and thus impervious to its effects)? And can someone become addicted to danger (in the sense of becoming dependent on the arousal it can produce)? We think the answer to both questions is a tentative "yes," and wartime situations often seem to produce this effect. In his book *A Bright Shining Lie,* Neal Sheehan (1988) notes that Vietnam War hero John Paul Vann became desensitized to the routine danger of living in a war zone, resigned to "fate," and addicted to the thrill of confronting new levels of challenge and danger. These characteristics ultimately led to his death. (He was killed flying a helicopter into an enemy zone against the advice of his colleagues.) Anyone who has been in a war zone and escaped unhurt is a prime candidate for desensitization, resignation, and addiction—as Kotlowitz (1991) found in his study of children growing up in one of Chicago's inner-city war zones. In our own studies, we have found similar responses to chronic danger among inner-city children (Garbarino, Kostelny, and Dubrow, 1991).

Most children can appreciate the thrill that comes with moderate danger and seek it out in their play (for example, climbing games on the playground). Some children even seem to thrive on danger. They seek the thrill of it (and may be incompletely aware of the possible ramifications for themselves and others). Still other children seek extreme danger as an expression of psychopathology—as explorations of childhood suicide make clear (see Orbach, 1988). They put themselves in jeopardy partly as a tactic designed to communicate with adults in their environment, sending the message "I am in deep trouble. Help me!" They may seek out danger as a response to self-loathing, having incorporated a message of personal devaluation (for instance, as a result of having been abused or neglected). Whether it is affirmation or self-punishment, this reckless danger-seeking behavior is a significant force in the lives of children living in psychologically unhealthy environments. Child victims of trauma may reenact the events surrounding the trauma, perhaps seeking to find an alternative outcome (Terr, 1990). But such reenactment may itself be dangerous (for instance, a child may reenact the trauma of a car crash by riding his bicycle into a wall).

In contrast, some children—usually through an unfortunate interaction of temperament and parental training—are paralyzed by the slightest hint of danger. We know of a timid seven-year-old boy who visited friends of his parents at their lakeside home and spent the entire time with his life jacket on, cataloguing the dangers to be found there, from the possibility of being bitten by the family's pet hamster to falling from the dock into the shallow water and drowning.

Children who live in objectively dangerous environments may present a more complex picture in this regard. What is the appropriate level of fearfulness for a child living in a neighborhood where violence is common? Is it normal in such an environment to be afraid to play on the playground? Would frequent nightmares be a normal "strategy" for unconscious processing of the environmental danger?

Children who grow up in dangerous environments, as defined by high levels of community violence, often present a curious mixture of bravado and fearfulness. They are often "tough on the outside and soft on the inside." In a classic account of this phenomenon (Davis and Dollard, 1940), a girl's extreme belligerent toughness and recklessness existed in tandem (and in dynamic relationship) with her extreme inner fearfulness. We have seen similar patterns in tough inner-city kids having their first experience at summer camp in the country. They often are aggressive and reckless when they are indoors but become timid and fearful in the forest. Others have observed this combination in boys as well as girls (see Kotlowitz, 1991).

A Framework for Understanding Injury

To proceed with an examination of children in danger, we need a social and cultural framework for understanding childhood injuries. This framework can then provide a context for exploring psychological issues associated with living in danger. Childhood injuries may be classified in four broad categories along a continuum reflecting the degree to which they are "random" or "inflicted": random accidents, preventable accidents, negligence, and assault (see Garbarino, 1988).

Random Accidents

When children are injured by accidental trauma, members of the community manifest a spirit of unmitigated sympathy toward the adults responsible for these injured children. At this end of the continuum, no one contends that these adults inflicted the injuries. Of course, the term *accident* is a social label, reflecting a community-based judgment that such harm is not someone's fault. Because it is a social label, the definition of what is or is not an accident is subject to historical change and contemporary variation across geographical, social-class, ethnic, and demographic lines.

Some accidents are loaded on the random end of the continuum—for example, deaths caused by a meteor striking the earth. Others conform to a systematic pattern in which poverty, race, or risk taking make some classes of people more likely than others to fall prey to harm; for example African-American children (who are likely to be poor) are three times as likely to die in "accidents" as are white children (who are less likely to be poor). Some injuries are random in the sense that the individual victim was not targeted, although the device causing the injury had the general purpose of causing harm (for example, if a child steps on a land mine, the injury is considered "accidental.").

As noted above, most automobile-related injuries to young children were once defined as random accidents but are now understood to be preventable. More than 90 percent of fatalities and 66 percent of disabilities are avoided through the use of child safety restraints (Margolis and Runyan, 1983). Thus, an event can be redefined as community understanding changes, or it can be defined differently from community to community and from culture to culture.

In the current climate in the United States, the analysis of gun-related injuries provides a kind of litmus test of individual and community thinking about the meaning of accidents. How do we define an injury to a child that occurs when the child is playing with a loaded gun found in the house? Is this an accident? And what about children hurt when guns are fired into the air as an act of celebration? Or when children are "accidentally" caught in the cross fire of a gang shoot-out? How do we define such "collateral" damage?

Preventable Accidents

When a knowledge base develops to demonstrate that informed caregiver and community action can significantly reduce the likelihood of specific accidental injuries to children, those events become redefined as preventable accidents. This redefinition is a social process reflecting the interaction of community concepts and scientific expertise about what is and what is not socially and technically feasible. For example, many ingestions of dangerous fluids by toddlers are understood to be preventable through the use of "child-proof" caps on bottles. The use of helmets can exert a significant preventive effect on childhood head injuries resulting from bicycle "accidents." Similarly, as laws and norms about gun safety change, more and more incidents are being moved from the category of random accident to the category of preventable accident—and even beyond, to the realm of negligence.

Preventable accidents are disproportionately common for children in urban war zones, where adult supervision is often marginal and physical hazards abound. These accidents elicit a spirit of regret but not official approbation toward adults responsible for the injured children.

Negligence

When children are injured because an adult has failed to meet the community's *minimal* standards for care and protection, we enter the realm of negligence. Consider the case of a young child who is injured while sitting on a parent's lap in the front seat of a car involved in a crash. Defined as a random accident thirty years ago, and a preventable accident fifteen years ago, such an injury is now defined as negligence in many communities. The same is true of many childhood injuries related to handguns. Some communities have laws that

make the owner of a gun responsible for any injuries occurring because a child gained access to the gun at home. Negli-
gence-related injuries may carry with them a spirit of anger,
indignation, and often legal retribution for the adults deemed
responsible.

Assaults

Assaults are intentional injuries inflicted on children. They
stand at the opposite end of the continuum from random
accidents. Physical abuse of children falls into this category,
as do injuries to children occurring as a direct result of community violence. Legally, even the accidental, collateral injuries of young children may qualify as assaults (for example,
being shot in a cross fire). The community's response to
assault-related injuries is often rage and vengeance directed at
those responsible, coupled with legal/criminal penalties.

Scientific, Ethical, and Policy Aspects

All of this may seem simple enough on the surface. But these
four categories can hide difficult issues of science, ethics, and
policy.

First, some intentional injuries are not socially defined
as assaults. For example, many Americans favor the use of
corporal punishment for children. Such "discipline" is often
exempted from the category of assault, even when it produces
specific injuries (which may be treated as "accidental" or "incidental" to discipline). A Louis Harris poll in the 1980s found
that only about 41 percent of adults believe that physical punishment "often" or "very often" leads to injury to a child. On
the other hand, 73 percent indicated that "repeated yelling at
and cursing a child" "often" or "very often" produce emotional harm. Other surveys indicate that a growing number of
parents reject the use of physical punishment with children
(National Committee for Prevention of Child Abuse, 1987).

Second, injuries may be classified as random accidents
because lack of evidence precludes assigning blame. Research

on sudden infant death syndrome (SIDS), for example, suggests that, at least among some families living in poverty, many such diagnoses may be better classified as preventable accidents, negligence, or even assault (Bass, Kravath, and Glass, 1986).

Third, some "intentions" may be unconscious and thus not directly accessible for review by caregivers. An adult may not directly harm a child but may create situations in which the child is exposed to elevated risk of "accidental" injury. Also, a child may seek out injury as a way of getting attention, expressing anger, or demonstrating self-destructive intent. Unconscious intent is a kind of wild card in understanding children and danger. Such intentions are real, but they must be inferred indirectly, a tricky business under the best of circumstances.

Fourth, community-level actions can increase or decrease the magnitude of individual responsibility for injury prevention, as well as the level of risk experienced. For example, if a community permits controllable toxins (such as lead-based paint) in the environments of children or if the community fails to control known child abusers (such as previously identified pedophiles), the protective task facing caregivers increases in difficulty and magnitude. If, on the other hand, the community seeks to defuse risk by assuming responsibility for providing safe environments (for example, by building pedestrian overpasses connecting playgrounds and residential areas, so that children will not have to cross busy streets), it decreases the burden on caregivers (Aldrich, 1979). Spontaneous random mouthing of objects becomes dangerous as adult supervision decreases and/or the presence of swallowable toys or toxins increases. After the introduction of safety caps on bottles, the percentage of child deaths from poisoning declined dramatically (Baker, O'Neill, and Karpf, 1984).

These same considerations apply to the issue of community violence. Is it tolerated? Do community institutions mobilize to prevent it? To control its perpetrators? As society does more to prevent harm, individuals who fail to apply available precautions or otherwise fail to do their (smaller) part are much more likely to be judged harshly and deemed inadequate or neglectful.

Trauma

What happens when a child is hurt, when danger is actualized in trauma? The dictionary defines trauma as "an injury, a disordered psychic or behavioral state resulting from mental or emotional stress or physical injury" (*Webster's New World Dictionary of the American Language*, 1968). The consequences can range from minor injury to death. The consequences of greatest concern are psychological and moral, since they establish the developmental meaning of physical consequences. The same physical consequences can have very different life-course effects, as a function of cultural, social, and psychological influences. Thus, for example, it matters developmentally whether a child's leg is broken by a parental assault or through play, whether in the course of running away from a fight or in the course of standing up for a friend. Of particular developmental interest is whether or not danger results in psychological disruption. The emergent field of traumatic stress studies is recognizing the importance of understanding the phenomenon of post-traumatic stress disorder as a response to childhood trauma (Eth and Pynoos, 1985). This disorder is now included as a category for official diagnosis in the American Psychiatric Association's *Diagnostic and Statistical Manual* (1987). We will discuss the meaning and dynamics of PTSD in inner-city children at a later point in our analysis (Chapter Four).

Conclusion

In this brief introduction, we have shown that the social context established for the child by the community and by caregivers affects the way in which children respond to growing up in environments made dangerous because of community violence. In other words, we have provided an ecological perspective on human development (Bronfenbrenner, 1979; Garbarino and Associates, 1992).

An ecological perspective highlights development as the interaction of an active, purposeful, and adaptive organism, on the one hand, with a set of nested social systems, on the other. This ecological perspective provides a framework for hearing the experience of children around the world who face chronic danger as a result of community violence. As always, by looking at children far away, we can gain a better perspective on children near at hand. Thus, we turn next to profile the experience of children growing up in war zones in other countries. We bring to this discussion the concept of danger (its objective and subjective dimensions), a preliminary appreciation for the relation of trauma to development, and a model of accumulative childhood risk.

2

Children in War Zones: From Mozambique to Chicago

Children living in war zones around the world and here at home can tell us a great deal about the dynamics of injury and danger. They can put us in touch with the inner world of childhood trauma. They can show us something about coping and resilience, their limitations and possibilities. They can reveal the process of social mapping that results in identity and world view.

But what children can tell depends on what adults are prepared to hear. We use the term *prepared* in two senses (Garbarino, Stott, and the Faculty of Erikson Institute, 1989). First, adults must be willing to listen to children express themselves as they seek to construct a narrative account of their lives. At the same time, adults must be willing to hear children struggle with the confusion that comes when they must make sense of what fundamentally does *not* make sense.

In our studies of children in war zones, we have not merely reviewed research and theory but also have journeyed to war zones around the world as well as examined those close to home. We have listened to children in Africa, Asia, Latin America, and the Middle East (Garbarino, Kostelny, and Dubrow, 1991) including Iraq and Kuwait (Garbarino, 1991). We think that a brief "clinical" sketch of children growing up in these war zones will do much to orient the professional who deals with children and families closer to home—in the war zones of Chicago, Los Angeles, Miami, New York, Detroit, Washington, D.C., and wherever else violent crime, gangs, drugs, and poverty catch children in the cross fire of community violence. As we examine the experience of Mozambican, Cambodian, and Palestinian children, we can search for lessons applicable to the American problem of community violence.

Mozambique: How Much Can People Bear?

Mozambique has been at war for most of its existence as an independent nation. The effects of the war have been devastating to economic, social, and educational gains made following independence in 1975. The war is undeclared. The conflict is between the government and a terrorist force with little indigenous identity or support. This force is composed mainly of kidnapped men, women, and children, and relies on outside, self-interested financial support to sustain itself.

The Mozambique National Resistance (Renamo) has waged a war in the rural provinces of Mozambique that has sent more than 4,600,000 people fleeing their homes to find safety. Severe dislocation has left half of the population unable to feed itself and has had a profound effect on the country's overall self-sufficiency. According to a 1989 UNICEF report, "Out of the estimated 600,000 Mozambicans who have lost their lives as a direct or indirect consequence of the war, some 494,000 are children" (UNICEF, 1989).

Teachers have been attacked. Their schools have been destroyed. In 1987, the province of Gaza had 120 schools; by 1990, only three schools remained standing after Renamo attacks. In Nampula province, Renamo forced 399 first-level primary schools (first to fifth grade) to close. This represents 35 percent of the school network in the province, and it affects the education of 36,000 children (United Nations and the World Bank, 1990). Here, as elsewhere, those intent on demolishing a community have targeted the schools for special attention.

The psychological cost of the war remains largely unmeasured, but by any standard it is enormous. UNICEF estimates that half a million children are at risk of severe psychological harm. In one study, twenty-four of the thirty-

five children interviewed (aged eight to seventeen) had witnessed at least one instance of violent death. Included in the
stories these children told were incidents of seeing people
drowned, burned, buried alive, and shot. Children themselves
have been tortured by the bandits. A study of 110 Mozambican
children (seven to twelve years old) who live in a refugee
settlement camp in Zambia documents that 15 percent had
been tortured or physically abused (McCallin, 1989). These
children may survive their physical wounds, but they will
live with the psychological consequences of being victimized.
Still other children are separated from their parents when
their villages are attacked by Renamo. The younger children
are sent into the bush to fend for themselves without their
parents. These children are sometimes found by the military
and brought to local orphanages.

On the day we arrived at United Methodist Church's
Inhambane Hospital, the hospital had one tank of diesel fuel
in reserve, and the ambulance would be able to make only
one more run to transfer patients to and from the hospital.
The emergency plan was to send hospital staff out to the road
to flag down drivers who might be willing to assist them in
transporting the wounded and sick. To complicate the situation even further, the hospital had run out of gauze, and
clean water was in extremely short supply.

There is a constant battle for survival. Priorities are the
basics: blood, food, water, and electricity. The children enter
the hospital in "revolving-door style." In one year, 800 children were admitted to the hospital. Hospital records are coded
to track *guerra,* or war-related injuries. Separate accounts are
kept for adults and children in this category. On the day we
visited, the hospital admissions book included the names of
fifteen children (aged five through fourteen) who had been
injured because of the conflict. An equal number of abandoned children were listed in the admissions book.

The surgeon put his arm under the shoulders of a nine-
year-old boy who lay on his side in a hospital bed. As the
doctor unwrapped the partially covered head of the child, he
explained that the child's head had been "carved up" with a

machete by a member of Renamo. A piece of the boy's cranium had been cut out, leaving a gaping hole that, as the surgeon explained, would never grow back together. In fact, the back of the boy's head would be extremely sensitive for the rest of his life, and he would not be able to sleep on his back because of the pressure it would cause.

In the next hospital bed was a boy of ten who suffered a gunshot wound to his leg. The bullet missed the child's tibia but left a deep wound that exposed the bone. The doctor turned the boy toward us so that we could see his injury. The child was in obvious pain. He did not look at us and was not able to focus on anything in the hospital room.

Another recent admission to the hospital was a father and his child. His wife, the mother of the child, had been killed in a recent bandit attack on their village. During the attack, the child's hands and feet were burned by the bandits. After witnessing his wife's murder and the torture of his son, the father managed to escape into the bush with the child. Soldiers later found them wandering in the countryside and brought them to the hospital in Inhambane. The child was recovering from his physical burn injuries, but both father and child were still struggling with the psychological effects of the experience.

We observed the faces of children. They showed little expression even when the staff attempted to elicit a response. The attending physician uses children's desire to interact as a barometer for their improved health. She said that when children begin to feel better, she can tell, "because they start to smile." In the week before we visited, five of the six new children admitted had died.

In addition to the physical injuries, more than 90 percent of Mozambiquan children suffer from malnutrition. Malnourished children are more susceptible to other diseases. They are also at risk for abnormal physical development. Research indicates that their central nervous system may suffer irreparable damage.

The psychological effect of the war on professionals is evident. When 80 percent of the new child admissions in one week die from war-induced causes, staff openly question their ability to remain strong. They cope by becoming psychologically numb. Said one supervisor, "Staff suffer, but they show little emotion. But if it's encouraged, I wonder how they will survive?" We have found this same sentiment in Chicago and elsewhere as professionals seek to protect themselves from drowning in the suffering that surrounds them. The unwillingness to express emotion is a major impediment to training programs, as we shall see in Chapter Nine.

On the day we visited the Inhambane Hospital, a group of school-age children who had been kidnapped by Renamo and rescued from the bandit camps by the Mozambique military had been brought to the orphanage. We interviewed these children to learn about their experiences with Renamo.

One of the boys had spent three weeks with the bandits. He had been tending the family's cattle with his brother when the bandits came. His brother escaped, but the bandits took him away to their camp. He said, "The bandits are bad; they kill, and they beat people." When we asked him what should be done to the bandits, he said, "They should be killed." This is a simple and direct form of revenge that we have heard from children—particularly boys—around the world and in our own city. When asked what he would want if he could have anything in the world, a little boy in Detroit, whose brother had been killed by gang members, replied: "A gun, so I could blow the head off the person who killed my brother."

Many of the children we interviewed in Mozambique were often quiet and sullen, particularly if they were separated from family. Frequently these children stared beyond us as we talked. What were they looking for? They displayed no joy or laughter during the time we spent with them. We asked some of these children to draw pictures for us as we have done in other war zones.

One boy drew a house and said, "No one lives in the house." Another child drew a picture of people walking, and said, "They don't know where they are going." Yet another child drew a picture of an upside-down person. These pictures illustrate the empty, displaced, and confused world of these child victims of Renamo. We have seen such pictures elsewhere, in residential treatment programs that deal with abused and abandoned children.

There are no boundaries between the war zone and the most private domains of a child's experience in Mozambique. For them, this is total war. The combination of horrible experiences and disrupted attachment relationships has set them adrift. Their aloneness is frightening—to them and to the people who are supposed to care for them. How much can a child bear? How much can an adult care?

Of the 110 children served in both day and residential programs at the Xai-Xai orphanage, 40 were orphans living in permanent residence. They ranged in age from nine months to fourteen years. The children's records indicated that their parents had been killed in the war or that they had been separated from their parents during village attacks by Renamo. Twenty-three of the children had been kidnapped or forcibly dispersed from their homes by the bandits. Many of these children had wandered the rural countryside alone. They were found by the military and brought to the center.

One young boy made a particularly strong impression on us. He had fallen on a land mine and lost both his legs at the knee. He was playing on a bridge that had collapsed, and government soldiers had mined the area under the bridge as a deterrent to Renamo attacks. Thus, in a sense, his injuries are "accidental"; he was not the target. After the incident, his parents separated. Neither parent wanted the responsibility for this child, and he was brought to the orphanage. He had no prosthesis and no wheelchair. Using his arms, he scooted around on the sandy ground. He smiled often and participated in all the center's activities with the other children. Somehow he had begun to fill in the gaping holes in his life. When the children formed a circle to play a tag game, he joined them, and he took part in an organized relay race. His school friends encouraged him and allotted extra time for him to get to the finish line. It was clear that staff gave him a great deal of support. When we asked him to draw a picture for us, he drew a picture of the man who had helped him after he was injured.

The loss of parents, home, and limbs has tested the limits of this child's resources as it would for any child—or any adult for that matter. And yet he can still smile and laugh with his friends. Why? We judge him to be what developmental psychologists have called a "resilient child." Existing research on resilience (Lösel and Bliesener, 1990) suggests that such strength comes from a combination of temperamental robustness, intelligence, positive early relationships, community support and encouragement, and role models for active coping strategies.

That he is managing is wonderful. But the strength he demonstrates in coping with catastrophic adversity predicts that he would have been a remarkable child had he been permitted to live whole, in peace. War squanders the gifts of children on mere coping, gifts that in peace can be the basis for creative opportunities.

We visited with a family who had been displaced several times by the war. The mother lives with her three sons and three daughters. Her husband left her after the second bandit attack. In 1983, the bandits invaded their village, forcing them to move. One of the daughters is mentally retarded. During the attack, the bandits broke this young girl's leg in what was apparently an act of gratuitous brutality. And they destroyed the village hospital, leaving the families without accessible medical care. As a result, the child's leg healed in a fixed position. She cannot bend her leg. There is a deep scar on her thigh where the bandits hit her with a machete. After the family settled for the third time, medical staff at the Inhambane Hospital attempted unsuccessfully to correct the problem. The child will never regain the use of her leg.

We asked her to draw a picture of where she lives. She sat with the leg straight out in front of her, bending deeply to reach the paper and pens we had placed near her. Her drawing was of extremely small human figures, positioned in one corner of the paper. What does it mean? Does she represent her physical limitations in her apparent inability or unwillingness to use the whole space? Is she representing what she has seen, the powerlessness of people and their inability to protect themselves? Is this what the small figures crowded in the corner mean to her? Is this what she is telling us? It seems so.

To the extent that we can get beyond the physical conditions of life, the malnutrition, the disease, the poverty, and the maiming wounds, we can and do see the spiritual challenge and the psychological neediness. Looking over our field notes, we find many references to the need for efforts to promote psychological healing for the children of Mozambique. These children need to be reunified with their families; they need simply to feel safe. On a more sophisticated level, they need to understand what life is all about; they need a positive identity and a belief in the future when the past has meant dislocation, terror, and deprivation. Children and childhood in Mozambique are under siege.

A study by the International Catholic Child Bureau in Geneva (McCallin, 1989) analyzed data from interviews with 110 mothers and one of their children between the ages of seven and twelve years, interviews that focused on their experiences with Renamo violence in Mozambique. All the families had left Mozambique because of the bandit activities and were living in a refugee settlement camp called Ukwimi in the Petauke district of Zambia. Some 44 percent of the women and 20 percent of the children had witnessed a murder. About 45 percent of the women and 19 percent of the children had witnessed or known someone injured by political violence. And 32 percent of the women and 15 percent of the children had been tortured.

In the same study, a group of 119 adolescent refugees from the same camp were interviewed. Among these adolescents, 42 percent had witnessed a murder, 44 percent had witnessed or known someone who had been injured, and 18 percent had been tortured. While these figures are horrifying, still more disturbing for us as Americans was the recognition that in some neighborhoods and housing projects in our own city, 33 percent of the adolescents have witnessed a murder.

The lessons of Mozambique are these. There are no limits to human cruelty. Some children have a remarkable capacity to cope. Adults who care for victimized children in large numbers, and over a long period of time, are themselves in psychological peril. We will bring these lessons to our efforts on behalf of children who live with American community violence.

Cambodia: Living Well Is the Best Revenge

Cambodia has experienced catastrophic communal conflict and war for nearly three decades. At first an interested bystander in the war that centered in Vietnam, eventually it was drawn into the conflict. As a result, there were massive bombings, widespread fighting, and eventually the takeover by the Khmer Rouge in 1975. In the years that followed the Khmer Rouge takeover, more than a million of Cambodia's eight million people (the Khmer) died in the savage and genocidal restructuring of Khmer society. Since the Vietnamese invaded in 1979, and overthrew the Khmer Rouge, hundreds of thousands more have died in a civil war that continued into the 1990s. Horrific violence was endemic under the Khmer Rouge, and the legacy is a generation of children and youth killed and maimed—psychically as well as physically.

And yet there is an amazingly positive theme that many Cambodian youth embody: "Living well honors those who died and is the best revenge." We came to recognize this theme in 1991, as we sat in an orphanage—a "children's city"—after driving out from Phnom Penh into the countryside. Two young boys, sixteen and seventeen years old, sat with us. They were brought forward in response to our request to have some kids draw pictures of Khmer life.

Both had the shy softness we came to associate with Khmer youth. Both were orphaned as young children in the Khmer Rouge disaster. One boy insisted that he does not remember his early years—quite plausible given what we have been told about those experiences and what we know about the symptoms of post-traumatic stress disorder. And yet he drew vivid pictures of what happened. His artistic talent was impressive. Where do the scenes he draws come from? The explanation is simple. He has seen the pictures drawn and painted by others, and he has heard the stories we have heard. He has been "indoctrinated" about the Khmer Rouge calamity as part of efforts by the current government to forestall a return to power of Pol Pot's Khmer Rouge.

What are we to make of such indoctrination? We suspect that such "stories," such personal narratives, are an important resource in helping people cope with trauma and disaster. They give social meaning to personal experience. They provide a basis for interpreting the present and acting in the future. Such stories can be fundamental to the process of coping with adversity.

Under Pol Pot, teenagers and children were recruited as enforcers and executioners. The film *The Killing Fields* documents the bestiality and brutality of these events. It has become the public narrative through which Americans understand the Cambodian holocaust. But it is only part of the story.

For the children who have reached Heaven in the United States with some direct link to their families, the dominant theme is deliverance. In contrast to children who left without benefit of family, and who have been relegated to orphanages or other institutions, children with parents appear almost messianic in their optimistic rebirth. They—and their parents—seem determined to make a success of their lives almost as an act of religious faith. They have survived, and have an obligation to make the best of their lives. Robert Coles (1986) observed these attitudes in his interviews with Cambodian refugee children and their parents. He writes: "I am thinking that I have never seen a group of children, in all the years of my work, who are more resilient and perceptive. Moreover, the parents of these children, no less eager to become adjusted to this country, to enjoy its possibilities, are as industrious and as caring as any mothers and fathers I've seen anywhere in the world" (pp. 266-267).

It is not that the children and adults who managed to emigrate to the United States or other rich, modernized countries are free of the horror. Nightmares and flashbacks and night terror and worries about "there" coming "here" are common. One child told Coles, "I wake up and I realize that I've been back there, and they're trying to kill us, all of us, the soldiers are" (p. 265). And a recent study concluded that even four years after they had left Cambodia, half the children manifested symptoms of post-traumatic stress disorder (Kinzie and others, 1986). But those with families were doing better than those alone. All share the experiences of victimization. They are all survivors.

Having survived death and destruction, many Cambodians feel a moral obligation to live well, to make a statement about the human spirit and about what matters and what one can do in the world.

We asked the director of an orphanage in Phnom Penh about revenge. She herself had survived the Pol Pot era by escaping to the remote countryside to live among a small band of mountain people. A teacher since 1960, she was widely known in Phnom Penh and realized that, to escape detection as a criminal (being an educated person was a capital crime), she would have to go where no one could know her fatal secret. Her husband—a sports star—was taken to a "reeducation camp." Her three children—the eldest of whom then was twelve—were separated from her and from each other. When liberation came in 1979, she found that the entire family had survived. But all had seen much horror and many times had feared that they would be among the unlucky ones.

Her experience as a teacher—and a survivor—prepared her to work in a newly opened orphanage to help children. That became her revenge against the Khmer Rouge. Her strong sense of mission is not uncommon among those who have remained in Cambodia despite the hard times and the political difficulties that accompanied the Vietnamese-dominated era from 1979 to 1989. She told us that, over the years, the children at the orphanage have spoken often of revenge— but revenge in terms of remembering, of determination to ensure that "the Pol Potists" can never return to power. The orphans are drawn—and directed—to work for the government, in the various ministries, or in the army. Such work must offer a sense of an active coping: build the country, make it strong as a way to protect yourself and honor those who perished.

We have looked for this theme in conversations with the children of America's inner-city war zones. With few exceptions, we find it lacking. Why? We suspect the reasons are several. For one thing, Cambodian children and youth are past the crisis—for now at least—whereas American kids seem mired in the problem of community violence. For another, American adults seem rarely to offer the political analysis that would turn the "problem" of community violence into a "struggle." What is it about? What sense does it make? Only in some religious efforts to make sense of the violence and give meaning to the life of inner-city children do we find anything like the ideological resources made available to Cambodian children.

Most Khmer children have triumphed over the madness we might expect to find among those who have been subjected to the terror of the Cambodian holocaust. But their very success reinforces our principal hypotheses about the crucial importance of a child's basic relationships as the foundation for resilience and recovery. Children who are "unaccompanied" are at greatest risk, as they are in Mozambique. They are doubly at risk not only because of their loss but because of the way it came about. For children to see their parents killed in front of their eyes—shot, beheaded, disemboweled, drowned, strangled—to have "lost" them in this way is too much to bear. As most clinical reports indicate, the children who actually witnessed such murders (or who were forced to commit them) are most likely to manifest functional problems—classic psychiatric problems related to trauma.

A child can reformulate a world without parents if other things are held constant. A child can reformulate a world in which horror is a fact, not a fantasy. But how are children to cope when both axes of reality warp at once? It is as if they were faced with an impossible problem of psychic algebra: solve the equation $X = Y$, in which both X and Y are suddenly unknowns.

This is Robert Coles confronting such a child: "As he talks and talks, I wonder that he is still alive and able to be coherent, never mind attend classes and get though week after week of this life. He saw both parents die before his eyes at age five. No wonder he is tired so often, and guarded, and fearful, and a 'problem' to his good and sensitive teachers, who also have their 'limits,' and who, accordingly, expect that a psychiatrist might come up with some new ways of putting into words what happens when unspeakable political tragedies are visited upon those who have to suffer them on the ground—as opposed to those who plan them in the government buildings of countries far removed, including our own" (p. 269).

The director of an infant development and rehabilitation center presents an interesting and illuminating perspective on the process of healing. The center enrolls abandoned and orphaned young children (from birth through age six), so none of these orphans is a direct product of the Pol Pot era. But the staff are. The center hires as caregivers teenage girls who were themselves orphaned as young children under the Pol Pot regime. "They often need special training," the director tells us. They need to work at figuring out what it means to mother a child, and to do so without the implicit knowledge that one who has been well mothered has acquired "naturally."

The director continues, "I tell them—think of what you would have wanted from a mother when you were a child, and give it to this child now." This particular form of "processing" traumatic experiences is, we believe, crucial to overcoming those experiences. It is clearly linked to the concept of positive revenge that often comes up in discussions with Khmer victims. Not "Do unto others as was done unto you," but, rather, "Do unto this child as you would have had done unto the child you once were." It is golden advice. Visiting with some of the young women and the infants they are caring for, we could believe that they take this advice very seriously.

These are individuals who have been hurt. That is clear from their stories, and even in the way they seem hungry for connection and approval. But these are also individuals who are healing themselves through the active process of caring. That may be the key to the very future of Khmer society: healing through caring. We often look in vain for this attitude in the victimized children of America. It is there, to be sure. But when it appears, it is notable for being unusual. Rarely, if ever, does it figure prominently as the foundation for therapy, education, or counseling. Instead, the more "natural" rules of violence are more evident. "Do unto others what was done unto you." "Be strong." "Save yourself."

Why does one care? What resources do Khmer children have to meet this challenge? Their Buddhist religion contains concepts and rituals that often prove helpful. Many Khmer mention the Buddhist emphasis on remembering and honoring the spirits of those now dead. This concept, they say, provides a useful sense of connection that can help comfort an orphaned child. As we come to understand the process of coping with trauma, this spiritual dimension takes on increasing importance as an explanation for those who succeed and those who don't.

Beyond the spiritual as a matter of individual world view, there is the spiritual basis for collective responsibility. The strength of extended family relations and the willingness of neighbors to take in abandoned orphaned children are based in part on this spiritual commitment to the interconnection of lives. From a psychological perspective, it gives those children a model of caring that is very useful as fuel for the coping process. It gives them a positive model of revenge. It tells them that the truest revenge lies in living well, taking care, honoring the memory of those who have been lost. And it stands as an indictment of our culture that this approach seems so alien to the problem. Although we have a similar theme in our culture, it is not often expressed, particularly among professionals who look to social science for their models of human development and intervention.

We must explore the potential value of this theme in our efforts to help children cope with violence in American communities. Without attention to this spiritual impulse, we fear that our intervention efforts will fall short of the mark.

Israel and Palestine: The Dilemmas of Ideology

The birth of Israel as a Jewish homeland in 1948 is inextricably linked to the history of the Palestinian people as "outsiders." Now, more than four decades later, as the political identity of Jewish Israelis (who number 3.5 million) has solidified, nearly four million people who identify themselves as Palestinians have no political homeland. This identity problem lies at the heart of the conflict that dominates life for Israeli and Palestinian children.

Like the Kurds, the Assyrians, and others whose historical home is part of someone else's country, Palestinians are dispersed as "visitors" throughout the Arab world and beyond; or they are concentrated in refugee camps in the states bordering Israel or in towns, villages, or camps within the West Bank and Gaza Strip seized and occupied by Israel during the 1967 war.

While Palestinian children and youth have lived with and been part of communal conflict—often violent conflict—for four decades, since December 1987 they have lived with an intensification of that conflict—expressed in the movement known as "the Intifada" ("throwing off" in Arabic). Children and youth are active participants in this struggle, which pits them against the Israeli army and police. If our visits in Cambodia taught us about the importance of belief systems in human regeneration, the time we spent with Palestinian children and youth during the Intifada deepened our understanding of ideology as a double-edged sword: it strengthens day-to-day coping but in the long run may sabotage conflict resolution.

In 1988, in a village near the city of Hebron in the West Bank, we interviewed a twelve-year-old Palestinian boy involved in the uprising. As we approached the town, we found him ready to attack the Israeli forces with a handful of rocks. Around his head was the traditional Palestinian head-dress (*kafiyah*), wrapped so that only his eyes were showing (to prevent identification). Once he discovered that our guides were reliable, and that we were not with the military or the secret police, he was willing to be interviewed. While we talked, villagers down the road prepared for a confrontation with the soldiers who were reported to be waiting nearby (and who had entered the village the day before in force).

This boy dramatizes the role of children and youth in the Palestinian uprising, and the nature of ideology as a double-edged sword. His sixteen-year-old brother had already been taken away to prison for opposing the Israeli army and police. His father stood nearby and expressed pride in what his sons were doing. When we asked the boy what he wanted to be when he grows up, his answer was this: "I want to be free in my homeland or I want to be dead." Ideology gives him the sense of "meaning" he needs to continue to struggle, *and* it increases the likelihood that he will be exposed to danger.

Palestinian children and youth are imbued with ideology. The drawings they made in response to our requests for pictures of what their life is like almost invariably featured Palestinian flags, often in ingenious ways—for example, the flag as the window of a house, the flag worked into clothing, or the flag attached to a balloon. A systematic content analysis of a collection of such drawings documents the pervasiveness of nationalism and struggle as defining characteristics of the way Palestinian children and youth identify themselves. Indeed, when asked to draw a picture of "where you live and what it's like to live there," a few children and youth simply covered the entire paper with a picture of the flag.

Some of the Jewish Israeli children living in West Bank settlements approached the task in a similar manner. For example, one Jewish child simply drew a map of "Greater Israel" (an enlarged Israel including all the land from the Mediterranean to the Jordan River) and wrote on it, "Israel is for the Israelis"). When posed with the same task, a group of "gifted" ten-year-old Israeli children in Haifa responded with a wide variety of images. Some reflected concern with an outbreak of automobile accidents and suicide attempts by local children, but many reflected political concerns. We almost never see such drawings in the urban war zone at home, where children don't have much political conscious-ness about their situation. Like their parents, like most Amer-icans, they regard "politics" mainly as simple partisan con-flicts, in which neither party offers a dramatically ideological interpretation of events and situations.

In her studies of Palestinian families, Punamaki (1987) has identified ideology as an important psychological resource. She found that mothers who were committed nationalists artic-ulated a clear ideological interpretation of the struggle of their lives and were able to serve as resources for their children. Ideology made them strong, and their children could lean on that strength. We observed this display of strength firsthand in "fanatic" mothers who were caring for young children in impoverished refugee camps besieged by Israeli security forces.

On the Israeli side, a study by Pines (1989) suggests that Israelis who have a right-wing rigid Zionist ideology find the Intifada less stressful than those on the left, who see the conflict with more empathy. The former respond with "justifiable rage" to the Intifada; the latter are profoundly troubled by the conflict between their image of themselves and their society as "humanistic" and the reality of the oppres-sion they represent in the West Bank and Gaza Strip.

Some Israelis and Palestinians have the courage to be open to the complexity and ambiguity of their conflict. They struggle intellectually to find an approach that acknowledges the political rights and claims, as well as the human rights and dignity, of both groups. But the forces arrayed against those who appreciate the complexity are often intimidating.

Children and youth *can* show some of the same com-plexity in their sociopolitical thinking. For example, in his study of the life of children living amidst political crisis, Coles (1986) found that children and youth, when interviewed in depth and over an extended period of time concerning their views, often provided a surprisingly sophisticated political-moral analysis. Simplistic questionnaires seldom reveal this sophistication.

Dehumanizing and extreme ideology flourishes in the absence of humanizing relationships in which social categories are personalized. Forming such relationships requires sympathy and connection and dialogue. Palestinian children's contact with Jewish Israelis is generally confined to soldiers, police, bosses, and aggressive settlers. Israeli children often regard Palestinians either as an abstract threat or as the "other" (Grossman, 1988). When pressed about whether they would like to meet Israeli children, many Palestinian children whom we interviewed were evasive and apprehensive. Their pictures of "where the Israelis live and what it is like to live there" revealed an idyllic landscape with birds flying and the sun shining (something that rarely appeared in their pictures of life for Palestinians). What is more, the younger children often expressed admiration at the "superhuman" qualities of the Israeli soldiers, who in winter stand in the cold for hours on end (and have thermal jackets unknown to the children), who get hot coffee all day from the amazing machines in their vehicles, and who in other ways display a technological superiority that seems almost miraculous to some children.

An analysis of the dreams of 643 eleven- to thirteen-year-old Israeli and Palestinian children, conducted before the Intifada began, reinforces this point (Bilu, 1988). This research reveals that Israeli and Palestinian children often dream about the conflict between their two peoples. In these dreams, children confront stereotypical images of "the other": Arabs as "terrorists"; Israelis as "Jewish oppressors." Most of these dreams involve violent and aggressive confrontations "and often end in death."

The children most affected by all this are those for whom the Intifada invokes moral dilemmas—most notably, the children whose families openly discuss the conflict posed by the pitting of national security concerns against ethical imperatives. In a classroom of ten-year-olds that we visited in Haifa, the teacher reported that the children engaged in political discussions at home; they came from politically "aware" families. When asked to draw pictures of "where you live and what it is like to live there," most of the children drew what might be called political cartoons reflecting their profound involvement with the Intifada as a moral and political issue. Their emerging identity was clearly bound up in resolving what the conflict meant for them personally and politically. Though they were estranged practically from Palestinian children, they had received a strong dose of hypothetical empathy and sympathy at home.

These Israeli children, like the articulate children whom Coles learned from in his study of children's political lives, have a strong need to "process" their experience (in a way that parallels their Palestinian counterparts "on the front lines" of the conflict). Because they live in a democratic society and in democratic families, many Israeli children experience this necessary processing. The prospects for Palestinian children are less sanguine in this regard. On the whole, they live in much more authoritarian families, attend authoritarian schools, and are faced with an authoritarian political climate (derived in part from living under conditions of occupation, in which they have no political rights and in which loyalty to the struggle is equated with loyalty to the organizers of the uprising).

Many people hope that these children's ability to process their experiences can be increased via a democratization of family, school, and community, achieved through the Intifada. The characteristic commitment of Palestinians to education is a crucial resource in this regard. But as the Intifada ground on through the late 1980s and into the 1990s, many observers saw a hardening, associated with the failure to achieve a political solution, the accumulation of trauma, and the concomitant rise of religious fundamentalism and fanaticism that promoted a simplistic and dehumanizing ideology. Rigid ideology helps adults stand up to the stress of political conflict and daily threat. But it also heightens and prolongs that conflict, particularly in the thoughts and feelings of the next generation. Herein lies the dilemma.

In the inner-city war zone, we find some parallels to this ideological problem. The conflict between Israelis and Palestinians is primarily political (although religion and ethnicity are its foundation). Northern Ireland has its mix of religion and social class. America has race—and its social-class connections. The urban war zones in America are primarily African-American and Hispanic. The origins, interpretation, and response to the problems of community violence are bound up in racism and discrimination.

As Gilligan (1991a) has persuasively argued, shame, diminished self-esteem, and negative identity play a crucial role in generating violence. Racism and economic inequality are engines of violence and hostility. Without a compelling ideology to counter the psychological effects of inferior social position (the rage, shame, low self-esteem, and negative identity), only violence and destructiveness will give any sense of satisfaction. We often look in vain in the American war zone for such a compelling ideology, although perhaps there are glimmers in the Black Muslims and (formerly) in the Black Panthers.

The ideology of the Intifada in its first two years was very much one of limiting the weapons of resistance (and was about 80 percent nonviolent, according to observers who analyzed tactics). Acts of defiance and solidarity prevailed. When we analyzed the dreams of Palestinian children early in the Intifada, we found that themes of mutual support and solidarity were the dominant images. Morale was high; cooperation reigned supreme. However, as years have passed with no clear political progress, the ideology of the Intifada has suffered. More and more, there are intragroup conflicts. In 1990, for example, Palestinians killed nearly as many fellow Palestinians (for "disloyalty" and "collaboration") as were killed by the Israelis. These acts must be frightening and demoralizing for children. Perhaps the situation we observe in American inner-city war zones is what happens when ideological struggle fails (as it did in the post-1960s in American race and class relations). Perhaps turning on itself is the next step for an oppressed community once the struggle against "the other" stops.

Chicago: Community Deterioration and the Rise of Gang Warfare

Inner-city neighborhoods in the United States have undergone a dramatic transformation during the past twenty-five years. There has been a steady increase in the number of parents and their young children living in poverty. Teenage pregnancies, out-of-wedlock births, and female-headed households have escalated. Unemployment and welfare dependency have reached new heights; violent crime and serious drug abuse are rampant. Furthermore, an exodus of the middle and working class from these neighborhoods has taken place, leaving behind an underclass living in concentrated areas of poverty (Wilson, 1987). With this exodus has come the virtual collapse of many mainstream community institutions, worsening poverty, and a corresponding cycle of violence. Drug abuse is both cause and effect of this deterioration.

During the 1970s, a large number of inner-city families were in a permanent state of poverty. In 1972, 44 percent of urban white families and 74 percent of urban black families were unable to achieve a yearly income of $11,446, the level established by the Bureau of Labor Statistics for a "moderately decent" urban life (Silverstein and Krate, 1975). During the 1970s, the underclass grew dramatically. The number of people living in concentrated poverty areas (areas where 40 percent or more of the inhabitants earned less than the poverty level) increased 60 percent. For the large industrial cities, the rate was even more staggering. For example, the population of New York City living in extreme poverty grew by 269 percent; in Chicago and Detroit, by 162 percent; and in Indianapolis, by 150 percent (Wacquant and Wilson, 1989).

Another major change during the 1970s was a dramatic increase in the number of female-headed families in the inner city. In 1977, 60 percent of inner-city families were headed by women, compared to only 30 percent in 1960. The lack of prosocial male role models in these families is a major challenge to the community.

By 1980, the number of people living in poverty in the nation's fifty largest cities increased by 12 percent. Furthermore, the number of individuals living in poverty areas (census tracts with a poverty rate of at least 20 percent) increased by more than 20 percent from 1970 to 1980, despite a 5 percent reduction in the total population in these cities during this period. At the same time, the total population decreased by 9 percent in the extreme poverty areas of the five largest cities, whereas the white poor population increased by 24 percent and the black poor population increased by 164 percent. These increases put tremendous pressure on what community institutions remain.

Wilson (1987) suggests that the exodus of the middle- and working-class population from inner-city neighborhoods has created an underclass that has become increasingly isolated from mainstream patterns and norms of behavior. Inner-city neighborhoods are now predominantly black; 39 percent of all poor blacks live in such neighborhoods, compared to only 7 percent of all poor whites.

These inner-city communities are ecologically and economically very different from what they were twenty-five years ago. The residents of highly concentrated poverty neighborhoods in the 1980s had little contact with people who have stable work histories, and little interaction with friends or relatives in the more stable areas of the city. In the past, these families and institutions provided mainstream role models for impoverished children, youth, and parents. Their presence helped maintain traditional values of education, work, and family stability, and buffered some of the worst effects of poverty (Musick, 1987). Thus, in the 1980s, an important social buffer that could reduce the devastating impact of prolonged and increasing joblessness that plagued inner-city neighborhoods was missing.

The number of female-headed families continued to increase in the 1980s. By 1984, 73 percent of all female householders resided in metropolitan areas. In 1983, in Chicago housing projects, 92 percent of the resident families were headed by females. Female-headed families are not only more likely to live in poverty; they are also more likely than two-parent families to be persistently poor. Some 61 percent of those who were persistently poor over a ten-year period were in female-headed families. In 1978, 51 percent of the whites and 85 percent of the blacks in inner-city, female-headed families had an income of less than $4,000.

All these conditions together conspire to transform poor neighborhoods into urban war zones. The lack of legitimate opportunities, the rage, the violent models offered by the mass media, the marginal role of positive role models, the ready availability of lethal weapons, and the emergence of a powerful and lucrative drug economy—all conspire to make the problem of community violence grow. Families struggle and crumble. Crime escalates. Gang violence and drug trafficking escalate.

Although there is a generally upward trend around the country, the highest rates of violent crime are found in the communities of the underclass. In 1983, more than half of the murders and aggravated assaults in Chicago occurred in poverty-stricken areas. As noted in Chapter One, in Chicago's Robert Taylor Homes housing project (which comprises .5 percent of the city's total population), 11 percent of the city's murders, 9 percent of its rapes, and 10 percent of its aggravated assaults were committed—rates twenty times what they are for the rest of the city.

According to the U.S. Federal Bureau of Investigation (FBI), 2,000 minors were murdered in the United States in 1988. This figure is 50 percent higher than in 1985. Among black males and females aged fifteen to thirty-four years, homicide is the leading cause of death (Secretary's Task Force on Black and Minority Health, 1985). Murders in New York, Chicago, Los Angeles, Detroit, and Philadelphia accounted for a significant percent of this increase (Chilton, 1987). Additionally, bystander shootings more than tripled in New York, Los Angeles, Washington, D.C., and Boston between 1985 and 1988 (Sherman, 1990).

But even these figures hide something important. Medical technology has improved so much in the last twenty years that many of those who are now wounded in incidents of violence would have died had they experienced the same injuries in the 1970s. This is important to remember when we compare the rates of serious assault in the mid 1970s and 1990 and note that these rates have increased by 400 percent in American cities such as Chicago.

The escalating level of violence associated with drugs, gangs, and the proliferation of lethal weapons is a growing concern for American society. Whole communities are being described as war zones, where gangs instill fear to control the daily lives of residents. For example, a gang in Chicago imposed an early-evening curfew on everyone who lived in a particular public housing building, threatening violators with being shot (Caseso and Blau, 1989).

Although gangs are not a new phenomenon on the urban scene, most observers note that they are fundamentally different today. There are more of them, and they exist in more communities. Gangs have increased adult involvement, are more organized, are active in more illegal enterprises, and use more lethal weapons.

In the first six months of 1990, Chicago police seized 8,289 weapons (Blau, June 10, 1990). According to the state attorney's office, "Thirty years ago, gangs had zip guns—single shot, homemade, primitive. Now these gangbangers have 'sprayers' and automatic weapons that simulate the weapons of armies" (Blau, June 10, 1990). Media confront us regularly with reports entitled "Growing Up Scared" (Zinsmeister, 1990), "Can the Children Be Saved?" (Morgenthau, 1989), and "Child in Wrong Place at Wrong Time Is Blinded" (Blau, April 6, 1990). These reports underscore the pervasiveness of the problem and point to inner-city environments as particularly dangerous.

In the United States, public housing developments are home to approximately 1.6 million children (National Association of Housing Redevelopment Officials, 1989). These environments include some of the most impoverished, highest-crime communities in the country. What is more, the violence and stress in these communities exist inside families as well as outside. Rates of child abuse and neglect are as disproportionately high as are the measures of crime and violence in the community at large.

In Chicago, over 100,000 children live in public housing (administered by the Chicago Housing Authority). A recent analysis of Chicago's police data (Reardon, 1988) revealed that the officially reported rate of violent crime victimization for residents of the housing developments was 50 percent higher than for the city as a whole (34 per 1,000 versus 23 per 1,000). These figures mean that children in public housing projects are twice as likely to be exposed as other children are. (Since the overall 23 per 1,000 victimization rate includes the housing projects, the overall figure is substantially inflated.) Similarly, the New York City Department of Planning and Health report the homicide rate in the Harlem community at 71.3 per 100,000 people; in contrast, the rate for New York City as a whole is 27.5 per 100,000 (Terry, 1990).

The rate at which children are exposed to violent crime in these neighborhoods is alarming. A visitor to a Washington, D.C., eighth-grade classroom asked the children, "How many of you know somebody who's been killed?" Fourteen of the nineteen children in the class raised their hands. When the children were asked how the killings had happened, they responded, "Shot, stabbed, shot, shot, drugs, shot" (Zinsmeister, 1990). A survey by Chicago's Community Mental Health Council found that nearly 40 percent of 1,000 Chicago high school and elementary school students had witnessed a shooting, more than 33 percent had seen a stabbing, and 25 percent had seen a murder (Kotulak, 1990). Los Angeles County law enforcement officials estimate that 10–20 percent of the annual 2,000 homicides are witnessed by dependent children (Pynoos and Eth, 1985).

In Baltimore, 168 teens (80 percent female, 20 percent male) seeking routine medical services at an inner-city health clinic were screened for exposure to violence. The teens indicated that they had been the victim of serious violence an average of one and a half times each. Twenty percent of the teens reported that their experiences constituted a serious threat to their lives (Zinsmeister, 1990).

In a sample of elementary school children in a violence-plagued area of Chicago, 26 percent had seen someone shot, and 29 percent had witnessed a stabbing (Bell, 1991). In New Orleans, over 70 percent of the children in one study had seen weapons being used, and nearly 40 percent had seen dead bodies (Osofsky and others, 1991). Another study of Chicago middle and high school students found that 35 percent had seen a stabbing, 39 percent had seen a shooting, and 24 percent had seen a killing. For 47 percent of these studies, the victims were friends, family members, classmates, or neighbors. Additionally, 46 percent of these students reported that they had personally experienced at least òne violent crime, ranging from having a weapon pulled on them to being robbed, raped, shot, or stabbed. What are the consequences of such experiences for children's development? Answering that question comes next.

Conclusion: Four Themes from the War Zones

As we review our field notes from the war zones we have visited, and the research and clinical reports available to us, we are drawn to four themes:

- The resilience of children subjected to chronic brutality, *if* they have sufficient psychological and social resources.
- The enormous challenges faced by adults who care for children in situations of community violence.
- Alternative concepts of revenge that flow from the cultural and spiritual resources of children and adults caught up in situations of community violence.
- Ideology as a motivator of children during times of crisis and stress.

We will return to these themes in Chapter Eleven. But first we must make clear why we believe it makes sense to approach inner-city children as we would the children of Mozambique, Cambodia, Palestine, and Israel.

3

The Developmental Toll
of Inner-City Life

Kotlowitz (1991, p. 46) describes the following unspeakably horrible act of violence on a fifteen-year-old boy known as Bird Leg:

> A single pistol shot echoed from below. Twenty-four-year-old Willie Elliott had stepped from between two parked cars and aimed a pistol at Bird Leg. Only two feet away, the boy froze like a deer caught in the glare of a car's headlights. The bullet tore through Bird Leg's chest. He clutched his wound and ran through the breezeway of one high-rise. "Man, I've been shot!" he hollered in disbelief. He appeared to be heading for the safety of a busy street. He didn't make it. The bullet, which had hit him at point-blank range, entered his chest and spiraled through his body like an out-of-control drill, lacerating his heart, lungs, spleen, and stomach. Bird Leg, struggling to breathe, collapsed beneath an old cottonwood, where, cooled by its shade, he died.

The horror does not end with the death of this child; the violence affected other children as well. A group of children saw the shooting as they played on the playground nearby. Bird Leg's thirteen-year-old sister heard the shot in their apartment above. His cousin Rickey saw him die under the cottonwood tree. And for Bird Leg's friend Pharaoh, who lives in the same public housing complex, Bird Leg's death followed a series of shooting incidents he had witnessed during a violent summer in the projects. By the end of the summer, Pharaoh's mother reported that he had developed a severe stutter, trembled at loud noises, and had become fearful and withdrawn.

Children growing up amidst violence are at risk for developmental harm. For some of these children, the consequences are devastating: developmental impairment, emotional trauma, fear, violence, and hatred (Goleman, 1986; Rosenblatt, 1983). In documenting the effects of chronic violence on children living in Beirut during the 1982 war, Macksoud, Dyregrov, and Raudain (in press) concluded that the repetitive nature of the traumas these children experienced had an additive effect. Not only the types of traumas but also the number of traumas and the extent of exposure were crucial factors related to developmental outcomes.

In dangerous inner-city neighborhoods, violence is an almost daily occurrence. Experience with chronic violence does not inoculate children against negative outcomes; instead, it tends to increase their susceptibility to developmental harm and post-traumatic stress (Pynoos and Nader, 1988). Moreover, the longer the violence continues, the fewer sources of support children have to draw on. All this is compounded in inner-city environments by poverty, family disruption, and community disintegration.

For many children, violent experiences are powerful stressors that increase their vulnerability to developmental harm. These stressors tax these children's resources, endanger their well-being, pose new limitations and new threats to the current situation, and present new obstacles to learning. Some experiences are so utterly devastating that some children become traumatized as a result (this extreme type of reaction is discussed in Chapter Four). But what of the less dramatic but equally important consequences to a child's overall development?

Factors Determining Responses to Violence

How children respond to the challenge of growing up in environments made dangerous because of community violence depends on their own inner resources and on the social context established for them by their caregivers and the community. An ecological framework helps us understand these risks through a model of development as the interaction of an active, purposeful, and adaptive organism with a set of nested social systems (Bronfenbrenner, 1979).

An ecological perspective on developmental outcomes looks to two kinds of interaction. The first is the interplay of the child as a biological organism with the immediate social environment of his family as a set of processes, events, and relationships. The second is the interplay of social systems in the child's social environment. Thus, one must look both *inward* to the day-to-day interaction of the child in the family and *outward* to the forces that shape the child's social contexts. It is the coupling of family risk with community violence that makes the inner city such an insidious environment for children.

The child's social context includes family, friends, neighborhood, church, and school, as well as less immediate forces—such as laws, institutions, and values—that constitute the social geography and climate of the child's physical environment. The child's experiences can be viewed as subsystems within systems within larger systems—"as a set of nested structures, each inside the next, like a set of Russian dolls" (Bronfenbrenner, 1979, p. 22). In seeking to understand children's development, we must always be prepared to examine the next level of systems beyond and within (Garbarino and Associates, 1992).

Escalona (1982) provided an early demonstration of the developmental consequences of the interaction of child characteristics and the social and economic forces constituting the child's environment. She found that environmental insufficiencies (low-income parents, ethnic-minority status, residence in deteriorated housing) adversely affected premature infants more than full-term babies. The combination of low birthweight *and* social and economic deprivation accounted for high rates of subsequent cognitive and social impairment among the premature children. Favorable environments provided effective buffers to constitutional vulnerabilities, and favorable constitutional factors helped protect children from environmental risks. Subsequent longitudinal and epidemiological research has documented that economic stress, lack of social integration, an impaired or immature parent, and a difficult infant can interact, placing the child in jeopardy of serious damage. As has now become evident, "community violence" must also be added into that equation.

An ecological approach is also able to highlight situations in which the actions of people with whom the child has no direct contact significantly affect the child's development. Children living in dangerous neighborhoods may not come in direct contact with the perpetrators of violence; yet they are affected when they can't go outside to play for fear of shooting incidents, or when they must sleep on the floor to be out of the range of random bullets coming through the windows of their home.

Age and Developmental Level

Age and developmental level are important factors in children's responses to community violence. As we noted in Chapter One, individuals who experienced an initial trauma before the age of eleven were three times more likely than those who experienced their first trauma as teens to develop psychiatric symptoms (Davidson and Smith, 1990).

Preschool children tend to exhibit passive reactions and regressive symptoms—such as enuresis, decreased verbalizations, and clinging behavior—as responses to experiences with violence. Head Start teachers report that, after a series of shooting incidents, some children have exhibited extreme clinging behavior, including being afraid to leave their teacher to engage in play activities.

School-age children display more aggression as well as more inhibition, and they develop somatic complaints, cognitive distortions, and learning difficulties as a result of experiences with violence. Nine-year-old Alonzo was entering his building in a Chicago public housing project when he was hit by a bullet meant for someone else. Since he was shot, he has become forgetful, has trouble concentrating, and has difficulty learning in school.

Adolescent responses to community violence are characterized by a "premature entrance into adulthood or a premature closure on identity formation" (Pynoos and Eth, 1985). They may also engage in acting-out and self-destructive behaviors, such as substance abuse, delinquent behavior, promiscuity, life-threatening reenactments, and other aggressive acts.

Multiple Risks

Permanent developmental damage is more likely to occur when multiple risks are present in a child's environment (Rutter, 1987). The risk of developmental harm from exposure to violence increases when that exposure is compounded by other biological, cultural, psychological, and social risks. Thus, developmental harm tends to occur when a child is subjected to cumulative stress from a variety of stressors throughout the course of development. A single risk, according to Rutter, is no more likely to cause developmental harm than no risk at all; when risk factors accumulate, however, the chance of damaging consequences increases dramatically, and when four or more risk factors occur, the risk increases tenfold.

For inner-city children, the risks of living in the midst of violence are compounded by the risks of living in poverty—risks that include malnutrition, unsuitable housing, inferior medical care, inadequate schools, family disruption, family violence, and maladaptive child-rearing patterns. Because many of the developmental consequences endemic to inner cities—for instance, poor school achievement, aggression, and self-destructive behaviors—occur almost routinely, the contribution of community violence to developmental harm is often overlooked (Bell, 1991).

Children who are poor have the odds stacked against them developmentally. Poor mothers are more likely than mothers with adequate incomes to have low-birthweight

infants, to be unmarried, and to begin child rearing as teenagers, experiencing all the attendant stresses and difficulties
(Kamerman and Kahn, 1988). The increasing geographical
concentration of poor families is relevant to child development because it represents a decline in the proportionate availability of individuals who are "free from drain," persons who
would be caretakers and sources of support for children (Collins and Pancoast, 1976). One result of the chronic stress of
living in poverty-stricken and violence-ridden communities
is that parents cannot meet the needs of their children.
Depressed, overwhelmed, and their own needs unmet, such
parents are not able to care for and nurture their children
adequately (Halpern, 1990c). Depressed or overwhelmed parents, who are already isolated socially because they live in
dangerous areas, may further isolate themselves and their children by not leaving their homes to seek out supportive networks for themselves and their children (Belle, 1982).

　　While mothers experiencing such stress are frequently
aware of the limited effectiveness of their child-rearing strategies, they often feel that they lack the physical and psychological energy to behave differently (Jeffers, 1967). In such
dire circumstances, parents easily transmit feelings of powerlessness, futility, and hopelessness to their children (Halpern,
1990c).

　　Poor mothers are also more likely to be abusive than
are nonpoor mothers (Gelles and Straus, 1988). Informal
reports from child abuse and mental health clinics suggest
that the children of adolescent mothers in poverty areas are
frequent victims of child abuse (Osofsky and others, 1991). In
Chicago, for example, the rate of child abuse in the poorest
neighborhoods of the city is four times the rate in more affluent areas (Garbarino and Kostelny, 1992a). A significant number of children in these communities experience violence both
inside and outside their homes. These children, who are
already vulnerable from experiencing familial violence and
are then exposed to community violence, are at increased risk
of developing behavioral and personality problems (Osofsky
and others, 1991).

What is more, the chronic and pervasive quality of poverty in the inner city makes it likely that risk factors will accumulate over time in the lives of children and their families, fostering an intergenerational transmission of poverty and its attendant risk factors and poor outcomes (Schorr and Schorr, 1988).

Parent-Child Relationship

One risk of living in such stressful environments is that mothers (or other primary caretakers) will be too depressed or overwhelmed to form a secure attachment relationship with their child. The lack of a secure, stable parent-infant attachment during the child's early life can result in maladaptive behavior patterns as well as psychological disorders later in life.

A relationship characterized by continuous threat of separation and lack of warmth and support jeopardizes the child's normal development. A child who has been unable to form a positive early relationship with a supportive adult may develop such characteristics as lack of guilt, withdrawal, mistrust, and an inability to form intimate, lasting relationships later in life (Bronfenbrenner, 1979). Rutter (1987) has found a relationship between insecure attachment and behavioral and emotional problems in school-age children. Furthermore, a mother under stress can transmit her stress to her infant through such subtle cues as her facial expression, the tone of her voice, and her posture (Anthony and Cohler, 1987).

Research on the mother-child relationship during war illuminates the mother-child relationship during community violence. According to these studies, the level of emotional upset displayed by the child's parents, not the war situation itself, was the most important factor in predicting the child's response to the war. In a study of mothers and children living in Beirut during the 1982 war, Bryce, Walker, Ghorayeb, and Kanj (1989) found that the mother's perception of the war's negative effects on her children was a stronger predictor of psychological disturbance in her children than the number of war-related experiences.

A study of Central and South American refugees found

that mothers who were depressed because of the disappearance or death of their husbands during the war could not protect their children from psychological disturbances (Allodi, 1980). In Belfast, during intense communal fighting, children who displayed the most psychological disturbances tended to have a parent who had exhibited psychological disturbances as a result of the violence. This finding suggests that the children were modeling their parent's distress or that the parent's distress impaired his or her ability to mediate for the child (Lyons, 1971).

Another example of communicated anxiety comes from a study by Ziv and Israel (1973), who compared Israeli children in settlements that experienced shelling and Israeli children in kibbutzim that did not experience shelling. While they found no relationship between a child's being shelled and a child's anxiety, they did find a correlation between a *parent's* level of anxiety and the child's anxiety.

Most children are able to cope with dangerous environments and maintain reservoirs of resilience as long as parents are not pushed beyond their "stress absorption capacity" (Garbarino, 1989b). Once that point is exceeded, however, the development of young children deteriorates rapidly and markedly. Reservoirs of resilience become depleted, day-to-day care breaks down, and rates of exploitation and victimization increase. Parental buffering can be very powerful. And yet some experiences are so overwhelming and traumatic for children that parents cannot mediate the trauma for them, as we shall see in Chapter Four, where we examine post-traumatic stress disorder as a clinical phenomenon.

Children's Responses to Chronic Violence

Children experiencing acute traumatic events lose interest in the world and try to avoid anything that reminds them of the event; they also manifest feelings of estrangement, constriction in affect and cognition, memory impairment, phobias, and impairment in performing daily activities (Osofsky and others, 1991). But what of children who experience situations of violence continually? Osofsky and her associates found a significant relationship between exposure to chronic community violence and stress reactions in a sample of elementary school children living in a high-violence community. Mothers noted changes in their children's behavior, reporting that the children became sad, angry, aggressive, and uncaring after exposure to continuous violence. Additionally, children also displayed sleep disturbances, disruptions in peer relationships, and erratic behaviors.

According to these researchers, the following outcomes can be expected in children living in chronic community violence:

1. Difficulty in concentrating, because of lack of sleep and intrusive imagery.
2. Memory impairment, because of avoidance or intrusive thoughts.
3. Anxious attachment with their mothers, being fearful of leaving them or of sleeping alone.
4. Aggressive play including imitating behaviors they have seen, as well as showing a desperate effort to protect themselves.
5. Tough actions to hide their fears.
6. Uncaring behavior resulting from experiencing hurt and loss.
7. Severe constriction in activities, exploration, and thinking, for fear of reexperiencing the traumatic event.

Psychological Disorders

Convergent research studies suggest that the more children are exposed to violent events, the more psychological disorders they manifest. In her study of Palestinian children living under Israeli military occupation, Punamaki (1987) found extreme anxiety, phobic reactions, aggressiveness, withdrawal, and enuresis in children exposed to violence as a result of the military occupation.

Terr (1990) noted that brief traumas have only limited

effects on children but that repeated traumas may lead to anger, despair, and severe psychic numbing, which in turn result in major personality changes. While some effects may become evident immediately, others may not appear until years later in the child's life. For example, children exposed to the stress of extreme violence under the Pol Pot regime in Cambodia did not reveal mental health disturbances until years after their horrendous experiences were over (Kinzie and others, 1986).

Regressive behavior—such as thumb sucking and loss of bowel and bladder control—has been noted by mothers of children living amid urban violence. Research in the area of "learned helplessness" suggests that the feeling of helplessness may be a realistic response under conditions where the stressors are unpredictable and uncontrollable (Peterson, Luborsky, and Seligman, 1983). Children living in constant danger also may display fear and anxiety in a variety of ways, ranging from excessive clinging behavior to continuous crying. For example, some children living in Kuwait under the Iraqi occupation in 1990–1991 cried incessantly and were unable to eat (Garbarino, 1991). Bell (1991) found that children's fear increased as the number of experiences of violence increased.

Another reaction to long-term violence may be denial and numbing. Terr (1990) found that children begin to deny reality when "disasters" continually occur. When extreme situations become unpredictable, these "battle-weary" children attempt to block out "disasters" by ignoring reality. Consider the case of seven-year-old Pharoah:

> As Lafayette and Pharoah played on the jungle gym in midafternoon, shooting broke out. A young girl jumping rope crumpled to the ground. Lafayette ran into his building, dragging behind him one of the triplets. Pharoah, then seven, panicked. He ran blindly until he bumped into one of the huge green trash containers that dot the landscape. He pulled himself up and over,

landing in a foot of garbage. Porkchop followed.
For half an hour, the two huddled in the foul-
smelling meat scraps and empty pizza boxes, waiting for the shooting to stop, arguing about when
they should make a break for their respective
homes. Finally, the shooting subsided and they
climbed out, smelling like dirty dishes. They
watched as paramedics attended to the girl, who
luckily had been shot only in the leg. Her frightened mother, who had fainted, was being revived.
It was at that point that Pharoah first told his
mother, "I didn't wanna know what was happening" [Kotlowitz, 1991, p. 40].

Just as Pharoah wanted to block out frightening reality,
children become desensitized when they must continually
guard against thinking about the reality of their situation
(Terr, 1990).

Grief and Loss Reactions

For children living amidst community violence, one of the
most devastating consequences is the death of a primary caretaker or other significant person. Studies of children whose
parents have died report that these children experience emotional reactions of hopelessness and despair, along with suicidal thoughts. Rutter (1987) also noted a number of studies
linking parental loss in childhood to later psychiatric disorders, especially depression. For example, Cambodian children who witnessed the violent death of a parent experienced
recurrent night terrors and somatic complaints (Kinzie and
others, 1986). But any parental loss can be traumatic.

Refugee children separated from their parents during
war exhibited severely disturbed behavior, with long-term
effects of anxiety and hostility dominating their development
(Ressler, Boothby, and Steinbock, 1988). Although these children remained physically healthy, their social behavior and
emotional health rapidly deteriorated. They showed develop-

mental retardation, destructiveness, and an inability to play. Children separated from their mothers before the age of three were retarded by age five in the cognitive and social domains (Langmeir and Matejcek, 1963).

When the death of a primary caretaker or other family member occurs, the child may not be able to resolve his or her grief. Young children especially have confusing and frightening grief and loss reactions (Osofsky and others, 1991). The necessary reminiscing about the person may be avoided, because such thoughts trigger anxiety regarding the event, especially when that event occurred in a violent way. Grieving may also be complicated or impeded by the child's rage and desire to punish the perpetrator (Pynoos and Eth, 1985).

Impaired Intellectual Development and School Problems

Children exposed to chronic community violence often develop problems related to school performance and intellectual development. Gardner (1971) found that children who had experienced violent events during their first six years of life could not learn in a normal classroom situation—possibly because the recurring threats in these children's environment constituted a "lifelong expectation of aggression, violence, exclusion, derogation, and defeat" for them. In order to deal with their fears of violence, the children employed defenses that were manifested as learning disabilities in the classroom. For poor children who already risk academic failure for cultural reasons, community violence is often scholastically the last straw.

Because children experiencing such violence in their environment believe that aggression is an expected style of life among people, their first impulse in any interpersonal relationship is either to respond with the same type of hostility or else to withdraw into a fantasy world to avoid such expressions, having learned that they consistently lead to punishment (Gardner, 1971). These defenses used in dealing with one's fears of violence may be labeled a learning disability. For example, the child withdraws into fantasy, which is often concerned with aggression or violent action; the child is over-active, with an aggressive, violent, or disruptive goal; the child actively seeks distractions; or the child actively stimu-lates peers to engage in distracting events (Gardner, 1971).

In a study of California children who experienced life-threatening situations or who witnessed injuries to others, Pynoos and Nader (1988) found that the majority of these children had serious difficulties in concentration and per-formance in school. They concluded that these difficulties occurred because the intrusion of thoughts related to violent experiences distracted the children and prevented them from concentrating on schoolwork. Other consequences related to exposure to violence are the development of forgetting as a defensive mechanism to help control spontaneous reminders of the event and fatigue from sleepless nights.

In a public school in a high-crime area in Chicago, chil-dren who had witnessed the murder of a close family member displayed behavior problems and poor academic performance (Dyson, 1989), and their collective behavior was disruptive to the entire class. Homeless children in New York living in a dangerous welfare hotel (where prostitutes and drug addicts also live and where violence and crime are rampant) were found to be deeply troubled, withdrawn, and hyperactive. Their angry, aggressive behavior often caused disruption in class, and they were ostracized by other students (Kozol, 1988).

A special issue is the association of school with danger in the minds of children. For example, as a result of the chronic violence in the Israeli-occupied territories, Palestinian parents say that school has become a locus of fear for many children as soldiers harass them on their way to and from school. Palestinian mothers report that their young children cry and scream in fear of going to school.

The same concerns apply to inner cities where children have to pass through gang territory on their way to school. Gang members harass children, extorting their lunch money and coercing them into joining their gang. Sometimes children must run for their lives when shooting breaks out. Tamara, an eleven-year-old girl living in one of Chicago's housing projects, was caught in the cross fire of two rival gangs on her way from school to the after-school program she attends a few blocks away. She described having to "hit the ground" and then scramble on her hands and knees to the safety of the after-school program. Although she escaped physical injury, she says she was "pretty scared." Unfortunately, this is not an isolated incident in Tamara's life in a dangerous community.

Schools themselves are no longer safe places for children. As the *Chicago Tribune* proclaimed, "Once Safe Havens, Schools Now in Line of Fire" (Wiltz and Johnson, 1991). In Chicago, as in inner cities across the nation, schools cannot protect children from harm.

> Students . . . talk of South Side classrooms where file cabinets are pushed against windows to block stray bullets and North Side schools where warring gangbangers sometimes throw each other down stairwells. In one schoolyard, prepubescent boys pause in their basketball game to debate if a booming noise is the sound of a backfiring car or gunfire, and a freshman girl describes a city bus rushing off in the middle of a drive-by shooting, leaving her scared and stranded on the corner across from her high school. . . . At Woodson North School . . . a teenage gunman invaded the grammar school's crowded gym and fired 12 bullets, turning the refuge into a shooting gallery [Wiltz and Johnson, 1991, p. 19].

During the 1990–91 school year in Chicago, police made 9,822 arrests on or near *school grounds*. Of these arrests, 9 were for murder; 153 for carrying guns; 244 for aggravated battery; 28 for aggravated criminal sexual assault; 51 for burglary; 218 for robbery; 11 for felony theft; 15 for auto theft; and 380 for carrying knives and other weapons (Wiltz and Johnson, 1991).

Luis, because he intervened in a fight outside his school, had a contract put on his life by gang members. He later developed excruciating pains in his stomach and was taken to a hospital emergency room by his family, who thought he was having an appendicitis attack. The doctor's diagnosis: "Completely scared." Luis was able to take his case to the board of education and was allowed to transfer to a safer school. As Luis said, "It's safe. . . . You go there to study. You don't worry about getting shot in school" (Wiltz and Johnson, 1991). Unfortunately, Luis's case is the exception, not the rule. Thousands of youth attend unsafe schools, but very few are able to transfer to safe schools.

Truncated Moral Development

Kotlowitz (1991, p. 73) describes the effect of Bird Leg's death on his cousin Rickey:

> Rickey had heard the lone gunshot and watched his cousin stumble and fall by the cottonwood and die. He then sat on a nearby bench and wept. For the next two days, Rickey stayed in his apartment, refusing to talk or eat. He vomited throughout the weekend. His mother worried that he was ill, but by Monday he started eating again and venturing back outside. The anger about Bird Leg's death, though, didn't subside; instead, it simmered and stewed within him. It was two years before he talked to anyone about watching his cousin die. "I felt like I lost a big brother. . . . Seem like I don't care no more. I don't feel sorry for people no more 'cause when they killed Bird Leg, the peoples who shot him mustn't of felt sorry for him. . . . Now, it seems like if I get in a fight, I don't care if I kill or something. I don't even care. It be like, we be fighting, we be fighting other people. Someone be telling me in my mind, "Hurt him, just don't worry about it."

As Rickey's response demonstrates, another risk of living with chronic violence is "truncated" moral development (Fields, 1987). Boys are particularly vulnerable to this consequence of living "at risk," as they are to most other risks (Werner, 1990). To develop advanced moral reasoning, children need to engage in issue-focused discussions and social interactions. These discussions, guided by parents or classroom teachers, enable children to use their reasoning capacities to formulate ideas about values and principles. If children are to advance, their moral teachers must lead them toward higher-order thinking by presenting positions that are one stage above the child's characteristic mode of responding to social events as moral issues. The child recognizes the difference, values the person demonstrating it, and seeks to emulate. For example, in some high-crime urban areas children may have the opportunity to make some money by carrying drugs. If children feel they should not do this because they may be caught and punished, an adult can illuminate other morally advanced reasons for avoiding such activities—for instance, the fact that drugs harm people. When all this happens in the context of a nurturant affective system, such as a supportive family, the result is ever-advancing moral development—the development of a principled ethic of caring (Gilligan, 1982). However, when both family and community block moral development, truncated moral development is the result.

Pathological Adaptation to Violence

For some children, repeated exposure to violence can produce what appears to be a functional adaptation to the violence but is actually a pathological effect. Although the adaptation is successful in the short run, it may prove detrimental in the long run. For example, some children develop a sense of "futurelessness," or a profound fatalism about their lives (Terr, 1990). They come to expect more violence directed at them and death at an early age (Bell, 1991; Osofsky, 1991). Participation in dangerous, violent activities loses its threatening character and takes on a special psychology for them, since they expect to die no matter what they do. Having a big funeral is the most that some children can look forward to. A journalist writing an article on families living in the Henry Horner housing project in Chicago interviewed one of its ten-year-old residents: "I asked Lafeyette what he wanted to be. He responded, 'If I grow up, I'd like to be a bus driver.' *If,* not *when* (Kotlowitz, 1991, p. X). This ten-year-old child could not count on making it to adulthood. Of course, thinking this way can well become a self-fulfilling prophecy, as kids flaunt danger and often pay the price in lethal encounters with bullets, knives, cars, and drugs.

In their attempts to cope with community violence, parents may engage in child-rearing strategies that impede their children's normal development. Inner-city parents and children growing up in poverty are exposed to different demands and experience more risks than economically privileged parents (Ogbu, 1985; Halpern, 1990a). Thus, child-rearing strategies that are adaptive for coping in these inner-city environments are quite different from child-rearing strategies practiced in mainstream society. Inner-city parents who are trying to help their children cope may demand unquestioning obedience while discouraging curiosity. What drives these child-rearing techniques? Survival. "Don't go outside to play; you might get shot." "Don't report to the police; you might get killed in revenge." "Don't talk to anyone; you might be victimized." Parents regard these strictures as necessary in the dangerous environments in which they live, since errors in judgment can have life-threatening consequences (Silverstein and Krate, 1975; Halpern, 1990c). But, while protecting her child from immediate danger, a mother who doesn't allow her child to play outside because she fears there may be shooting incidents is denying the child a chance to engage in social and athletic play. The restricted opportunities of the urban war zone can make for restricted development.

Similarly, parents of children in high-crime environments may manifest their fear by imposing an extremely restrictive and punitive style of discipline (including physical assault) on their children. In their efforts to protect the children from the influence of negative forces, such as gangs, in the neighborhood, these parents often employ harsh, restrictive measures to suppress the self-assertive tendencies of children—especially boys—so they won't get into trouble with teachers or police. Unfortunately, this approach is likely to heighten aggression on the child's part and endorse an acceptance of violence as the modus operandi for social control (Scheinfeld, 1983). The ironic result is greater susceptibility to the negative forces abroad in the community.

Parents may cope with danger by adopting a world view or persona that is dysfunctional in "normal" situations. Some adaptations to chronic danger, such as emotional withdrawal, may be socially adaptive in the short run but become a danger to the next generation when their children become parents and adopt similar maladaptive parenting procedures. This phenomenon has been observed in studies of families of Holocaust survivors (Danieli, 1985) and in the parenting patterns of adults who were abused as children (Egeland and Farber, 1984; Gelles and Lancaster, 1987). In all these examples, the parental adaptation is well intentioned and may appear to be practically sensible, but its side effects may be detrimental in the long run.

Identification with the Aggressor

One way to feel safer is to align yourself with those who frighten you, and children's early adaptation to violence may lead to a process of identification with the aggressor. They model themselves and their behavior on those powerful, aggressive individuals and groups in their environment who caused the danger in the first place. Joining a gang (whose activities include assault, robbery, rape, and even murder) is one type of identification with the aggressor. Children who experience recurring violence will themselves feed into the cycle of violence, victimization, and fear (Bell, 1991). In violent communities, a gun is a status symbol, and using it gets positive reinforcement.

Exposure to violence also increases the likelihood of the child's engaging in future violence and other antisocial acts. Observing violence may lead to an acquisition of that behavior if the child identifies with the perpetrator and the outcome of the violence (Bandura, 1973). Six-year-old Christopher's brother was shot to death at age fifteen in inner-city Detroit. When asked what he would like if he could have anything in the whole world, Christopher did not need time to think. Without hesitation he responded, "A gun . . . so I could blow the person's head off who killed my brother" (Marin, 1989).

Conclusion

Child development is in part about the child's emergent social maps. Cognitive competence and emotional orientation define and shape those maps in response to environmental experience. The "normal" development of children suffers when the conditions of life are themselves "abnormal." We consider life in the urban war zone to be abnormal. That is why the urban war zone is a hotbed of antisocial and self-destructive behavior. These developmental consequences are not the only result of living amidst poverty and community violence. Beyond these developmental outcomes are a set of clinical outcomes, which find their focal point in the diagnosis of post-traumatic stress disorder.

4

Clinical Outcomes:
Post-Traumatic Stress Disorder

Dana attends a community-based preschool center in a high-crime inner-city neighborhood in Chicago. Six months ago, Dana was in her house with her family when a car raced past the front porch, its driver spraying bullets through the open car windows—a "drive-by shooting." Her twenty-year-old cousin was shot in the head. He staggered into the house and fell several feet from three-and-a-half-year-old Dana, bleeding profusely.

Four-year-old Dana draws pictures of herself and her family in sessions with her counselor. One drawing appears to be a view from above, looking down on some people lying on the floor.

Dana's counselor asks her to tell stories, using picture cards. One card shows a child on the floor, with another child standing over her. Dana responds: "Somebody shot her. Go in the house and leave her. Hair is coming out, or is it blood? No, hair is black, blood is red. Blood is coming out her head. She's dead." When Dana looks at a picture of adults standing in a room, she sees a funeral. She tells the counselor, "Somebody died. The mama died, the daddy died, little boy got no daddy, a cousin died. Probably got hit by a car or shot. Shot the little cousin in the park. They don't want to hear that noise. The son is crying because the little cousin died going across the street. They shot him. The boys came across and shot him. Shot the big boys. He don't want them to ever come back."

When Dana looks at a picture of a man and a woman arguing, she tells the counselor, "The daddy had to put on clothes. They pick up the baby. They put shoes on feet so glass don't cut them, don't bleed, like when someone shot them."

Dana's Drawing: Family Lying on Floor.

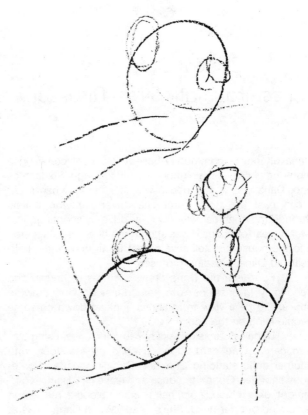

A traumatic event, such as the shooting witnessed by Dana, is marked by two key elements: surprise and piercing intensity (Terr, 1985). It is "an event that is outside the range of usual human experience and that would be markedly distressing to almost anyone" (American Psychiatric Association, 1987, pp. 250-251). A significant aspect of trauma is the life-threatening nature of the event. The routine and predictable negative events of childhood—such as divorce and illness, distressing as they may be—are not ordinarily within the framework of "traumatic events."

Traumatic events include natural disasters (floods, tornadoes, and earthquakes), accidental man-made disasters (car accidents and fires with serious injuries), and intentional man-made disasters (kidnappings, murders, and war). Research indicates that intentional man-made disasters are particularly harmful: "The disorder is apparently more severe and longer-lasting when the stressor is of human design" (American Psychiatric Association, 1987, pp. 250–251).

Accidents of nature and mistakes in judgment can often be justified by one's religious beliefs and understanding of human error. However, acts of intentional evil, person against person, undermine a child's basic trust in humanity and may create a lifelong inability to develop close, trusting relationships. A young girl whose brother, mother, and grandfather had been killed in three incidents of violence in Northern Ireland was asked whether the deaths had altered her belief in God. She answered: "Not in God. In man" (Rosenblatt, 1983).

Individuals are affected by the nature of a disaster and whether they are exposed directly or indirectly to it. They can be primary victims or (like the Irish girl) secondary victims of a traumatic event, and thus of psychological trauma. When a crime is perpetrated against a child, the child is a primary victim. When a child has witnessed an event in which someone else is victimized, or has a relationship with the primary victim, that child is a secondary victim (Society for Traumatic Stress Studies, 1990). Victimization occurs when there is "serious threat to one's life or physical integrity; serious threat or harm to one's children, spouse, or other close relatives and friends; sudden destruction of one's home or community; or seeing another person who has recently been or is being seriously injured or killed as the result of an accident or physical violence" (Ochberg, 1988).

Although individual responses to traumatic events differ from child to child—depending on a number of factors, such as age, prior experience, and available support systems—the consistency of core response is clear: heightened anxiety, generalized fears, and loss of self-esteem (van der Kolk, 1987). Some children respond with withdrawal, avoidance, and denial. While these responses are self-protective, the isolation removes them from full participation in the world of family, school,

and community, and thus exacerbates their emotional problems. Others respond with self-blame and feelings of helplessness. Still other children develop angry, hostile behavior
patterns and act out their aggression.

In 1976, twenty-six schoolchildren (five to fourteen
years old) were kidnapped in Chowchilla, California. The
kidnapped children were at different developmental stages
when the event occurred. However, all the children showed
some degree of collapse in their earlier developmental achievement. Furthermore, four years after the event, all the children
suffered symptoms of what is now known as post-traumatic
stress disorder (Terr, 1983).

The age and developmental level of the child will affect
that child's response to traumatic events (see Chapter Three).
As illustrated earlier, children are more vulnerable to trauma
when the trauma occurred prior to age eleven than when the
trauma occurred as teenagers (Davidson and Smith, 1990).
When trauma occurs in early childhood, the risk of severing
significant bonds of trust is high.

Even in studies of adults, age is a significant factor in
persistent symptoms of PTSD among Vietnam veterans (van
der Kolk, 1987). Men who experienced combat at 18.3 years
developed subsequent feelings of helplessness or loss of inner
control more often and with greater intensity than did the
members of the control group, whose average age was 21.5
years. Furthermore, given a great deal of time and support to
heal from the traumas, the younger men had more difficulty
healing and moving on.

Children's previous experience with trauma and victimization may lead to their subsequent participation as a
victimizer. In his study of 1,035 high school and middle
school students, Bell (1991) found that 73.7 percent had witnessed robberies, shootings, and stabbings, and 46.5 percent
had been primary victims of violence. When asked to report
on their participation in crime, 22.7 percent said they had
committed a violent act. The analysis of this data suggests a
significant correlation between children who are primary victims and their subsequent involvement as perpetrators of
crime (Uehara, Chalmers, Jenkins, and Shakoor, forthcoming).

Research on Trauma: Historical Background

Terrifying life events, especially when experienced in early childhood, have been linked to mental health problems in adulthood ever since Sigmund Freud developed his psychoanalytic theory in the 1920s. However, as Freud's adult patients recalled early childhood events, he found these recollections colored by childhood fantasies and misperceptions of what occurred. Subsequently, Freud focused his attention on the adult's *interpretation* of childhood events (van der Kolk, 1987). At this juncture, the impact of the external event lost significance in psychoanalytic theory (Terr, 1990; van der Kolk, 1987).

However, Freud's original definition of psychological trauma underscores the importance of exposure to outside events that are sudden, intense, and overwhelming to the individual. He described the sense of utter helplessness that floods an individual when faced with a traumatic event (Freud, 1926). Caught off guard and unable to control the effects of trauma by means of defensive techniques and resources, the individual is rendered powerless. If that individual's belief in inner control is not restored, "learned helplessness" or a sense of victimization may become a habitual response (Seligman, 1975; Horowitz, 1976).

Until the last fifteen years, there has been little research on the effect of external trauma or environmental trauma on children. Additionally, the effect of chronic versus acute trauma has received little attention. Ironically, it seems that more research has been conducted on the effect of television violence on children than on the effect of real violence on children.

In 1943, Anna Freud and Dorothy Burlingham documented their observations of World War II orphans at the Hampstead Nursery in England. They were interested in learning about the effect of children's wartime experiences on development. During the London blitz, these children had been exposed to bombing, house demolitions, and loss of family members. Freud and Burlingham focused on whether the children had experienced these events in the presence of or separated from a familiar adult. They concluded that children who remained in the care of their parent or a parent surrogate were able to cope with exposure to frightening events. The adult's presence seemed to buffer children's stress.

However, this pioneering study leaves unexplored the status of the adult's mental health and the subsequent inter-generational effect of trauma on children. This relationship becomes clear in studies of survivors of the Nazi Holocaust and their children. Parenting styles adopted in response to the parents' concentration camp experiences affected their children, who were not directly exposed to the events (Danieli, 1985). For example, family members who defended against further trauma by psychologically closing out the world were devoid of emotion and expressed low tolerance for stimulation (Danieli, 1988). Children found their parents unable or unwilling to respond to their emotional needs, and often searched for role models outside the family. Bowlby (1984) suggests that a parent's low frustration tolerance, low self-esteem, and diminished capacity for empathy elicit insecure and anxious attachments.

The Hampstead study contains detailed descriptions of the children's post-trauma play or reenactment of the traumatic event. For example, Bertie's father was working in London when an air raid began. He was killed. Bertie's mother was so distraught after the event that she suffered a complete mental breakdown and was institutionalized. Bertie was "orphaned" at age four and brought to the nursery. In the months that followed, Bertie played a bombing game for hours at a time. He would build paper houses, bomb them, and set them up again. Bertie, as well as other children at Hampstead, worked to gain control of these events through storytelling. Bertie rescued his father in the stories he told the nursery workers (Freud and Burlingham, 1943).

In 1956, a group of children were attending an after-noon movie in Vicksburg, Mississippi, when a tornado struck the theater. Researchers distributed questionnaires to a sample of schoolchildren, of whom some had been in the theater when the disaster occurred, and they interviewed their parents. The study concentrated on such factors as the children's proximity to the event, whether they or someone they knew had been physically injured, and the psychological stability of the children's parents. The researchers concluded, as did Freud and Burlingham, that children who had stable caregivers were more likely to recover psychologically from the event (Bloch, Silber, and Perry, 1956).

Research on survivors of Hiroshima (Lifton, 1967), German concentration camp survivors (Eitenger, 1980; Krystal, 1968; Danieli, 1988), and Vietnam War veterans (Wilson, 1988b; Lifton, 1973; Figley, 1985) provided ground-breaking work on the short- and long-term effects of exposure to traumatic events and the psychological sequelae of the experience. This research began to describe the phenomena of psychic numbing and survivor guilt.

In 1972, following a flash flood that wiped out the community of Buffalo Creek, West Virginia, children were interviewed systematically by researchers for the first time. Through art, stories, and projective tests, preschool children voiced their perception of the disastrous event and demonstrated their altered feelings of self-confidence and control in response to the event (Newman, 1976). From this study comes a first-draft sketch of post-traumatic stress disorder (PTSD) in children: numbing, play reenacting traumatic events, diminished future orientation, guilt, fear, lowered self-esteem, and impaired intimate relationships.

Terr's (1979) study of twenty-six children kidnapped on their school bus in Chowchilla, California, clearly documents children's reaction to an acute traumatic event. Ranging in age from five to fourteen years at the time of the incident, the children were driven in the bus by their captors for eleven hours and then "buried alive" in a previously buried truck trailer for sixteen hours. The event was unique: the children were rescued, no child had suffered serious physical injury, and the children had been completely separated from their parents. Terr's analysis focused on the psychological effect of the event on children. She observed reenactment of the kidnapping in dreams and in play. During the first year following the kidnapping, the children's dreams contained the exact details of the event, a flashback of the kidnapping. Four years after the kidnapping, the children continued to have repetitive dreams that were more "obscure" in the sense that the details were more deeply disguised (Terr, 1983). For example, Leslie was seven years old when she was kidnapped. She had repeated dreams that she was in a hole with an alligator that bit her (Terr, 1985).

The children of Chowchilla played a game called "kidnap tag" on their school playground. Some of the children played modified versions of the game at home with their siblings (Terr, 1983). During the four years following the event, Terr found that eighteen of the twenty-six kidnapped children played repetitively. For the nontraumatized siblings and playmates who were drawn into their play—and, thus, into the details of the kidnapping event—the possibility of a contagion effect was strong.

The research documents cognitive and perceptual changes, time distortions, and heightened sense of vulnerability among many of the children (Terr, 1985). Four years after the event, 92 percent of the kidnapped children "suffered from severe philosophical pessimism, the sense that their futures would be greatly limited" (Terr, 1983, p. 1547).

Studies of children who live in situations of armed conflict and children who live in dangerous high-crime neighborhoods in the United States are beginning to document the effect of exposure to traumatic environmental events of a chronic nature (Garbarino, Kostelny, and Dubrow, 1991; Eth and Pynoos, 1985; Osofsky and others, 1991). Preliminary findings indicate that children do not become accustomed to environmental violence. Chronic environmental assault on children's physical and psychological well-being may instead diminish their capacity to cope with the stresses. Beyond the "normal" developmental consequences discussed in Chapter Three, they can and do suffer from PTSD as a clinical syndrome.

Children's Responses to Traumatic Events

Research on children who live in dangerous environments establishes a global picture of the kinds of traumatic events to which children are exposed in their day-to-day lives. In Chapter Two, we reviewed some of these events as they occur in the war zones of Mozambique, the Middle East, and Cambodia and in the war zones of American cities. We return now to the urban war zone.

Urica was only six years old when two men broke into her family's apartment, high on cocaine and seeking drug money. In the struggle that ensued, she witnessed the stabbing murder of her mother and her younger sister. The child witness was stabbed forty-eight times and left for dead by her assailants. But she was "playing dead," a performance that saved her life. Her thirteen-year-old cousin discovered the scene the following morning and reported it to relatives.

Stressful life events affect children's learning and psychological well-being. Young children have little control over the environmental danger that surrounds them in the inner-city neighborhood—on the streets and in their homes. However, to survive, they cope. But coping often reveals the depth of the challenge they face. Some children seek resolution by reenacting or drawing pictures of what happened. Other children attempt to forget experiences with violent events. Many seem to be jumpy and hypervigilant. Teachers and parents observe these and other changes in children's behavior and in children's ability to learn in response to traumatic events. Together, these symptoms often meet the criteria to assess the presence of PTSD: reexperiencing the event, numbing of responsiveness, and symptoms of increased arousal (American Psychiatric Association, 1987).

Reexperiencing the Event

Victims reexperience traumatic events in dreams, flashbacks, intrusive memories, and distress when confronted with reminders of the event. In young children, themes or aspects of the trauma are likely to be expressed in repetitive dreams and play.

Children's dreams reflect both cognitive processing of information and an effort to contend with life's issues. Thus, their dreams may provide an indication of what is "left over" from conscious, overt processing during awake time (Garbarino, 1989b). Dreams, like play, indicate the child's attempts to gain control of events.

Bertie's repetitive house-bombing play was described earlier. Following his father's death, Bertie also had dreams about his father, in which he fantasized his father's safe return home. In one dream, Bertie's father hid in an impenetrable bomb shelter during the attack and later returned home by train. In another dream, Bertie was able to locate his father and rescue him before the fatal bomb exploded (Freud and Burlingham, 1943).

The children of Chowchilla had repetitive dreams of the kidnapping incident. These dreams often expressed the child's core fear, his or her greatest concern about the event. For example, one eleven-year-old girl had been terrified that she would be asphyxiated while "buried" in the school bus. She dreamed repeatedly that one of the other children in the bus smothered to death. Her dream contained the element of her deepest fear, and she assigned the tragedy to another child (Terr, 1990).

Children in Kuwait, when interviewed immediately after the end of the Gulf War (Garbarino, 1991), revealed numerous repetitive dreams in which they reexperienced their worst experiences—for example, seeing a father abducted or witnessing the execution of a neighbor. A ten-year-old girl who had seen the body of an executed neighbor dumped in their alley said she had the same dream at least once a week. In this dream, the neighbor is sitting on her head and asking, "Why don't you cover me up?"

The themes of children's play are not random (Waelder, 1976). They come from within and represent the children's innermost thoughts and concerns. It is in play that children deal with complex psychological difficulties (Bettelheim, 1987). Repetition of traumatic themes in children's play is an indication that they are reexperiencing thoughts about disturbing events (Terr, 1981).

In a training session with elementary school teachers serving a large public housing project in Chicago, a teacher reported the following incident. During an assigned writing task, she discovered one first grader and a friend crawling under the tables with homemade guns in hand. She asked the "leader" what he was doing. He said, "Oh, it's OK, teacher, we won't kill anyone. We're just robbing a house." The child's preschool teacher was also present at this session. She told the group that this boy's family home had indeed been robbed while he was a student in her class. She observed that following the incident "he became quiet and moody."

For some children, their play, art, storytelling, and social interactions are laced with themes of the event shortly after it occurs.

> Sheila was almost five years old when she was shot in the hand. The circumstances of the shooting remain unclear to the staff of her local preschool program. She was with family members when it happened, and they were preparing lunch at the time she was shot. In the months following the incident, Sheila's teachers have observed her playing "shooting" during lunchtime. She "shoots" at the other children, saying, "Pow, pow, pow!" When asked, Sheila acknowledges, "Yeah, we're playing shoot guns."
>
> Sheila's preschool program employs a full-time counselor to work with children and families on issues of violence prevention and intervention. As part of her work, the counselor asks children to draw pictures of themselves and their families. When Sheila is asked to draw a picture of herself, she draws detached fingers and hands with large fingers. Another self-portrait is a large, empty rectangle. There are no eyes or other facial features.
>
> In play sessions with the counselor, Sheila is the doctor and her counselor is the patient. The patient has been shot in the finger. Sheila sets up an IV and takes the patient's blood pressure; in the process, she applies strong pressure to the patient's finger. When the patient protests, Sheila responds by increasing the pressure, saying, "Be quiet; lay still; you be quiet." Sheila tightens her grip on the patient's finger and continues, "You're big enough to hurt yourself; you're big enough to take this." Sheila stops the procedure and opens the playroom door. Looking down the hallway, she beckons for help, saying to an imaginary assistant, "You hold her still; let me work on this finger." Sheila uses a probing action to "work" on the finger. It is terrifying to watch this. Imagine how it feels to the child to live it?

Sheila's Drawing: Picture of Fingers.

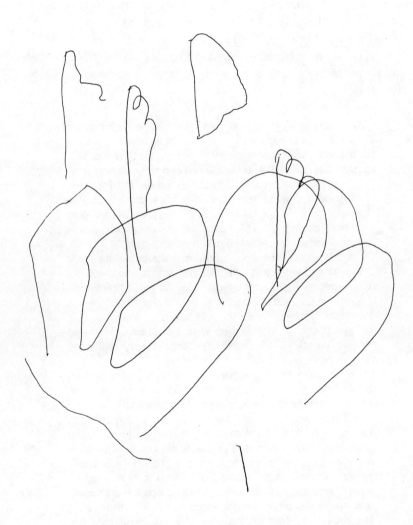

Sheila's Self-Portrait.

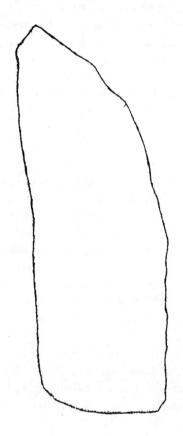

Numbing of Responsiveness

To cope with a dangerous environment, adults and children wear psychological blinders as protective gear. The process of desensitization includes both conscious and unconscious attempts to avoid all thoughts, activities, and symbols of traumatic events, and thus avoid being flooded with the powerful feelings that come back when the traumatic events return. Though desensitization is a powerful survival strategy, the danger is in spillover to other domains of social, emotional, and cognitive development—a generalized numbing of feelings.

Urica's grandmother worries about her granddaughter's response to witnessing the murder of her mother and sister. She reports that Urica says she is not afraid of anything. Perhaps the little girl is revealing her efforts to avoid reexperiencing the fear she felt during the attack by a generic refusal to feel fear. Additionally, her grandmother is concerned about the community's response to environmental violence. To illustrate her concern, she cited an incident of shooting at her public housing development. When the shooting started, "Nobody ran; nobody moved" (Marin, 1989).

Children's responses can become numb at an early age. One mother observed the reactions of her youngest daughter to shooting incidents in her inner-city neighborhood. When she was two years old, the girl was very frightened when she heard gunfire outside. She would throw herself on the floor of the apartment, saying, "Mama, I'm scared." The little girl developed bad headaches and stomachaches in the wake of these incidents. Her mother took her to the doctor, and he confirmed that the physical symptoms were related to psychological stress felt by this child. He prescribed Tylenol. After a year, the mother noted that her daughter became "immune" to the shooting. The child's headaches and stomachaches ended, and when shooting started, she told her mother matter of factly, "Well, Mama, we have to get down on the floor."

The numbing response is also evident in victims' loss of interest in daily activities, and in their inability to remember or accurately recall aspects of the trauma. In Cambodia, for instance, adult victims of the Pol Pot regime reported that they could not remember the sequence of events following their capture and expulsion from Phnom Penh. Additionally, they still struggle when faced with tasks of memory and concentration (Garbarino, Kostelny, and Dubrow, 1991).

Another element of the numbing response is to avoid all thoughts and activities that remind the victim of the event. For example, a social worker at a local community service agency recalled the day she and her young children found a dead man on the stairs leading to their high-rise public housing building. The man had been murdered. For years after the event, they all avoided the staircase. By choosing an alternative route to the apartment, they tried to avoid being reminded of the incident.

Some children react to trauma by losing previously acquired developmental skills. They may begin to wet the bed or suck their thumbs; they also may acquire speech problems and have difficulty learning in school. Urica's grandmother notes that her granddaughter began to suck her thumb after her mother and sister were murdered and she was stabbed. Her grades have slipped. Alonzo's mother reports that since he was shot, he bites his nails and he stutters. The children of inner-city war zones frequently exhibit these regressive and "nervous" symptoms (Kotlowitz, 1991).

Symptoms of Increased Arousal

Paradoxically, and perhaps as a signal of what the children are trying to avoid, along with numbness comes increased arousal. Sleep disturbances, irritability, inability to concentrate, angry outbursts, hypervigilance, and exaggerated startle response are observed among children who are exposed to traumatic events. These reactions indicate the intensity of the child's struggle to master the forces set loose in his or her inner experience by the confrontation with outer trauma.

Dyson (1989), a social worker with Chicago public schools, found that exposure to violence had a significant impact on learning and behavior problems in school. In her case studies of six children with learning and behavior problems from one classroom on Chicago's South Side, she found that all these children had a close family member who was murdered. Their experiences affected their individual ability to function in the classroom, and their collective behavior was disruptive to the entire classroom. Urica is aggressive toward her classmates. Alonzo has trouble concentrating, is forgetful, and has difficulty learning in school (Marin, 1989).

Victims of trauma have difficulty modulating anxiety as well as aggression (van der Kolk, 1987). Increased anxiety and generalized fears are common among traumatized children when they are confronted with reminders of frightening events. Some children generalize fears. A three-year-old plane-crash survivor screamed as he entered his therapist's office; the psychiatrist was wearing the same colors as the flight attendants' uniforms from the doomed plane (Terr, 1990). In another related example, the director of a Palestinian kindergarten in the Gaza Strip recalled that all the children began to scream when United Nations staff entered the school building in uniform. Teachers had to calm the children before the staff could distribute the toys they had brought.

Mothers report exaggerated startle reactions in their children. For example, five months before we interviewed her, one mother and her five-year-old daughter were caught in a gang shoot-out while crossing the playground. When we interviewed her, the mother reported, "The child still shakes when she hears a balloon break or some other loud noise." Furthermore, other parents and teachers who live and work in gang-infested neighborhoods report that they and the children startle at the sound of cars backfiring or garbage dumpster lids crashing. They attribute this reaction to the numerous shooting incidents they have encountered.

Spiritual and Philosophical
Consequences of PTSD

How does trauma affect the underlying structures of knowledge and self? What are the spiritual and philosophical symptoms of PTSD?

Loss of Security

In any society, children are the most powerless, and therefore the most vulnerable. Infants attach themselves psychologically to the adult caretaker (usually a parent), who provides a safe base from which they can explore their surroundings. Within this relationship, children construct a personal representation of how life proceeds, developing a pattern of expectation for the future (Bowlby, 1973). Additionally, these early bonds help children understand themselves in relation to other people. Within this framework, children develop confidence that others will be helpful to them and, therefore, that they should cooperate with others. PTSD challenges and often displaces these positive social maps.

What has been destroyed for children traumatized by community violence is the idea of home, school, and community as a safe place. The traditional bastions of safety have been destroyed by external violence, which dictates every aspect of children's lives. Danger replaces safety as the organizing principle. "The essence of psychological trauma is the loss of faith that there is order and continuity in life. Trauma occurs when one loses the sense of having a safe place to retreat within or outside oneself to deal with frightening emotions or experiences" (van der Kolk, 1987, p. 31).

Following exposure to a traumatic event, the process of psychological healing is best aided by restoring a sense of safety and trust to the individual (van der Kolk, 1987). This is extremely difficult in the high-crime neighborhoods of inner-city America. Decisions about where children can play, which walking route to take to school, and what time to come in and out of the house are dictated by the possibility of encountering a dangerous situation. During interviews with mothers who live in high-rise public housing apartments, they listed the strategies they have developed to protect their children from the violent environment. The rules reflect a preoccupation with safety. Children are instructed: stay away from windows; go in the closet, the bathtub, or get on the floor when shooting starts; and stay together all the time (Dubrow and Garbarino, 1989). The impetus for developing these rules is clear. One mother stopped the interview to point out the bullet hole in her kitchen wall next to the refrigerator. The bullet had come in through her apartment window while she was inside with her children. It was a stray bullet, but she emphasized, "Bullets don't have eyes."

For preschool children, the local community-based classroom is not always a safe place. When shooting started outside the classroom window one afternoon, a Head Start teacher reported that she instructed all twenty of the children to get down on the floor. A similar incident occurred when rival gang members staged a shoot-out within range of the local public elementary school. Using the public-address system, the school's principal instructed all staff and children to leave their classrooms and "take cover" in the building's main hallway until the shooting stopped. Even playgrounds, a primary source of fun and neighborhood socializing for most of America's children, are dangerous places in some inner-city communities. Frequent gang shoot-outs across the playground in one Chicago public housing development prompted mothers to teach their children a playground survival skill: Get under the slide when the shooting starts.

Recall seven-year-old Pharaoh. He was playing with his older brother when he was caught in the middle of gang cross fire. He dove for the safety of a nearby garbage dumpster, but a young girl who was jumping rope on the playground was shot in the leg. Pharaoh and his brother hid until the shooting stopped and emerged physically unharmed. When Pharaoh arrived home, he told his mother, "I didn't wanna know what was happening" (Kotlowitz, 1991). This motivation can have clinical ramifications.

General Sense of Loss

Loss is a significant theme in cases of trauma. One single event can result in any of the following losses: loss of people (death), loss of physical capacity (injury to people), loss of protection (including loss of adult's ability to protect a child and loss of safe places to retreat), loss of control, loss of hope (diminished future orientation). A child who witnesses the murder of a parent may experience all these losses at once. With loss comes damage, trouble, disadvantage, and deprivation. Loss increases the child's sense of vulnerability and can cause chronic sadness and depression (Pynoos and Nader, 1988).

Children who live in the urban war zone experience the death and injury of relatives, friends, and neighbors more often than children who live in safer neighborhoods (Dubrow and Garbarino, 1989; Zinsmeister, 1990; Terry, 1990). In Detroit, six-year-old Chris lost his best friend when his fifteen-year-old brother was shot and killed. In Chicago, Robert Jones was struck in the head by a bullet fired by one gang member at his rival. The injury caused Robert to lose his ability to see.

Rochelle and her sister Leah live together in a two-flat apartment building in a high-crime West Side neighborhood in Chicago. They both became mothers when they were teenagers and are now in their early twenties. Rochelle is married and has a four-year-old daughter, Ann. Leah lives with her boyfriend and her four-year-old son, Chris. Both children attend the same local Head Start program.

Seven months ago, the children's uncle, fifteen-year-old Tai, was found shot. He died in what appeared to be a suicide. However, family members suspect that the death was in fact murder: a gang-ordered killing meant to appear to be suicide. The family members recognize that questions about the cause of death keep the incident "alive," and they continue to feel dissatisfied about the investigation. At least one young family member, a cousin, openly expresses his anger, saying that he will find out who killed Tai and seek revenge.

The incident occurred while the children were at school. Tai was rushed to a local trauma center, and the family was notified. Rochelle, who was pregnant, was at home, and Leah was attending a GED (high school equivalency) class in the same building as the Head Start program. The teachers reported that Leah, visibly upset, rushed to the classroom to get Chris, saying that something was wrong with Uncle Tai. Leah took Chris to the hospital, where he saw Tai lying on a gurney. Chris recalls that his mom was crying a lot. He remembers her telling him, "Tai is dead." When we asked Chris if he thinks about Tai, he responded, "Yes, I wanted to know when he was coming back."

Rochelle's daughter, Ann, was present when Leah took Chris out of the classroom, but she remained in school for the rest of the morning session. Ann's thirteen-year-old cousin arrived to pick her up. She told the teachers what happened. When Ann got home, she asked her mother what happened to Uncle Tai. Rochelle reports that she stayed calm and told Ann that Uncle Tai died and went to heaven.

After the event, Rochelle continued to take Ann to school every day. Chris's attendance became sporadic. His teachers report that he seems depressed. He became very quiet and sullen after Tai's death. Tai was both an uncle and a friend to Chris. He often picked Chris up from school. The teachers report that Chris appears to be waiting for Tai to pick him up at the end of the day.

During separate counseling sessions, Chris and Ann were asked, "What happens when someone dies?" Chris responded, "They go to the hospital. If they are still dead, they go to church. They are put in a casket. You come to the church to see them. Then they leave. The family is going to have to find him. The boy is going to have to find him. I look for Tai."

Ann said, "Go to heaven. They don't come back alive. They stay up with God. They get their wings from them. They [the family] feel mad, they cry a lot, very sad."

Chris and Ann's drawings are qualitatively different. Seven months after his uncle's death, Chris's self-portrait shows sadness and anger. By his own account, it is a "crying face," a picture of "how I looked when Tai died." There is a tear falling from one of Chris's eyes, and his prominent teeth fill his open mouth.

Chris's picture entitled "When I get scared" contains a figure that looks very much like a ghost. Following Tai's death, Chris's grandmother, Tai's mother (who lives in the first-floor apartment with Rochelle), sealed Tai's room and would not allow anyone to go into it. The family members report that strange things started to happen. The microwave oven and the radio would go on, and Tai's clothes were strewn across his room. They sensed a strong "presence."

When Chris was shown a picture of a child and a man, he said that the boy has "feelings about ghosts, wondering about the man, wondering about if he is a super boy turning into a monster, dreaming about ghosts in the house, having bad feelings about his mother."

Chris's Self-Portrait: "How I looked when Tai died."

Ann's Self-Portrait.

Chris's Drawing: "When I get scared."

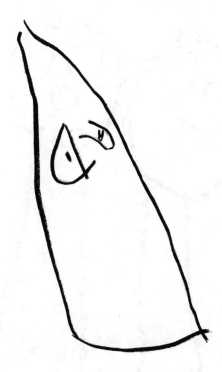

Ann drew a picture of "my family." She pointed to each figure saying, "This is Chris, this is Jennifer [new baby sister], and this is my mom."

Ann's Family.

Interviews with three Chicago inner-city school-age girls illustrate feelings of loss one year after exposure to trauma. Loss is a prominent theme in the discussion.

Elizabeth (age twelve), Nancy (age ten), and Kathy (age eight) attend a community-based after-school program near their home. Their mother was caught in the cross fire of two rival gang members as she walked on a busy Chicago street in the family's neighborhood with her sister-in-law.

None of the girls witnessed the event, but all three struggle with the losses it represents, including the loss of innocence. Six months after the incident took place, Elizabeth drew a picture entitled "Guy shooting my mom," and Kathy drew a picture of "dad bringing mom home from the hospital." Elizabeth's drawing weaves the event of her mother's shooting into the fabric of her everyday life. A family barbecue, playful running in the neighborhood, and swinging on the swings in the park surround the image that depicts a "guy shooting my mom." Kathy's picture recalls the important event of her mother's arrival home following hospitalization to treat the gunshot wound. In the drawing, mom has emerged from the family car wearing a prominent bandage on her neck, and Kathy and her sisters stand in line to greet her.

The oldest and youngest children seem to have processed and integrated the incident more fully than Nancy, who is the middle child. Her responses are a source of clinical concern. Her eyes well up with tears whenever she discusses it. She is aware of the emotions that are evoked around discussions before she has them, saying, "It makes me cry to think about it." We learned from Nancy that the family had been on a trip to Mexico to visit relatives during the Christmas holidays. Nancy chatted for a while; then she told us that they had dug up her grandfather's bones while she was there, and had put them in a church during a service. She said that her grandmother wanted this to be done and that it was traditional in Mexico.

Then she told us that she now has one cat but had previously had five dogs and nine cats. When we asked her what happened to the other animals, she said that her father said it was too many and got rid of them. While in Mexico, her uncle had killed a goat (to eat). She lamented, "I really liked that goat a lot!" She noted several times that either she or her grandmother cried about these things.

Nancy also talked about her mother's injury. She prefaced the conversation with the fact that she would probably cry. First, she relayed all the details, the facts as they did happen. Then she said her mother had died but had

Elizabeth's Drawing: "Guy shooting my mom."

Kathy's Drawing: Dad bringing mom home from the hospital.

come back (from the dead). When we asked her how she knew this, she said her mother had described the experience to her. She said her mother needed a new voice (it is slightly different than it was before the accident).

Kathy, the youngest, told us twice that her father lied to them about what happened to their mother. He was afraid to tell them what happened, so he told them that she had a bad headache and had to go to the hospital. She said, also twice, that Blanca, the school social worker, told them the truth.

When we asked the girls what should be done to the man who hurt their mother, all three responded that he should have done to him what he did to their mom or he should be killed. The spirit of vengeance is here, even among these sweet little girls.

Blurring of Distinctions Between "Friend" and "Enemy"

For children who live in Chicago's dangerous neighborhoods, the perpetrators of environmental violence are the gang members who plague the community. Children know that the business of the gangs is drugs and guns and power. But they also know that gang members are family members. The distinction between who is enemy and who is friend is often challenging. For a young child, the problem is finding a path to trust when "my uncle" is both the person who comes to my house and watches television with me on Sunday afternoon and the person who shot the neighbor last night in a gang confrontation.

When we asked Juan what was dangerous about his neighborhood, he quickly responded, "The man who does voodoo. He's from Cuba. I have to walk by his house on my way to school and to empty the garbage. He's always drunk. He curses at the kids. Guns are dangerous. My sister got shot in the head last year. The bullet went in her forehead and came out the top. My mother almost had a heart attack when they told her. I was there. She started to shake and cry. She fell on the floor. It took all of us to lift her from the floor. My sister was shot by mistake. They were shooting at my brother. If you want to come to my house to see my sister, she'll lift up her hair and show you where the bullet went in. She was lucky!"

Juan is twelve years old. He lives with his mother, stepfather, and three brothers and two sisters in a West Side neighborhood that is laced with gangs, drugs, and violent crime. Juan knows the inner workings of the gangs, because his two older brothers, seventeen and twenty years old, belong to a prominent local Chicago gang. His twenty-year-old brother is currently being held in detention while he waits for trial on breaking-and-entering charges. When asked about the circumstances of his brother's arrest, Juan explains that his brother was "framed." The details are complicated; but, according to Juan, the robbery was committed to get cocaine, and a gun was "planted" on his brother by his accomplices as he lay passed out (drunk) on "look-out" duty.

Juan's brother is his hero. He always has money, expensive cars (Mercedes and BMW), and girlfriends. However, the most important role his brother plays is that of protector. By Juan's accounts, his brother has shielded his family from an abusive father, who beat Juan's mother and tried to beat the children. On many occasions, Juan's brother physically stopped the father from hurting them. His brother also promises to take him and his family to Puerto Rico, where it is safe (safer than his current neighborhood).

Although Juan participates in a drug education program and says that he realizes the danger of drugs, he must deny this reality to maintain a positive image of his brother, who provides critical physical and emotional support. Children of gang families acknowledge the crimes of rival gang members but psychologically dismiss the infractions committed by members of their own families.

We asked Juan to recall the worst thing that ever happened to him. He told us that when he was eight years old, the day before his ninth birthday, he saw his two cousins get shot. He and his cousins were on their way home in the car. The teens were in the front seat of the car and Juan was in the back seat. The cousins had taken Juan with them to a party, where they had been drinking. On the way home, they decided to pull over and sleep off the alcohol to avoid a confrontation with their mother, who was waiting up for them. Juan, too, fell asleep on the back seat of the car. As he recalls, he suddenly woke up, and "A guy was holding a gun to Sammy's head and he pulled the trigger. Then he shot Manuel. There was blood. I don't know what happened. I got out of the car. I asked a man for help. He called the cops." Manuel is a paraplegic. Sammy did not survive his injuries. Juan was present when Sammy's mother was told that her son was dead. He remembers that she started to cry uncontrollably. Juan said, "she had a heart attack [literally]; how would you feel if your son was shot?"

There was no birthday party to mark Juan's ninth year. There was, however, a funeral for Sammy. According to Juan, the funeral was held in a rival gang's "hood," but the funeral home was filled with Sammy's gang. Juan said, "This made the folks [other gang factions] nervous!" A gang funeral has distinct characteristics. Juan explained that everyone except the family has to leave the sanctuary as gang members surround the coffin. They "throw" the gang sign in unison and say the gang prayer. Gang members place a banner over the body. Juan recalled the banner: "Rest in peace, Sammy." There was a certain pride in Juan as he remembered the unity and recognition of his cousin's death. He spoke of the strength of their numbers and their ability to frighten the rival gang members.

Michael, one of Juan's friends, expressed a similar view when asked what was dangerous in the neighborhood. He said, "Gangs are good for kids. They protect their hood." We asked him to tell us how this protection works. He responded, "If a stranger comes into the hood with a gun, they'll [hood gang] take it away." We asked, "How careful do you have to be?" Michael said, "Real careful. You have to keep one eye open all the time [he demonstrated by winking]. The best thing to do is don't join a gang. I'm going to finish high school, get a college degree, a master's, and be a fireman."

Juan has dreams about Sammy. He dreams that his cousin is alive and that he is coming back. Juan recalled an especially vivid dream from which he awoke. He went to his mother and told her about it. She lit candles in the house and made cocoa, and they stayed up all night waiting for Sammy.

Juan has been encouraged to think about Sammy's "return." He said his pastor told him, "When a kid sees a murder, the guy comes back, in another body, and he always remembers the kid." Juan looked around saying, "Sammy could be here right now. He's probably one of my friends."

During a summer camping session, Juan was feeding one of the horses. He held out the hay, and the horse grazed enthusiastically. All of a sudden, Juan stopped and pointed to the two round indentations above the horse's eyes. These indentations are a normal part of horse anatomy that deepen with age. Juan said, "Looks like bullet holes!"

In Cambodia or Nicaragua or Mozambique under conditions of civil war, people of the same race and culture torture and murder each other. Part of the special pain (and savagery) of civil war comes from this contradiction—the contradiction of people being at war with "their own." The child in the urban war zone faces an even more complex task of reconciliation, because there are no political guidelines. "Autogenocide" is a confusing reality for children, who are pressed to understand the idea of same people but different spirit (Rosenblatt, 1983). We suspect that the child faced with the ambiguities of the urban war zone is at risk for many of the same clinical problems as the victim of domestic violence, where similar problems of definition exist.

Studies of abused children suggest that, to survive the psychological consequences of being abused by one's parent, children must split representations of individuals into the good and bad person. More than deciding which people to trust in life, these children are faced with the complex task of identifying personalities of the same individual and relating to them discriminately. Research indicates that these adult-child interactions are strongly associated with the development of multiple-personality disorder (Fish-Murray, Koby, and van der Kolk, 1987). The child's efforts to pacify a contradictory world in which friend and foe are intermingled may lead to splitting off portions of oneself. If these splits "harden," the person can develop more than one identity or multiple-personality disorder.

Institutional Response to Child Victims
of Psychological Trauma

People never become comfortable with the experiences of having their lives threatened or with the unpredictable nature of crime in the inner city. They do adapt, however. Large numbers of families are isolated by the risk of harm in the environment, finding safety within the confines of their apartment walls. While employing this method of protection for themselves and their children, mothers describe the environment as a prison, and this is no country club prison. Having made that analogy, we feel compelled to offer some commentary on the social realities of traumatized children in the urban war zone.

On May 20, 1988, Laurie Dann entered a second-grade classroom in the Hubbard Woods School in the affluent suburb of Winnetka, Illinois, carrying a gun. She wounded six children and killed an eight-year-old boy. The incident shocked the small suburban community, which had recorded only two homicides over the past thirty years (Page, 1988). Two days later and approximately ten miles away, in the Henry Horner public housing development in Chicago, a nine-year-old boy was shot by a nineteen-year-old man "armed with a large-barreled firearm" (Montana, 1988). The child was critically wounded and brought to the county hospital. His friends and neighbors were shocked. In 1988, Chicago police crime statistics for Henry Horner Homes recorded 266 *reported* aggravated assaults with weapons.

Media attention to the Winnetka incident was immediate and dramatic. The story was front-page news for days. The Horner incident was reported in a short column buried inside the paper on the day after the shooting. Violence and trauma in Winnetka were big news; violence and trauma in Horner were routine.

The professional concern demonstrated for the psychological well-being of the children of Winnetka was extraordinary. The adults in the Winnetka community recognized the probability of short- and long-term psychological conse-

quences of the event for themselves and the children. They
had access to support services in the community and the economic ability to acquire assistance from nationally recognized
psychiatric experts. These experts in the field of psychic
trauma helped the children and adults in the community cope
with the psychological consequences of this traumatic event.
Local schools also mobilized professional resources on behalf
of their students. None of this happened in Horner.

In the United States, the communities with the greatest
need for support and guidance often have the least resources.
Psychic trauma does not occur in a social vacuum. For example, 37 million Americans are without health insurance
(Chollet, 1987). Studies indicate that 64 percent of the
employer-sponsored health insurance plans provide no mental
health coverage. Distressing is the fact that among Medicaid
(government-funded health care program) recipients, most of
whom are poor minorities, mental health facilities are increasingly less accessible, and options for care are limited (McGrath,
Keita, Strickland, and Russo, 1990). The public mental health
system continues to concentrate limited resources on people
with chronic mental illness. Mental health services for all children who witness and are victims of environmental violence
are critically needed.

Institutional support for people who live in communities like Horner is dismal. They receive little external valida-
tion for their experiences or recognition of their efforts to
cope with the situation. Racism remains an underlying factor
in public policy inaction on their behalf. For example, in a
recent survey based on 1,732 interviews of households across
the United States, 56 percent and 50 percent of the respondents
said that blacks and Hispanics, respectively, are more "vio-
lence-prone" than whites (Smith, 1991). Many are ready to
"write off" inner-city kids as a lost cause. This attitude can
itself lead to a self-fulfilling prophecy. PTSD and the other
clinical outcomes of life for children in the urban war zone
demand a powerful response from community institutions
lest they perpetuate an ever downward spiral in the succeed-
ing generations.

5

Resilience and Coping
in Children at Risk

While the developmental consequences of living in chronic violence can be devastating for some children, and all children pay a price, not all children experience developmental harm or clinical outcomes. Consider the case of Anita.

> Anita lived in the projects in Chicago until she was seven years old, at which time she moved with her mother, brother, and grandmother to a house a few blocks away. In both her apartment and her house, she was unable to sleep because of the gang shootings at night; and her brother was repeatedly beaten by gang members until her mother sent him to live with an aunt in another city. She was not allowed outside at night because it wasn't safe. She remembers the drug dealers lurking in the doorways, the used needles in her alley from the addicts, the prostitutes she passed on her way to school. She remembers the time she was in a car with her mother when a man smashed the car window and tried to steal her mother's purse. She remembers the funeral of her nineteen-year-old cousin, who was killed when shooting broke out between gangs.
>
> Anita, now twenty-one, is a senior with an A– average at a prestigious East Coast college. She has been accepted at several law schools and plans to continue her studies after college. She has a boyfriend and several close girlfriends. She is on the student council and active in her church. She is resilient.

Child developmentalists have estimated that up to 80 percent of all children exposed to powerful stressors do not sustain developmental damage; some children even make use

100

of the challenge and grow stronger (Rutter, 1979; Werner, 1990; Fish-Murray, 1990). These children develop a high degree of competence in spite of stressful environments and experiences. Who are these "resilient" children? What shields them from the damaging effects of day-to-day violence and victimization?

As we saw in Chapter Three, the context in which violence occurs is very important in understanding developmental outcomes in children. Will the child succumb, or will the child rebound? The outcome depends on the interactions of each individual child with the various social systems in his or her environment. A child's individual characteristics and early life experiences, as well as protective factors in the child's physical and social environment, contribute to resilience (Anthony and Cohler, 1987). These characteristics and protective factors can buffer a child's response to constitutional risk factors or stressful life events (Masten and Garmezy, 1985).

Character Traits of Resilient Children

Werner (1990) found that the developmental level of a child is a factor in resilience; that is, older children are better able to cope with stress than younger children are. As noted in Chapter Four, children who were older when they experienced their first trauma had far fewer symptoms than children who were under eleven years of age when they experienced their first trauma.

Research on stressful early experience suggests a series of ameliorating factors that lead to resilience (Lösel and Bliesener, 1990). Among individual characteristics are cognitive competence, experiences of self-efficacy and a corresponding self-confidence and positive self-esteem, and temperamental characteristics that favor active coping attempts and positive relationships with others (characteristics such as activity, goal orientation, and sociability) rather than passive withdrawal.

Character traits developed in early childhood can buffer children from severe stress and trauma. Resilient children are active, affectionate, cuddly, good-natured, and easy to deal with as infants, and have few feeding or sleeping problems. They are humorous, confident, and competent. They are realistic, flexible, and, as a result of repeated successful coping experiences, confident of their own inner resources as well as support from outside resources (Murphy and Moriarty, 1976). Some resilient children even display competence beyond their developmental level. Resilient children also generate a high degree of attention and warmth from their caregivers (Werner, 1990).

Adding to this catalogue of characteristics observed in resilient children, Anthony and Cohler (1987) describe them as popular with peers and adults, well regarded by themselves and others, and active on their own behalf. Furthermore, they have a strong sense of personal control, take responsibility for their own actions, and exercise self-discipline. Resilient children also have the ability to endure extreme pressures, as well as the capacity to recover quickly from a temporary collapse, with or without outside help, and to resume normal levels of functioning (Redl, 1966). When confronted with stress, they attempt to master the stress rather than retreating from or defending against it. This coping process involves interacting with the environment in a flexible and purposive manner, and is oriented toward present reality and future planning. Faced with potent stress, people who cope well are able to retreat to safety, to take time out to recuperate, to comfort themselves, to play traumatic experiences out, and to use fantasy to transform unpleasant reality into more tolerable situations (Anthony and Cohler, 1987).

Murphy and Moriarty (1976) include in their characteristics of effective coping behavior withdrawing from stressful situations, postponing an immediate response, finding better and more manageable situations, restructuring the environment, accepting both the good and bad as part of everyday life, and working toward maintaining optimal conditions of adjustment, security, and comfort.

Resilient children are able to manipulate and shape their environment, to deal with its pressures successfully, and to comply with its demands. They are able to adapt quickly to new situations, perceive clearly what is occurring, communicate freely, act flexibly, and view themselves in a positive way. Compared to vulnerable children, they are able to tolerate frustration, handle anxiety, and ask for help when they need it (Anthony and Cohler, 1987).

Finally, resilient children have the capacity to make sense of the stressful and traumatic events confronting them. This "representational competence," the ability to understand clearly what is occurring in their environment, helps children master the stress (Anthony and Cohler, 1987). Our observations of children in war zones confirm the importance of this last characteristic, "representational competence." The ability to make sense of threatening experiences is crucial and, as we shall see, is a foundation for building intervention programs.

Environmental Protective Factors

In addition to individual characteristics, a number of protective factors from the environment can buffer stress and trauma for children and lead to resilience (Lösel and Bliesener, 1990): a stable emotional relationship with at least one parent or other reference person; an open, supportive educational climate and parental model of behavior that encourages constructive coping with problems; and social support from persons outside the family.

During infancy, a secure attachment relationship between the child and the primary caretaker contributes to resilience. This attachment results from the initial behaviors both mother and child bring to the relationship and emerges through their recurrent interactions. While initially all infants become attached in some manner to their caregivers, regardless of how they are treated by them, the quality of the attachment relationship differs according to the quality of care the infant receives. The knowledge that a caregiver is accepting, sensitive, available, and responsive gives the child a strong feeling of security and confidence and contributes to resilience (Anthony and Cohler, 1987). In turn, infants who have a positive mood and adapt easily will contribute to the parent's feeling of efficacy.

The attachment relationship is a potent determinant of the child's social, emotional, and cognitive development (Garmezy and Rutter, 1983). If this relationship is supportive, stable, and affectionate, development most likely will proceed along a normal path. Solnit (1983) has found that an optimal parent-child relationship with positive early experiences promotes ego resilience and gives children a sense of self-worth and hope for a favorable future. Ego resilience enables a child to recover from and cope with risks resulting in stress and trauma. Many children who have experienced deprivation and neglect do not have the ability to cope with the present or to foresee a future bright enough to justify postponing immediate gratification. In order to cope with the world of school and work, children need to have a sense of being valued and a feeling of coherence.

As we saw in Chapter Three, one of the most traumatic experiences for a child is the loss of a primary caretaker. However, a secure early attachment can buffer much of the trauma of such a loss. Studies of refugee children orphaned by war report that the ability to recall earlier, positive experiences with their parents was an important buffering factor for older children whose parents were killed. Here we see "representational competence" again. The idealization and identification with parental and cultural values acted as a protective factor for these children in their new environment (Ressler, Boothby, and Steinbock, 1988). However, children who lost both parents before the age of five exhibited many psychological disturbances. These children evidently did not have an opportunity to internalize the values of their parents or their culture. Continuity of values, language, and cultural ties helps to buffer long-term psychological consequences, and early loss tends to exceed the capacity of the child for representational competence.

Children separated from their families, particularly their mothers, are placed at increased psychological risk. But when separation is followed immediately by an attachment with another supportive adult in a stable environment, the immediate symptoms—such as enuresis, anxiety, and fear—do not necessarily evolve into long-term psychological disturbances (Ressler, Boothby, and Steinbock, 1988).

Parents as Models of Resilience

Resilient children have parents who are "models of resilience," available with reassurance and encouragement during adversity, helping their children understand and process stress and trauma (Anthony and Cohler, 1987). Children are most likely to endure the emotional stress and physical disruption of war and chronic violence if they can remain with their primary caretaker and be taken care of in a stable, routine manner. Researchers conducting studies of children under extreme conditions during World War II emphasized that the emotional state and behavior of mothers are the main mediators between children's psychological functioning and traumatic experiences (Freud and Burlingham, 1943; Janis, 1951). Parental resilience tends to predict child resilience.

While 25–50 percent of the children who were evacuated from cities in England during World War II (while their parents remained) manifested neurotic symptoms, very few children who remained behind with their families displayed neurotic symptoms. The security provided by parents apparently compensated for the traumatic effects of the war (Freud and Burlingham, 1943).

For the few children who had remained with their parents and displayed psychological symptoms, the symptoms lasted only a short time. Because they do not fully comprehend inherent danger, younger children often exhibit only minor symptoms of anxiety when they are able to remain physically close to at least one parent and when parents are able to remain calm themselves.

Of those children who were evacuated, those who had strong, positive relationships with their parents prior to evacuation had fewer psychological disturbances than children who did not have good relationships. Bowlby (1980) has noted that while separation during infancy and early child-hood has serious consequences for psychological development, a child's capacity to bear separation between the ages of five and eight is related to the quality of care received as an infant. Resilience becomes internalized.

In times of unusual stress, children have an increased need for intense physical contact with parents, since their predominant fear is separation from them (Ressler, Boothby, and Steinbock, 1988). Fraser (1974) observed that in Belfast a child's response to violent rioting depended largely on the degree of emotional security the child had before and during the stressful event and the psychological resources available from the child's primary caregiver and immediate family. The stressful experience itself was secondary. In another study conducted in Belfast, during extended periods of intense fighting in neighborhoods, Lyons (1971) reported that only a small percentage of those seen for psychiatric disturbances were children. Presumably, they were protected from such disturbances because they were able to remain close to parents at home.

A study of Lebanese mothers and their children in Beirut during the 1982 war indicated that mothers who were psychologically healthy could be effective mediators between war experiences and the psychological functioning of their young children (Bryce, Walker, Ghorayeb, and Kanj, 1989). Interviews with children and parents in Kuwait in the aftermath of the Iraqi occupation confirm these findings. Physical proximity was important for young children, and parents often had entire families sleeping together to promote feelings of security (Garbarino, 1991).

During situations of chronic danger, family bonds take on major importance. In Germany after World War II, many refugee families perceived themselves to be united by a common destiny and clung together (Ressler, Boothby, and Steinbock, 1988). Children who remained with parents, even in concentration camps, revealed less psychological disturbance than did children who had been separated from their families. Separation from parents was more traumatic for children than the actual exposure to bombing and witnessing of destruction, injury, and death from air raids.

Other Family Members

While the primary caretaker is an important factor in buffering stress and trauma for children, other family members can also protect a child from developmental harm. In her study of children at risk, Werner (1990) found that secure attachments in infants were related to the presence of a supportive family member, but not exclusively the primary caretaker. The extended family can lessen stress, encourage coping behavior, and facilitate the child's working through of stress and trauma by providing additional adult nurturing and positive models of identification.

If a parent is incapacitated or unavailable, other significant people in a young child's life *can* play an enabling role, whether they are aunts, uncles, grandparents, or other extended family (Werner, 1990). Even caregiving by older siblings proved to be a major protective factor for children at risk, though it is more effective as a protective factor when it is supplemental rather than substitutive (Werner and Smith, 1982).

Despite enormous risks from their physical and social environment, most resilient children had the opportunity to establish a close bond with at least one person who provided them with stable care, so that they were able to develop a sense of basic trust (Anthony and Cohler, 1987; Werner, 1990). This person accepted them unconditionally, regardless of temperamental idiosyncrasies, physical attractiveness, or level of intelligence. Children need not be passive recipients of this compensatory care. Resilient children are skillful at finding substitute parents if their own parents are unavailable or incapacitated. These alternate caregivers serve as role models, demonstrating that difficulties can be overcome by individual effort and with the support of family and friends (Werner, 1990).

The Role of the Community in Resilience

Social support from the community plays a powerful role in the resilience of children. Children need coherent experiences and the help of concerned, competent adults to meet new demands, to cope with new stresses, and to achieve new levels of organization. Social support has been defined as "information leading the subject to believe that he/she is cared for and loved . . . esteemed and valued . . . that he/she belongs to a network of communication and mutual obligation" (Cobb, 1976). Although stressful events can disrupt significant social relationships, some social networks are able to maintain children's belief that they are secure and cared for. This belief affects the degree of stress children experience, as well as their subsequent psychological adjustment.

Social support systems that act as potent protective factors in the lives of resilient children are friends, neighbors, and teachers who provide emotional support, encourage self-esteem, and promote competence. These supportive individuals are especially effective when they can supply a caring, stable, and structured environment for a child (Werner, 1990). Resilient children usually have one or more close friends whom they can rely on for ongoing emotional support (Garmezy, 1981). Many studies have noted that resilient children enjoy school (Kellam, 1975; Werner and Smith, 1982). Of special importance is a preschool or primary school teacher who is a positive role model for the child. The presence of such a teacher forms the basis for our approach to intervention, discussed in Chapters Six to Nine.

A high degree of social support from one's community has been correlated with less stress and illness, while little social support has been correlated with increased stress and illness (Caplan and Killilea, 1976). In a study of children growing up in Topeka, Kansas, researchers found that the stability, cohesiveness, and continuity in neighborhoods and families contributed to children's resilience as well as their ability to cope (Murphy and Moriarty, 1976).

Competence, confidence, and caring can flourish, even

under adverse circumstances, if young children encounter persons who provide them with a secure basis for the development of trust, autonomy, and initiative. Social support in the form of a socially coherent community can do much to enhance the resilience of children. Of course, the urban war zone is likely to lack precisely this important resource. Indeed, the socially and psychologically rich do get richer while the psychologically poor get poorer.

Community influences go beyond the interaction of the child with individuals from the community. They also affect the degree of support and guidance given to parents so that they can become effective partners in the child's development. Community factors influence whether or not parents adopt an "activist" ideology that provides philosophical, moral, spiritual, and political support for the active coping that helps children develop and express resilience (Garbarino and Kostelny, 1992b). For example, research conducted in two economically impoverished Chicago communities found striking differences in child maltreatment rates as a function of the amount of social support in a community: the socially rich community, with strong informal support networks and community activism, had more positive parenting and less child abuse and neglect than did the socially impoverished community (Garbarino and Kostelny, 1992a).

Communities can also provide activities that offer experiences of self-efficacy for parents and children. For example, the Missouri Parents as Teachers program (*Fortune Magazine*, Spring, 1990) involves parents in active and developmentally enhancing relationships with their children from the first weeks of life. This type of program reduces the risk of developmental impairment to the child and bolsters resources for resilience.

Community influences are important also in providing the "open, supportive educational climate" that is itself a source of resilience for children. Communities can do much to set the tone and the context of individual parenting decisions. The cultural blueprints provided for schools—curriculum, ambiance, and the like—can translate into a setting for children that encourages active processing. Or the schools can be rigid and authoritarian in ways that compound the problems faced by traumatized children.

The community also can foster moral development in children. Situations of chronic danger can stimulate the process of moral development in children through its political, educational, and religious institutions. As we have seen in Chapter Three, families can provide the emotional context for the necessary "processing" to make positive moral sense of danger, and even of trauma. However, communities must then stimulate higher-order moral development by presenting a democratic milieu for children—for example, by having issue-focused discussions in schools.

In order for parents or other caregivers to be effective supports for children, the community must sustain the basic infrastructure of family life, including parent-child attachment, parental self-esteem and identity, and stability of routine caregiving arrangements (Bronfenbrenner, 1986). If parents, or other significant caregivers, can sustain a strong attachment to their children, can maintain a positive sense of self, and can have access to basic resources, children will manage, although it may be at great cost to the psychic and physical welfare of those parents, who may be "used up" caring for their children.

In some villages in the Sudan—where there was drought and where most fathers were absent for long periods of time working in the cities—children appeared normal because they were cared for by their mothers, who themselves had access to food, fuel, water, and basic medicines (Garbarino, 1988). From a child's point of view, there was a semblance of normality in day-to-day life, even in the midst of national crisis. Stresses are more likely to lead to growth, rather than defeat, if the child is in a predictable physical and social environment.

Ideology

Ideology can also explain the resilience of mothers and their ability to buffer stress for their vulnerable young children

(Bettelheim, 1943; Punamaki, 1987; Bryce, Walker, Ghorayeb, and Kanj, 1989). Ideology contributes to resilience because it gives substance and meaning to dangerous events and sustains the ability to function under extreme conditions (Murphy and Moriarty, 1976). In his observations of life in Nazi concentration camps, Bettelheim (1943) noted that those who bore up best were those with intense ideological commitments—commitments that offered meaning impervious to day-to-day brutalization. Contemporary research has offered further documentation of this finding. A recent study in Israel reported that ultraorthodox Jews suffered less from stress than more secular Jews as a result of the current Palestinian uprising (Pines, 1989). Ideology is a psychological resource, even while it may be an impediment to negotiations and solutions.

This ideological dimension emerges repeatedly in accounts of families under stress. Political and religious views, especially when they are held with extreme intensity, can shape the consequences of experience. Strong religious beliefs in families have brought stability and meaning to children's lives, particularly during times of hardship and stress. For example, ideology mobilized the social and psychological resources of Palestinian mothers—who, with their children, were exposed to chronic violence—and enhanced their ability to buffer stress for their children (Punamaki, 1987). For Palestinians living under Israeli occupation in refugee camps, where every feature of day-to-day stress and physical deprivation is met with an ideological response that mobilizes social and psychological resources, "the psychological processes of healing the traumatic experiences drew strength from political and ideological commitment. Nationalistic motivation was present at all stages of the stress process: the meaning and harmfulness of an event as well as sufficiency of one's own resources to cope with stressors were approached in the wider social and political context of a victimized and struggling nation" (Punamaki, 1987, pp. 82–83).

The determined struggle to persist dominates Palestinian culture and community life (Grossman, 1988; Shipler, 1985) and is responsible for the resilience of children in the face of awesome stress, such as was experienced by Palestinian families under siege in the refugee camps in Lebanon (Cutting, 1988).

Punamaki (1987) found that mothers' experience with violence mobilized them into actively coping with the stress by engaging in political activities; this active behavior in a traumatic situation mediated the impact of traumatic events on their children's emotional health. Palestinian mothers whose children experienced many violent events but had no psychological disturbances strongly believed in their ability to control their lives, were actively trying to change the traumatic situation, had religious beliefs, and availed themselves of social support.

Where do we look for such ideological resources for parents and children in the urban war zone? Until we can answer that question, our ability to promote resilience in these lives will be limited at best. We will return to this issue in Chapters Six to Nine.

Conclusion

What about Anita, the Chicago girl with whom we began this chapter? Why and how did she make it? She grew up among chronic danger. She experienced loss. Why did she become a success story? We believe that she succeeded because she embodied and experienced several key factors.

First, Anita possessed individual characteristics correlated with resilience—intelligence, self-confidence, popularity with peers and adults.

Second, several key elements in her environment served as protective factors. While Anita had a stable emotional relationship with both her mother and her grandmother, her relationship with her grandmother was primary. Her grandmother provided a nurturing, supportive environment in the midst of the violence around Anita. For example, her grandmother established a neighborhood watch for Anita on her way home from school. Neighbors would call Anita's grandmother if Anita did not pass by their house at her usual time, and a search party would go out looking for her.

Anita's mother also served as a model of resilience for her. When Anita's father left her mother, shortly after Anita was born, Anita's mother moved in with her mother and returned to school. Anita's mother obtained a degree at a city college, received additional training as a medical technician, and then began working full-time at a hospital downtown. Her goal was to get out of the projects, and she was able to do so a few years after she began working. Anita embodied her mother's determination and her striving toward education as a way out. As Anita proclaimed, "After law school, when I'm making my own money, I'm going to live in the suburbs where it's nice and quiet and boring."

Third, several of Anita's teachers took a special interest in her. She was a good student, and her teachers liked and encouraged her.

Fourth, when Anita moved from the projects to her house, she was moving into a different social environment. Although it was only a few blocks away, and still plagued by drugs and violence, her new home embodied a strong, informal social network that was lacking in the projects, where there was a climate of social isolation. In her new home, neighbors watched out for her as she came home from school. Her family and neighbors organized a block club to try to do something about drug dealers and neighborhood crime. Anita had a sense that conditions were not hopeless, that change could occur.

Thus, in spite of multiple risks in Anita's environment, there were also several protective factors that helped her triumph against the odds: her grandmother, her mother, her teachers, and the support network in her community.

There are limits, of course, to resilience and protective factors. As we saw in Chapter Four, in our discussion of post-traumatic stress, some experiences are so overwhelming and traumatic that no amount of individual strength or protective factors from the environment can buffer them. Yet, even under the most "objectively" horrible circumstances, some children do better than others. Although they are changed by their experiences, and although they must invest enormous energy in the agenda of survival and coping, they do bounce back rather than breaking. So, for most children in the urban war zone, finding ways to enhance resilience makes good practical sense.

6

School as a Refuge:
The Importance of Early Intervention

Contemplating the threats to child development posed by chronic community violence, one is tempted to throw up one's hands in despair. Where do we begin? How do we start? Is successful intervention in school settings (by "school" we mean a broad range of settings, including child-care and pre-school programs) a realistic possibility? More questions arise than are answered when we look for descriptions of "successful" interventions that prevent developmental harm or improve outcomes for children in jeopardy. Easy confidence dissolves on every count before the gravity of the problem— the central issue being the deprivation and dysfunction of poor families mired in deteriorated inner-city environments and lodged in the legacy of racism. The current excesses of community violence may be only the most recent symptom of the problem. How is any intervention "program" to deal with the enormous negative momentum of this downward-spiraling cycle?

The following comments from researchers and practitioners at every level of analysis—from public policy to individual treatment—describe the context in which any serious discussion of intervention on behalf of children living amidst community violence must take place.

In *Small Futures: Children, Inequality, and the Limits of Liberal Reform,* de Lone (1979, p. 25) comments: "Many aspects of children's policy in this country have been more an effort to *use* children to resolve deep-seated tensions and contradictions in adult society than a genuine effort to help children themselves. By and large, the effort has failed on both fronts."

Or, from Halpern's essay "Fragile Families, Fragile Solutions" (1990b, p. 646), these comments: "When well conceptualized and implemented, services do have a role to play in sustaining, helping, and, in some instances, enriching the lives of poor children and families. Services can help families cope with poverty-related stresses, for example, the difficulty of securing health care or child care. They can help facilitate self- and situational awareness and adjustment to a difficult life situation. *But if there is one thing that program experience and evaluation research has taught us it is that services tend to have modest effects on participants' lives"* (italics added).

William J. Wilson states: "In the 1960's only a hard-core group of conservative observers would have endorsed the view that social programs to help the truly disadvantaged inevitably fail. In more recent times, and especially during the years of the Reagan presidency, this view has been adopted by many who represent the political mainstream" (Wilson, 1988a, p. ix).

Summarizing children's traumatic experiences involving alcoholism, divorce, incest, separation, and mental illness, Cottle (1980, p. 166) states: "Often, it strikes me that the children actually remained relatively unchanged; their burdens have not been lifted; the weight of the past, in Kafka's words, continues to influence their behavior and outlook."

Rutter (1979, p. 48) echoes this theme: "On the whole, the benefits that follow our therapeutic endeavors are pretty modest in the case of severely deprived children."

But Schorr and Schorr, in their volume *Within Our Reach* (1988, p. xxvii), come to a somewhat different conclusion: "If the superb health, education, and social services described in this book, now provided to a fraction of those who need them, were more widely available, fewer children would come into adulthood unschooled and unskilled, committing violent crimes, and bearing children as unmarried teenagers. Fewer of today's vulnerable children would tomorrow swell the welfare rolls and the prisons. Many more would grow into responsible and productive adults, able to form stable families and contributing to, rather than depleting, America's prosperity and sense of community."

Similarly, in her review of the literature on protective factors and resilience, Werner (1990, p. 109) concludes that "most resilient children are able to use the school experience profitably as a refuge from a troubled home environment."

These comments from Zigler (1990, p. ix) also suggest that the question of successful early intervention (for example, Head Start) has been "put to rest": "In regard to economically disadvantaged children, a consensus now exists among behavioral scientists, policymakers, and even taxpayers that *early intervention is a cost-effective method for combating the effects of poverty experienced early in life*" (italics added).

How are we to reconcile the starkly contrasting conclusions arrived at by these writers: those who say that intervention is too weak to make much difference, and those who offer hope? For practitioners working in these communities, who live out the reality of translating hope into successful intervention on a moment-by-moment basis, confidence and direction are hard to come by. The valiant rhetoric of an earlier time often is swallowed up in faint-hearted pronouncements—empty-sounding words evoking the sense of defeat that lurks in the shadow of programmatic failures to improve the chances for the children who walk in the door every morning. Thus, despite the allegedly "wide acceptance of the value of early childhood intervention," epitomized by programs like Head Start, today, more often than not, the "nothing really works" syndrome had taken hold of even the most stalwart and, heretofore, idealistic reformer (Zigler, 1990, p. ix; Wilson, 1988a, p. ix). This is part of the context in which we must address the needs of children as they cope with community violence.

Economic and Political Basis of "Failed" Interventions

It would be idle to deny the abundant evidence of apparently "failed" solutions. Nonetheless, we believe that the failure to improve the chances for multiply disadvantaged children and

their families derives, primarily, from the pronounced esca-
lation of underlying economic problems. This economic deterioration itself is the result of "deep-seated tensions and
contradictions" in political institutions and public values (de
Lone, 1979, p. 25). We do not accept the proposition that
intervention is intrinsically futile. Instead, we believe, social
interventions have been expected to remediate problems for
which they were not designed and for which they have not
been provided adequate resources (de Lone, 1979, p. 25; Halpern, 1990b; Grubb and Lazerson, 1982, chap. 5; Wilson, 1988a;
Zigler, 1990). "Programs" will not substitute for social reform.
Zigler (p. xiii) puts it this way: "The problems of many families will not be solved by early intervention efforts, but only
by changes in the basic features of the infrastructure of our
society. No amount of counseling, early childhood curricula,
or home visits will take the place of jobs that provide decent
incomes, affordable housing, appropriate health care, optimal
family configurations, or integrated neighborhoods where
children encounter positive role models."

In fact, from an ecological perspective, the social forces that shape children's lives from birth make it virtually
impossible for them to emerge from these high-risk environments unscathed and with "normal" hope for the future
(Meers, 1973; de Lone, 1979; Halpern, 1990b, 1990c). What,
then, is an appropriate goal for our efforts? Put most simply
and directly, our goal is to prevent the buildup of risk factors in the lives of inner-city children. We intervene to keep
the challenge facing these children within the limits of their
ability to cope. We seek ways to help them survive. Much
as we would like to make the world new for them through
some magical program, we know we cannot accomplish
that. We will console ourselves with helping them survive
emotionally.

The scope and complexity of the problems facing children and families who live in the extreme deprivation of
inner-city environments, coupled with the disheartening picture painted by current research, suggest that it would be
foolhardy to overpromise or oversell the claims of social inter-

ventions to produce long-term societal benefits (Halpern, 1990b; Zigler 1990, p. xiii). Confidence and direction remain elusive (Anthony and Cohler, 1987, chap. 13). These caveats notwithstanding, *we steadfastly refuse to deny our experience of positive outcomes for children "at highest risk" who are enrolled in well-designed and implemented early childhood programs, conceptualized and developed at a time when resources were more adequate and better matched to the task at hand.* These programs are crucial to a larger strategy of complementary efforts to keep children afloat developmentally.

Accordingly, in our efforts to help children exposed to chronic violence, we adopt a realistically defined concept of intervention that promises neither "too much nor too little" but speaks with cautious optimism (Zigler, 1990, p. xi; Sameroff and Fiese, 1990; Wilson, 1988a; Comer, 1980). This confidence derives from the parallel conclusions of the field research of others and our own experiences in more than a decade of work with publicly funded Head Start and day-care programs that serve over 700 preschool children each year in some of Chicago's most disadvantaged neighborhoods. None of these programs is a demonstration project.

Intervention in Multirisk Settings

Sameroff and Fiese (1990, p. 119) begin their discussion of the prevention of children's psychosocial disorders with this statement: "The two greatest myths identified by Rutter (1982) were that there are single causes for disorders and . . . that these causes can be identified by treating the child as an individual." In our work in inner-city communities with children exposed to chronic violence, we have eschewed these myths. We believe in the notion of multiple causation and cumulative effects, and in the further assumption that "behavioral outcomes are the result of the mutual effects of context on child and child on context" (Sameroff and Fiese, 1990, p. 119; Rutter, 1982; Anthony and Cohler, 1987). We therefore assume that the majority of children attending day-care, Head Start, school-age, and public school programs in severely disadvantaged communities are at risk for developmental harm because they have an accumulation of high-risk factors in their lives (see Chapters One and Three). However, no single clustering of risk factors predicts developmental arrest or permanent harm (Sameroff and Fiese, 1990). Different factors may add together to produce different outcomes.

These conclusions suggest that we should broaden the basis of intervention *beyond* a universally applied, single-focus strategy—for example, helping children exposed to community violence—so that it encompasses both the diversity and the idiosyncratic clustering of each child's problems, coping mechanisms, and protective factors. Accordingly, we speak of supporting children and preventing developmental harm from these two *interdependent* perspectives: (1) the need to base individual treatment on the premise of multiple causation and variable, cumulative risk (see Chapter Three); and (2) the need to intervene in the *child-rearing context*—or, in this case, the school caregiving and learning environment (Sameroff and Fiese, 1990, p. 119; Comer, 1980; Meers, 1973).

In choosing early childhood preschool and primary school settings as the basis for our discussion of intervention, we do not mean to suggest that other arenas for intervention are less important (for example, community-based approaches, such as tutoring programs, "neighborhood watch" groups, "Helping Hands," "Whistle Stop," and family support interventions. We assume that such approaches are integral to a well-conceived network of interfacing interventions. Nor do we mean to suggest that the preschool and early primary focus is developmentally more significant than others. Rather, at this preliminary stage of our research, these are the areas about which we are able to speak with greater authority, conviction, and experience. On the other hand, while we have limited the details of our discussion to early childhood and primary school settings, we believe that the underlying principles have significance for other situations where other interventions are planned.

The School as a Protective Factor

Contrary to the pessimism that continues to shroud the role of the school in ameliorating outcomes for disadvantaged children, our work in the field and our review of the literature suggest that a renewed understanding of the role of the school as a caregiving environment is critical. Not only are schools one of the most continuous institutions in children's lives (Wallerstein and Kelly, 1980, chap. 15) but "after the family, schools represent the most important developmental unit in modern social systems" (Comer, 1980, p. 268). Furthermore, as a public institution, schools are more accessible than the family—or indeed, the "infrastructure"—as an appropriate unit of intervention. Accordingly, we believe that school settings represent a significant context—a secondary caregiving and learning environment—that can be influenced and shaped to play a vital role as a protective factor in children's lives.

We observe that, despite the overwhelming pressures in the environment, 75–80 percent of the children can use school activities as a support for healthy adjustment and achievement *when schools are sensitive to them and their burdens.* We base our intervention on the premise that these children are developmentally normal and have the potential for school success when they are provided with a carefully designed, developmentally appropriate, and facilitative school experience. These positive experiences foster the development of coping and self-esteem, thereby reducing the potential for developmental delay or arrest from biological or psychological trauma. In such a setting, the "barriers to developmental potential" are removed (Musick and others, 1987, p. 250).

The supportive school-based intervention we envision is discussed in Chapters Seven and Eight. The special role of adults and the role of training, supervision, and consultation are the subject of Chapter Nine. The particular significance of play and art curricula will be discussed in Chapter Ten.

Individual Needs of Children at Risk

When we speak to teachers and staff who work with the children who live in these neighborhoods, we are acutely aware of the limitations inherent in a one-dimensional, single focus (for example, violence, drugs, gangs, sex), universally applied. In every training session we have conducted to discuss the consequences of community violence, teachers, administrators, and support staff immediately present a daunting list of other problems facing these children: "What about the eight-year-old child in my class who was raped last week in her home?" "What about the little girl who says she doesn't like him 'to touch her that way'?" "What about the children who are playing 'shooting up' in the doll house corner?" "What about the child who brought $100 of drug money that he took from his mother's purse?" "What about the child who is setting fires?" "What about a child who looks like he's 'on something'?" Frequently the problems are interwoven, presenting a confused, overwhelming picture that defies confident assessment. The concerns of these teachers and staff are well founded. On any given day, one child—or a number of children—may be facing a wide range of different problems, each claiming the attention of every ounce of physical and psychological energy—and cognitive capability—that can be brought to bear on the most rudimentary requirements of physical and emotional survival.

Individual Responses to Risk and Trauma

As we noted in our earlier discussion, a single potentially traumatizing event resulting from community violence will not *automatically* result in developmental arrest or delay. More specifically, psychobiological trauma resulting from external events (for example, rape, domestic violence, substance abuse, divorce, incest, or community violence) does not necessarily lead to either internalized psychopathology or developmental harm (Meers, 1973). Therefore, although psychological symptoms and regressive, adaptive behaviors in reaction to external conflicts may be present and indicate the child's need for support (see Chapter Four), they may or may not signify PTSD.

Nor can we assume that an environment characterized by chronic violence categorically predicts a given outcome.

The meaning and subsequent impact of the event, as is the case with other risk factors, will depend on the balance between stressful experiences and protective factors that exist for each child and, from an Eriksonian perspective, the compensating factors in the environment and the culture overall (Erikson, 1950). When they exist, these factors serve, in effect, to "cordon off," "immunize," "buffer," or "neutralize" the impact of situational assault.

In his summary of the current findings of risk research, Cohler (in Anthony and Cohler, 1987, chap. 13) notes that the lack of definitive data calls into question our ability to predict how adverse life circumstances—such as separation and loss, psychiatric illness, poverty, or abuse—will affect an individual child's development. Cohler particularly emphasizes the discrepancy between the "lived experiences" of individuals faced with extreme adversity and the theoretical constructs on which predictions of impairment are frequently based. The result of longitudinal studies showing that "lives are not as ordered and predictable as had previously been assumed" leads Cohler to stress the importance of studying persons' own accounts of their lives, or "personal history" (pp. 398–399). Central to this discussion is the way in which individuals understand and interpret the meaning of misfortune. Consequently, in our research and interventions, we focus on the stories that children and adults create, tell, revise, and retell to explain their experience in the inner city.

The discrepancy between theoretical constructions (in the absence of systematic empirical data) and "personal history" is especially well illustrated in the work of Coles (1964) and Cottle (1974, 1980). Both have recorded at length the responses of many children and adults to a wide range of extreme situations (for example, historical events, such as the integration of southern schools or busing, and problems more directly related to the family: substance abuse, incest, divorce, mental health, and physical and sexual abuse). Similar accounts are found in the work of other researchers who, like Coles and Cottle, have sought to understand the personal experiences of individual children and adults living out the reality of extreme adversity on a day-to-day basis (Meers, 1973; Peck, 1987; Moriarty, 1987; Anthony and Cohler, 1987).

The complex interweaving of risk and resilience—mediated by developmental age, ideology or personal meanings, and social and personal resources—is particularly well illustrated in the stories of Ruby (Coles, 1964, pp. 74–86), Genie and Virgil (Meers, 1973, pp. 410–411), Vreni (Anthony and Cohler, 1987), and Jim and Sam (Peck, 1987). In Coles's story "Down from Chicago" (1964, pp. 216–223) and Cottle's account of a suicidal child (1980, pp. 192–208), the contrasting significance of alcoholism in the life of each child illustrates the importance of "meaning" (also "interpretation," "personal narrative," "myth") in the ways in which individuals manage adversity. In each of these stories, the meaning of a particular event for a particular child and his or her family is very specific. Because of this specificity, interventions must be focused, individualized, and responsive to the significance of the event in that child's life.

In their numerous accounts of the children they have followed for many years, Cottle and Coles repeatedly emphasize the danger of generalizing responses based on preconceived developmental or social formulations, which, in the end, frequently turn out to be inadequate to the task. Both of these researchers have sought to remain "tentative" or "vulnerable." Coles speaks to the danger—in fact, the impossibility—of putting people in neat boxes. Similarly, Cottle (1980, pp. 5–6) suggests that we "let the stories tell themselves," allowing children "to describe in their own words how their lives are led," so that we "experience them in a more complete sense"—not as anecdotes or "postcard" illustrations of some larger conceptual issue that is "so appealing and so often wrong."

Personal Meanings of "Community Violence"

Over and over again, as we listen to the stories of these children and their families, we are struck by the inadequacy of the term *community violence* to describe the circumstances of their lives. As an overarching concept, it becomes an abstraction that dramatically underestimates, glosses over, and trivializes the intensely personal, frequently tragic, and complex meanings of these events in the community. As in any war zone, every act of violence may also have personal significance. But, as we have seen in Chapters One and Two, the stories in high-crime communities reveal much more conflict over right and wrong and the meaning of personal loss or gain in a given family. A brother who is shot in a gang shoot-out does not command the same community regard as a brother who is shot in a war.

The stories of Robert in the preface and Juan in Chapter Four particularly reveal the insidious and twisted ways in which "community violence" becomes part of the family experience. The following accounts have similar implications.

> For Johnny, the same gang shoot-out that his brother was involved in resulted in the death of this child's "janitor friend." But Johnny also has new "high tops" because there is more money around these days. Johnny idolizes his brother, who now wears a lot of "big gold," but he is worried because his brother also seems pretty scared and doesn't go to school much anymore. Johnny's mother cries a lot, and Johnny spends most of his time daydreaming in school.

> Bessie has become more and more withdrawn in the months following her mother's death. Her mother was shot on her way home from the store by an estranged boyfriend. A reneged drug deal was also involved. The boyfriend had been kind to Bessie, and she was fond of him.

> Anthony's mother has not returned home because she is hustling drugs. Her prolonged absence scares him. As night approaches, he begins to think about the lady who was shot in front of the church where he attends a Head Start program.

In each of these situations, the events of so-called community violence are deeply intertwined and enmeshed in the well-being of each family—in ways that seem to be short-changed or missed by the emotional distance that this term recalls.

Walking Home from School: Individual Notions of "Safety"

We turn now to our personal experience with a group of elementary school children. Since many of these children had said that they were "bothered" by gang members on the way home from school, we decided to set up a "buddy system" to enhance their sense of "safety." As we explored the individual circumstances of several children whom we wished to support with this strategy, we discovered that "feeling safe on the way home from school" meant different things to different children.

> For six-year-old Antonio, "safety" on the walk home from school means taking a very indirect route, walking a long way around the parking lot where he and his brother were caught in cross fire a year ago. Antonio still has a bullet in his leg. According to his family, the bullet can be used to identify the gun and, perhaps, the person who shot it. For Antonio, the question of safety is rooted in that event.

> For eight-year-old Marcel, getting home from school safely means rounding up four unruly brothers and sisters and putting them on the bus that will take them to the West Side, where their mother is living temporarily because she has a new job in that neighborhood. In a recent Chicago Housing Authority (CHA) "building sweep," these children were evicted from their aunt's overcrowded apartment near the school (where they were living as a result of their mother's new job), because they were not "on the lease." They are not supposed "to tell" where they live these days, for fear of having to change schools.

> For three other children, "crossing gang turf" determines the route they take home.

> For Tamika, a child who has a confirmed diagnosis of gonorrhea, home is not a safe place, because that is where her sexual abuse occurred. She prefers to avoid going home.

A similar situation exists for Shanelle, whose mother, uncle, and their respective acquaintances use drugs and are known to be extremely violent. Teachers and school staff tend to be afraid of this family.

Ramona has long hustled whatever she can steal on the streets. She has learned to survive there.

Sonita, a sexually precocious, emotionally disturbed ten-year-old also does not want to go home; she would rather follow the older boys.

Darnell is a likable, responsible twelve-year-old who struggles to keep his academic standing as a good student. But he also has a best friend who is spending more and more time after school with a gang. He tries to avoid gang involvement without loss of peer support.

Jerome is a very young, frightened, teenage father. Confused about his new role, he shifts between trying to assume a more adult role, consistent with his new status as a father, and those roles more appropriate to an adolescent boy. Increasingly, he is spending more time with a new group of friends involved in gang activity.

Tiny, waiflike Maria is less scared of the walk home than she is of entering her building alone. She has nightmares of the elevator doors crushing her.

Clearly, these children have quite different notions about risk, different perceptions and understandings of "safety," different coping strategies, and different developmental needs. Thus, our regimented "buddy system" seemed bound for failure. Nor were we particularly successful in engaging parents in these efforts. Moreover, as the children get older, decisions about what to do after school and getting home safely straddle the uneasy line between developmental push, the personal circumstances of their family histories, and the reality of life in these communities. A "buddy system" arranged by adults, for example, did not seem particularly well suited to the developmental needs of the school-age boys,

who wanted to appear strong, confident, and self-assured—at
any emotional cost. However, these boys frequently selected a
friend or group of friends to walk home with—for better or
worse! These comments by Deborah Meier, principal of Central Park East Secondary School in New York City, underscore
the complexity of this issue:

> The thing that is so hard for outsiders to under-
> stand . . . is the utter routineness of violence in
> the lives of so many of the children.

> Violence is normal in the lives of today's adoles-
> cents . . . Even worse, it is glamorous and appeal-
> ing. In advisory meetings, where people are frank
> and open, the boys will acknowledge that their
> ideal of manliness exudes violence . . . to be a
> man is to sneer in the face of the weak. To let
> your guard down is an invitation to danger or
> cruel jests, at the very least. Weakness [is] equated
> with sissiness. To be a thoughtful person is to
> invite a rep for being a homosexual.

> Middle-class kids often see this conforming
> cruelty as a temporary necessity of adolescence,
> whereas working class and poor kids seem more
> prone to the view that this is the way the world
> is [quoted in Raspberry, 1989; p. 4a; cited in
> Wood and Long, 1991, p. xi].

Finally, while all these children could benefit from the
more benign environment that a "buddy system," "Helping
Hands," or "neighborhood watch" might offer, we have seen
that the personal problems and solutions to dysfunction at
school, both social and academic, would be different for each
child.

Nonetheless, as part of an organized system of interventions stemming from school- or community-based initiatives,
such efforts can convey a message of personal worth to chil-

dren. These strategies would suggest to children that they deserve care and concern, that adults are in charge and are capable of protecting them. Such a message from the school, acting in its capacity as a caregiving entity, speaks to one dimension of our two interrelated goals (Meers, 1973). In fact, it might prove to be "the first straw" in helping children hold on as they struggle in the face of nearly overwhelming challenges "out there."

At the same time, if our goal is also to intervene and support children who *show evidence* of being at risk for developmental harm by their dysfunctional performance at school, the shortcomings of a generalized, nonspecific intervention are clearly indicated in the stories told above. We have tried to show that even when the nature of the problem looks the same (for example, fear of being "bothered" on the way home from school), the solution (for example, a "buddy system" to help children feel more secure) may not be responsive to a given child's needs. While potentially traumatizing for every child exposed to the event, the bloody, gang-related killing of a neighbor—or the question of "safety" on the way home from school—will raise different issues requiring *individual* solutions for each child. These solutions will depend on the entire range of mediating variables we have discussed throughout this book. Professionals cannot estimate the cumulative effect of these variables unless they know more about the child's history and are involved in a relationship with the child that would allow them to discover its meaning (Meers, 1973).

Researchers such as Coles and Cottle, who have listened to many children like the ones in our stories, caution us to listen to each story, to try to understand its meaning for a particular child, and to understand both dysfunction and intervention from the perspective of each child's individual needs—at a given moment, in a given situation. We also must be able to shift our attention and adjust our responses as children's needs change over time, when they move on to new concerns or revisit ("rework") old ones from a new developmental perspective. These suggestions parallel our own experience and form the basis of our discussion of the ways in which we can help teachers respond to children more effectively through training, consultation, and supervision (Chapter Nine).

Conclusion

The intervention we have proposed in this chapter is primarily supportive, educational, and preventive. We suggest that the "school" be regarded as a significant unit of intervention. We also contend that the majority of "at-risk" children in school are developmentally normal—not pathologically disturbed—and have the potential for school success when schools are sensitive to them and their burdens.

As we steer away from single-issue, curricular interventions that focus on the most negative aspects of these environments—gangs, sex, drugs, violence, and so forth—toward more positive, educationally based, and individually focused interventions, we emphasize the role of caring relationships with significant adults as the principal agent of change and source of support. Through training, consultation, and supervision, we can help adults provide a developmentally appropriate and facilitative classroom experience that is also responsive to the social and emotional problems these children bring to school each day.

A developmental approach suggests that "teaching" about violence, gangs, substance abuse, and so forth, is handled best, for the youngest children, as these concerns emerge in context—in the immediate, day-to-day interactions between children and teachers in the classroom—rather than as a subject for formal instruction. For older children, a more organized approach to these issues is appropriate.

We contend that a school-based intervention of this nature is not only therapeutic and healing but also a legitimate function of institutions whose purpose is primarily "educational." We see teachers not as therapists but as positive role models for children in a caregiving environment that promotes mental health. Perhaps the following comments best summarize our goals: "A school that is able to address student needs in an orderly way—first with attention to social and psychological comfort and trust and then through academic and intellectual growth—is in the best position to prepare students for success living in the complex society of today and tomorrow" (Comer, 1980, p. 267).

In making this case for a school-based intervention to improve outcomes—to "change the odds"—for children at highest risk, we do not in any way intend to divert attention from the overwhelming significance of the economic and political basis of failed interventions (Schorr and Schorr, 1988, p. xx). In the continuing absence of economic supports for children and families who live with severe deprivation, interventions such as we envision are bound to have marginal effects on the long-term prospect for improving optimal functioning. Nor is it clear that economic supports alone are sufficient to optimize human functioning. What is needed is an "integration of thoughtful noneconomic and economic strategies," which, if they were adopted, "would eliminate the problems of persistent poverty in a relatively short period of time." With such strategies in place, "the life chances of high-risk children and their families would noticeably improve" (Wilson, 1988a, p. xi).

In the end, the caveats and qualifications aside, our hope for children through a school-based intervention is perhaps best captured in Patsy Walker's words. In *Children's Secrets,* Cottle (1980, pp. 257-266) recounts her almost unbelievable story, which includes a family history of the most profound abuse and neglect, incest, prostitution, drugs, and incarceration. Speaking to Cottle about her decision to abandon a successful and lucrative career as a prostitute, get a job in a cleaning store, return to high school, graduate from college, and at age twenty-six enter graduate school, Patsy says this:

> There *is* a kicker in all this. I mean, I have a little sort of secret to confess. S-C-H-O-O-L. See what I'm getting to? A child grows up in what

you could call two homes. Home where he's
born, and home where he goes to school. One
fails him, he's got the other. It can work either
way. But if both fail, he can call the music to an
end. I was up to calling my own music to an end
several times there myself. Family didn't do too
much good, and I wouldn't have thought the
schools were going to be any different. But they
did their job. I didn't think so at the time, but
they were grinding away, all those evil little
school machines; putting all those facts in my
brain.

Recalling two, almost incidental, comments from two of her
teachers, she says:

My secret was not so much liking everything we
did in school . . . but I did like some of it, and a
few of the teachers. Not a lot of them, but you
don't need a lot of them. Fact is you only need a
few. . . . 'Cause what they both were telling me
was, okay, you want to make a secret out of it,
that's cool. But we could either forget you and
let you fall away like everybody else, or we can,
like I say, plant a little seed in you.

That's what both of them did, too, plant
little seeds. Took a long, long time for those seeds
to grow into something, but they did. . . . What
they were telling me, see, was you can play the
game, but we want to tell you we'll support you
playing a whole 'nother game if there ever comes
a time you feel you might be ready. Maybe they
were daring me. And the school, see, it stunk like
it always stunk. Nothing changed. Wasn't like
the day after they spoke with me everything was
perfect again, and my mother was all good and
my father flew out of prison. No magic. But the
seeds. Two funny old ladies, two funny little

seeds. So school didn't fail out like everything else. Didn't teach me all that much, but how the hell could it? Teachers knew they were in a losing battle right down the line. But like, what they did was plant those time capsules of theirs, kind of like they were saying, Hey, you might like to see what's inside you one of these days. Might like to find out there's more than one way to go in this world, game or no game. Fact, they never did say, think about it. Neither woman did. They just took a chance. Probably took it with lots of kids. Damn strange, school. Damn strange somebody seeing inside you to where you keep your secrets, where they *know* you keep your secrets. I had a secret, too, going with my school. Used to say to myself: School, get me a ticket out of this life. And baby, make it one way!

At the other end of the service spectrum, we conclude along with Comer—for the sake of the Patsy Walkers, Ramons, Juans, and Roberts of our acquaintance—that schools have a significant role to play and we "can't wait for the millennium" (1980, p. 268).

7

Ramon and His School:
A Case Study

Our vision for the role of the school as a protective factor in the lives of disadvantaged children is underscored by the following comments:

> There is a regrettable tendency to focus gloomily on the ills of mankind and on all that can and does go wrong. It is quite exceptional for anyone to study the development of those important individuals who overcome adversity, who survive stress, and who rise above disadvantage. It is equally unusual to consider the factors or circumstances that provide support, protection, or amelioration for the children reared in deprivation. This neglect of positive influences on development means that we lack guides on how to help deprived or disadvantaged children. It is all very well to wish for the children to have a stable, loving family which provides emotional support, social stability, and cognitive stimulation. But we are almost never in a position to provide that. . . . Would our results be better if we could determine the sources of social competence and identify the nature of protective influences? I do not know, but I think they would. The potential for prevention surely lies in increasing our knowledge and understanding of the reasons why some children are *not* damaged by deprivation [Rutter, 1979, p. 48].

134

Here and in Chapter Eight, we present the story of Ramon and describe the child-care program he attends. We then discuss those aspects of the program that seem particularly effective in providing help for this child from the perspective of developmental theory and practice and the research literature on effective schools and resilient children.

Ramon

Ramon is a four-year-old child who attends a publicly funded day-care program operated by a private social service agency in the city of Chicago. He is one of five siblings who have been in this program over the past ten years; as a consequence, the center staff are quite familiar with the circumstances of his family life. All the children have had difficulties of one kind or another; and, as time goes on, the cumulative effects of the family's problems seem to emerge earlier, and with more profoundly negative consequences, for each child.

When we saw Ramon at the center several months ago, we were struck by a seemingly new symptom of the family's recurrent difficulties, which result from a violent, alcoholic father and a somewhat disorganized and increasingly beleaguered mother who is only marginally able to protect her children from the emotional impact of incidents such as the one described below. During the ten- to fifteen-minute observation, Ramon—furtively, compulsively, trying to hide his hand as if he were hoping to stop it or to have it not show—kept making a gun and shooting it, over and over and over again. Almost every action he made—picking up a piece of Lego or his fork at lunch—related in some way to shooting a gun.

In addition to a history of intermittent, violent outbursts by the father and a periodic pattern of "leavings" by the mother, the most recent event in Ramon's troubled life was his "kidnapping" by his father's family. The child was taken at night, from his home in Chicago, to Puerto Rico. Then, under similarly mysterious circumstances, he was "returned" two months later.

Several days preceding the observation, Ramon told his teacher that his father had aimed a gun at his brother's head the night before. When the social worker discussed this matter with Ms. Ramirez, she stated that her husband had been drinking but that he was only "waving the gun around." She went on to say that the gun was not loaded. Obviously, this child's behavior in the classroom can be attributed to something more than the usual aggressive fantasy play of a preschool child. And, certainly, incidents like these, which we believe occur on a fairly regular basis, in and outside his home, have all the earmarks of potentially traumatizing events. For Ramon, the potential for harm is heightened by the fact that his physical and psychological safety has been seriously abrogated by his immediate family, in his own home, during the earliest years of his life (Meers, 1973; van der Kolk, 1987). From an ecological perspective, we are also reminded that the lines between domestic and community violence are increasingly blurred (Chapter Six).

Ms. Ramirez works regularly at a local fast-food restaurant chain. Despite his alcoholism, her husband also seems able to hold a job. She feels physically threatened by her husband, and from time to time there are light bruises on her face or arms. Her family lives in the Dominican Republic, and she is unable to call upon them for help or support of any kind. Since she does not want to return to the Dominican Republic, she relies on her husband's income, health benefits, and "benevolence" for the family's livelihood. Neighbors caught in a similar web of community and familial dysfunction, often characterized by violence, have few resources for helping one another and, like Ms. Ramirez, struggle on alone.

In the past, on several occasions, Ms. Ramirez has gone to counseling sessions at a neighborhood outreach agency offering bilingual services. She also leaves her husband periodically but always returns to the children, who remain in their father's "care," on these occasions. For the most part, the younger children attend school fairly regularly—largely because of the center's supportive vigilance regarding their attendance and general well-being (health, clothing, weekend care, and so forth) as a safeguard against the family's regressive tendency toward abuse or neglect.

The after-school care of the older children, however, remains a matter of concern. Since these children are no longer in the program, the center is less able to ensure that the parents will adhere to minimal standards of care and safety. Intervention is limited to "interested concern" about the well-being of the older children, "our graduates"—and, indeed, if the pattern holds, to the next generation of parents at this center. The center keeps in touch with the older siblings, who return with the family for holiday celebrations, to see their younger brothers "graduate," and, as they get older, to visit from time to time on their own.

Throughout many years of work with this family, Ms. Ramirez has tried to respond to suggestions that she provide better care for her children and obtain help for herself. In situations that suggested borderline abuse or neglect, she complied with requirements made by the center to enhance her children's safety and security. Her husband, on the other hand, refuses involvement with the center. On the whole, Ms. Ramirez probably does the best she can. It does not seem likely that she will leave her husband, and the family will probably continue to function as it is now functioning until a more serious crisis precipitates change. Ms. Ramirez is not a happy woman, but she is also not depressed; the children, however, do not do as well.

Like many of the children we see, who come to school each day struggling with the painful realities of their daily existence (problems of alcoholism, drugs, suicide, rape, poverty, domestic and community violence, physical and psychological abuse, and parental neglect), Ramon and his siblings exhibit periodic episodes of aggression, alternating with periods of depression and gloomy withdrawal. These children frequently display low frustration tolerance and heightened sensitivity to insecurity, anxiety, or fear, which may result in flight, panic, or diffuse destruction. They are often impulse-driven and have low resistance to temptation and are easily overwhelmed in groups. They are particularly vulnerable to high levels of excitement and find it difficult to use sublimation or to restrict their behavior in developmentally appropriate, socially acceptable ways. The inner controls that they might have developed in a more sensitive and responsive early nurturing environment are incomplete or missing.

Ramon's story is a typical story that might apply to many of the children served in programs like these, varying only in the specific details and intensity of the problem. Violence is frequently an underlying theme. But if a case such as

Ramon's—which raises the question of neglect, emotional abuse, and potential trauma—were reported to the state's protective services agency, these children probably would not receive help. Given the unmanageable caseloads and the more pressing problems of many abused and neglected children, this agency might regard Ramon's problems as minor. We are then compelled to ask: "Where does this leave Ramon and children like him?" And what of his neighbors and peers, for whom Ramon's father is part of the problem of community violence?

Two months after our observation of Ramon, during a follow-up visit to the center, we visited Ramon's classroom. We sensed that Ramon was immediately aware of our presence—unlike the past visit, when the consuming preoccupation with "guns" flooded him, shutting out awareness of the outside world. On this occasion, Ramon's sensitivity to our presence continued throughout the visit. He checked and rechecked our whereabouts repeatedly—every few minutes. In this program, the children are informed in advance when visitors are expected in the classroom, or, if a visit is unexpected, the visitor's presence is acknowledged and explained to the children. In this way, a feeling of safety and security about the integrity of their play space is conveyed to the children by the teacher. During this visit, the other children looked up at their teacher's announcement of our presence and returned to their play. After this initial glance, no other child in the classroom gave evidence of Ramon's hypervigilant behavior.

On the other hand, Ramon's behavior was not so driven that he was unable to play. During the free-play time, he worked with the Legos and then sat at a table and completed a puzzle the teacher selected for him. There was the barest hint of a smile on his face as he finished a task and moved on to something else. He listened to the story at circle time, and when he left his lunch table to get "seconds," there was a small skip in his gait as he carried the empty bowl to the serving cart.

Much to our surprise and relief, Ramon looked a lot better. His behavior was certainly not carefree, as evidenced by his nervous, somewhat anxious "checking out" of our whereabouts—echoes of the "kidnapping" event.

Nevertheless, given the family history and his earlier symptoms, his behavior on this visit seemed to suggest his beginning ability to rebalance in the context of program adjustments developed to respond to his particular needs at this time (Chapters Eight and Nine). Despite a slightly subdued demeanor and the level of anxiety described concerning our presence, he was able to eat with enjoyment, and he was able to play.

A tentative, emerging sense of pleasure characterized Ramon's behavior. There was no sign of the earlier gun behavior. And yet, in discussion with the social worker and director, we were told that there was not much change at home. It is possible that Ms. Ramirez interceded in some small way to act as a buffer for the children against their father's use of the gun as a result of the center's discussion with her. On the other hand, given her fear of him and what is known from the history of interpersonal relationships in this family, it is not likely that Ms. Ramirez was able to do much.

Ramon is but one example of the impact of chronic violence that community service providers see pervading every dimension of these children's lives. These are the children who are not likely to be seen by any other helping agency. There are no "Hubbard Woods" (see Chapter Four) mental health teams ready to rush in to help children like Ramon whenever they experience or witness acts of serious violence. More often than not, the Ramons of these communities are the "normal" children in the day-care, Head Start, school-age programs, and public schools serving disadvantaged children. And yet, despite the potential for long-term developmental harm based on the accumulation of risk factors in their lives (Chapter Six), these are the very children who are least likely to receive the therapeutic interventions that they need. The problems of these children, reaching "a new level of deviance and disturbance never before seen by educators" (Wood and Long, 1991, p. xi), are the daily fare of the teachers and other adults who work with children and youth in these communities.

Ramon's Day-Care Center

The center is funded by the state of Illinois and by the city of Chicago, though the Department of Human Services, to provide full day care for children (between three and five years old) of low-income families who are working or in educational programs. The center is housed in a small building in a very marginal and troubled West Side neighborhood. It is a neighborhood of boarded-up and graffiti-covered buildings, uncollected garbage, potholed streets, and littered sidewalks; a neighborhood where rats and roaches share the streets and abandoned buildings with gangs, junkies, and drug peddlers; a neighborhood that increasingly wavers on the edge of racial conflict and turf wars as black families from the projects to the east move west into Hispanic neighborhoods. Street violence is the norm. Inflamed, increasingly, by racial conflict, the violence intrudes regularly upon the center's existence.

Hiring and retaining qualified staff present serious obstacles. Cars belonging to staff and parents are vandalized and sometimes stolen. Purse snatchings are common. The six-foot cyclone fence surrounding the playground has been stolen twice. Bars on the windows and doors, peepholes, and buzzer systems have become a way of life. Increasingly, parent meetings have to be held before dark, so that families and staff can leave the center safely.

More often than not, the neighborhood "tot lots" are unusable because the shattered glass that carpets the broken concrete surface and the stench of urine preclude even the most diligent teachers' efforts to sweep and clean the area every day for the children's use. In addition, the use of these areas by gang members, drug addicts, alcoholics, or the homeless makes them unacceptable as play spaces for the children. (In some neighborhoods, the police direct these individuals to the tot lots to keep them off commercial thoroughfares!) Increasingly, teachers are reluctant to use these play areas if they are out of sight and hearing of the center itself. They question their ability to protect the children adequately in

the event of some unpleasant occurrence with a street person, and they feel equally threatened for their own safety.

One glance at the neighborhood is often enough to discourage prospective applicants from following through with their scheduled interviews to apply for positions at the center. In follow-up contacts with "no-show" applicants, the center has learned that many candidates do not even bother to get off the bus or "el" when they see the neighborhood. Reports in the newspapers of "drive-by" shootings in these troubled neighborhoods—a new phenomenon—will ultimately have the effect of dissuading applicants from even picking up the phone to inquire about an advertised vacancy. This problem is very familiar to service providers who have struggled for years with the problems of hiring staff to work in the well-publicized "notorious" housing project communities—neighborhoods where taxi drivers refuse to go! If the address of the program is posted in the newspaper ad, prospective applicants do not even bother to call—no matter how bad the job market, or how reputable the hiring agency.

This neighborhood is *not*, however, a high-rise housing project setting, where community violence and deprivation reach even more extreme levels. While drug trafficking is a common sight on the streets around the day-care center, and some of these children may live on the upper story of a crack house, overall, this neighborhood is safer and has more intact working families and better social and economic resources than the housing project communities of our experience. There are fewer men standing idly in groups on every street corner in the middle of the day; children playing in the neighborhood tot lots tend to be accompanied by an overseeing adult; people on the street walk purposefully, as if their lives had meaning and direction. There is more energy.

Traveling through the neighborhood on summer days, one can also see freshly painted walls and porches alternating with the more typical boarded-up buildings. Every other block or so, exuberant masses of marigolds, phlox, and zinnias, tended carefully by the occasional homeowner, stand in heroic defiance against the graffiti, weeds, and litter. These tiny city gardens and freshly painted walls proclaim a different set of values and standards. Energy and resources have not been depleted to the same degree that the downward spiral of social and economic disadvantage has affected the housing project communities. The fact that a community needs assessment supports the existence of a publicly funded child-care program for working families in this neighborhood speaks to this issue.

Staff

This forty-child center is administered by a director, a social worker, and a part-time secretary. Each classroom of twenty children is staffed by a head teacher and two assistant teachers.

Despite high professional standards and strong management, this is not a "privileged" educational setting. The annualized cost per child in 1989 was approximately $4,200, the result of combined public and private funding. The ratio of public to private dollars at that time was approximately 4:1, with an ever-increasing need to raise voluntary dollars as public funds have continued to shrink.

The average salary for a head teacher (1989) with *at least* an Associate of Arts degree in early childhood education, is below $14,000. The average salary for the director—who must have *at least* a bachelor's degree (often a master's degree), plus five years' experience (often much longer)—is below $20,000. A social worker with a bachelor's degree earns less than $14,000; a social worker with a Master of Social Work degree and more than fifteen years' experience may earn less than $20,000. And, unlike public school and Head Start teachers, the day-care center's staff work twelve months per year. An ongoing program of supervision and staff training begins with the first hiring interview and continues throughout a teacher's employment in the program (see Chapters Eight and Nine).

The average turnover rate in these programs is less than the 41 percent national average (1989), but it has steadily increased to 20–25 percent annually in the last several years as a result of funding cuts that precluded raises for staff for several years. The long experience, considerable expertise, and commitment of a dedicated professional staff notwithstanding, this is obviously not a well-endowed, laboratory school setting in a safe, welcoming neighborhood and an enriched educational environment.

Theoretical Basis for Programming and Curriculum

For the past fifteen years, the Virginia Frank Child Development Center (CDC) of the Jewish Family and Community Services of Chicago has provided consultation to the Lutheran Social Services of Illinois day-care, school-age, and Head Start programs. The inspiration and guidance provided by the center is acknowledged here. Although this program is not a replication of the Virginia Frank therapeutic program, the "developmental curriculum," "subgrouping," and "attachment teacher" concepts originally developed by CDC in its therapeutic nursery program have been adapted to meet the needs of preschool children in full-day, community-based programs.

The theoretical formulation that provides the basis for practice focuses on interaction and is developmental, borrowing from psychodynamic theory (notably, the theories of Erik Erikson, Margaret Mahler, John Bowlby, René Spitz, and, more recently, Daniel Stern) and the cognitive theories of Jean Piaget, L. S. Vygotsky, Jerome Bruner, and Michael Cole. Accordingly, this program assumes (1) the central role of human relationships in caregiving and learning; (2) the inseparability of cognitive and affective development (mediated by significant adults); (3) the importance of individualizing to support the child's optimal development; and (4) the need to view the child in the context of the family and community.

In implementing these principles, the program recognizes the standards for developmentally appropriate practice established by the National Association for the Education of Young Children (Bredekamp, 1987). When special plans are

developed for children such as Ramon, a wider range of theoretical approaches may be employed under the guidance of a
consultant (for example, approaches based on principles of
learning theory: drives, motivation, reinforcement, and so
forth).

The children's program that emerges from these principles assumes that children entering group life move through
a sequence of stages that parallels movement through the
expected developmental stages of the preschool child. (Developmentally appropriate adjustments in the program design
would be made for older children.) These stages have both
cognitive and affective dimensions. In Phase I, the issues
relate to attachment, dependency, and the establishment of
basic trust; in Phase II, issues of separation and autonomy
predominate; in Phase III, issues reflect the child's emerging
appreciation of social interactions with peers and developing
confidence in previously mastered abilities and learning new
skills (consolidation and initiative). This program is then
individualized to meet each child's particular needs and
circumstances.

A developmental approach to families with young children also provides the theoretical underpinning for work with
parents. This formulation suggests that, as children move
through normal developmental phases, related conflicts are
revived in parents. Programming is adjusted in response to
these emerging developmental issues for children, parents,
and staff.

Organizational Structure

The overall administration, program, and curriculum design
are conceived as a structural and functional whole, whose
specific features, goals, and processes are interrelated. Together, they are grounded in the assumption that *the ongoing
relationship with a significant adult—in this case, the attachment teacher—is the most significant mediator of a young
child's affective and cognitive development.* Administrative and
programming decisions reflect this theoretical priority. (For

example, see the section headed "Subgrouping and Attachment Teachers.") The interweaving of administrative, programmatic, and curricular goals with teaching and social
work practices—based on the central role of human relationships—provides the basis for intervention outlined in Chapter
Six (that is, the need to view the child and the school caregiving context along with the family as the combined unit for
intervention). The significance of this "context" as a protective factor for at-risk children is further discussed in Chapter
Eight.

Subgrouping and Attachment Teachers

In accordance with the theoretical basis for practice described,
two features of the children's program deserve mention. The
first is the subgrouping of each classroom of twenty children
into three consistent groups of six to seven children each.
The second is the provision of three consistent "attachment"
teachers (one head teacher and two assistant teachers) for each
classroom of twenty children. Together, these features and
their related programmatic counterparts (for example, the
organization of space, the use of equipment and materials,
scheduling, and curriculum) provide the basis of the caregiving and learning context we have described. These features
function as the school equivalent of a family—operating, however, within a framework that assumes the greater psychological distance appropriate to a school setting. From the
perspective of maximizing each child's optimal development—and preventing developmental harm in the case of at-
risk children—these program features help to ensure that each
child and his or her family will be offered a basic educational
program of activities and an individualized program of
services.

   In addition, these features support opportunities for
therapeutic interventions centered on individual children in
small-group school settings. Special plans and individualized
responses to each child are always possible. Accordingly,
through the development of a close relationship to a consis-

tent attachment figure, the program provides a physical and psychological structure for each child that supports normal development and enhances the child's resilience in distress. These program features are described in more detail below.

Subgrouping. Each subgroup in a given classroom is a semi-independent unit under the supervision of the head teacher. As noted above, each subgroup of six to seven children has its own attachment teacher. It also has its own space. Within this space, the subgroup children have their own chairs, their own place at the table, and a place for personal belongings. They nap close to their subgroup. These personalized spaces are not interchangeable.

The subgroup provides a home base, from which children can venture into the more challenging and demanding social environment of the larger classroom arena. During a ten-hour day, the subgroups function as described when all three attachment teachers are present: at all meals; at naptime; for all routines, such as toileting or dressing to go outside; at morning circle or greeting times; for teacher-directed activities; and for story time. During the early-morning and late-afternoon program, during free play and outdoor play, the children spend time together with the other children and teachers in the larger, twenty-child group setting.

Children return to their subgroup and special teacher for comfort, privacy, and the easy familiarity of the small group and space. Like a family, each subgroup has a "life" of its own: its own events and celebrations (for example, birthdays and farewells), its own projects (making a card for a sick child in the subgroup or a welcome-back sign for a vacationing teacher), its own history (pictures and scrapbooks of the subgroup children, teachers who have left the program, or favorite rituals), its own routines (calendars, birthday charts, and helper charts)—its own shared meanings. The program of activities in each subgroup is individually tailored to meet the specific needs of those children as a group. Most important, these children "wait for a turn" among only six or seven children instead of among twenty children—a turn to be a "helper," or to "be first," to get their teacher's attention, to have a private conversation with her, or to sit on a warm and comforting lap. These arrangements are better attuned developmentally to the needs of a preschool child.

Attachment Teachers. The attachment teacher is a responsive, caring adult who is trained in early childhood education. This teacher's primary responsibility is to develop a close relationship with each of the *six or seven children— rather than twenty children*—in her care. This relationship provides the basis for the child's affective and cognitive growth, which will be supported through a specific plan of activities to address individual needs.

Teachers are hired for a particular subgroup. Except under unusual circumstances, they are never reassigned to another group, nor are they interchanged from one group to another in the course of the day-to-day program. If reassignment becomes necessary (for example, if an assistant teacher has completed a degree and is promoted to a head teacher position), the subgroup children with whom the teacher has an ongoing relationship remain with that teacher or the promotion is deferred until a number of these subgroup children leave the program to go to kindergarten.

When a teacher is absent, the children go to their regular "substitute subgroup" and "substitute attachment teacher." These substitute groupings are also preplanned and consistently implemented. Children's places are not interchangeable in the substitute subgroup. Children who have been in the program for sufficient time to have experienced the absence of their teacher on several occasions can readily tell you who their regular teacher is, where they sit every day, and where they sit when their teacher is absent.

Children do not leave their subgroupings at the "beginning of a new year," "for math or language," "when they reach four," or on the occasion of any other developmental milestone. Nor are subgroupings combined when attendance is low—when one subgroup has very few children on a given day.

These administrative and programmatic arrangements are designed to ensure that each child experiences a deeply felt sense of place, of belonging, of being wanted, and of being cared for. This is the first step to be achieved in the successful implementation of a developmental curriculum: the establishment of basic trust with a primary adult in a predictable, nurturing environment. As children's functioning in the daily program parallels their progress through each of these early developmental stages (basic trust, autonomy, initiative), the role of the attachment teacher and planning of daily activities are adjusted to reflect each new developmental challenge. The subgrouping and attachment teacher constructs are *organically related* to the implementation of these goals.

Directors and social workers attempt to place children in a subgroup that seems well matched to the child's personality and developmental needs as they have emerged during a careful intake process. In spite of the realities of contract compliance and funding, this process works remarkably well—largely because of the consummate skills of experienced social workers and directors committed to the goals of this program for the children and families served.

In unusual situations, a decision is made to change a child's subgroup. Before such a change takes place, careful plans are made with the family and both attachment teachers to ensure the child's best possible developmental adjustment to the new subgroup and new attachment teacher. These plans include visits to the "old" teacher and subgroup companions, and an official "moving day" with Mom, teachers, and perhaps a special friend assisting. Frequently, the "old teacher" will continue to visit the child in the new subgroup until the child is able to relinquish this emotional tie on his or her own.

Parent Program

A close, mutually beneficial relationship between the parents and the center—the *sine qua non of responsible child care*—begins at intake and continues throughout the family's enrollment in the program. Parents are routinely encouraged to participate in the program in whatever way they can—through informal discussions with staff, through visits to the center or participation on field trips, during conferences, or in activities such as parent meetings, workshops, or center committees.

Unfortunately, however, despite the sophisticated skills of the social work staff, parents sometimes cannot or will not develop a strong relationship beyond complying with the most rudimentary requirements of the intake process (documentation of eligibility, health, and developmental history). Frequently, these parent lead such stressful lives that they have little energy left over at the end of the day for participation in extra activities. Other parents are reluctant to become involved with the center because of an instinctive distrust of mainstream institutions by minority communities—even when those programs are staffed by minority professionals who represent these communities. In other cases, avoidance of the center may have its roots in more complex psychological issues. Increasingly, where serious levels of substance abuse and addiction are concerned, parents are unresponsive and unapproachable. This lack of response is not unusual in inner-city programs and occurs most frequently in precisely those families where the problems are most extreme—where the children show the greatest evidence of dysfunction. In these cases, the center is frequently called upon to manage the child with its own resources and with less than desired participation by the parents.

Special Needs: Staffings and Consultation

Regular weekly "staffings" with the director, social worker, and classroom teaching team provide an ongoing forum for discussing the special problems that emerge for children as they enter group life for the first time, as they encounter new developmental challenges, or as they struggle to cope with the troubling dimensions of their own multiproblem families. Children with problems like Ramon's, for example, are brought up for discussion at a regular weekly staffing.

As the problems that these children bring to the center have multiplied in number and severity over the past five years, these staffings—which include biweekly observation and consultation with an early childhood specialist who has a background in mental health—have become the most crucial and effective intervention strategy for helping at-risk children function successfully in the day-care setting. These collaborative, problem-solving sessions are directed to helping the classroom team help a child manage the day-care experience more effectively.

As a vehicle for training and a support mechanism, these staffings are as critical for the staff as they are for the children who will benefit from them. In the course of developing specific plans to help children, the staff also receive support for their concerns. This mechanism provides an outlet for the enormous frustration, sense of helplessness, diminishing confidence, and lack of satisfaction that are often the result of working with children whose problems are so difficult to resolve.

Work with the family to develop a comprehensive plan for the child parallels, complements, and supports the work with the classroom team. If necessary, plans are made for additional evaluation and/or referral to an outside agency. Together, the education director, the social work supervisor from the central office, and the program consultant from an outside agency collaborate with the center's director, social worker, and classroom teaching staff as a *multidisciplinary team* to ensure that the best possible plan is made for the family within the context of the agency's goals, funding limitations, public mandate, and available resources. This process is an integral and highly effective component of the program's services that helps it retain many children in the center who would otherwise require another placement. Likewise, it is the most crucial mechanism for ensuring ongoing, meaningful staff development, training, and support.

8

Developing Supportive Settings
for Children at Risk

Ramon's story, told in Chapter Seven, is important because it highlights the role of the school as one vehicle for helping children who are exposed to conditions of chronic violence. With so many children experiencing similar difficulties, it is critical to understand the ways in which the school program can support and complement a child's self-righting tendencies, inherent strengths, and potential for resilience. The child-care program Ramon attends provides a wonderful example of this small but real miracle that can occur for children. (As noted in Chapter Six, we use the term *school* to refer to a broad range of school settings, including child-care and preschool programs.)

In her review of the literature on protective factors and resilience, Werner (1990) notes that most resilient children are able to use the school experience profitably, as a refuge from a troubled home environment. To help us better understand the role the school plays in the lives of resilient children as an external source of support, we draw on several important studies (Rutter, Maughan, Mortimore, and Ouston, 1979; Comer, 1980; Schweinhart and Weikart, 1983; Wallerstein and Kelly, 1980; Tharp and Gallimore, 1988). In particular, we shall discuss its effectiveness as a social organization when it provides (1) an opportunity to develop strong relationships with adult role models in a "nurturing setting that combines warmth and caring with a clearly defined structure . . . and explicit limits that are consistently enforced" (Werner, 1990, p. 113); (2) an organized and predictable environment with "clearly defined and consistently enforced standards, rules, and responsibilities" (Hetherington, Cox, and Cox, 1982; cited in Werner, 1990, p. 110); and (3) developmentally appropriate opportunities for enhancing self-esteem and coping skills through academic and/or social achievement (Werner, 1990). We also discuss the significance of the overall school "culture" ("climate," "ethos," "milieu") and its organization as a social context for caregiving and learning.

In describing those features of Ramon's program that contribute to the development of resilience in children exposed to conditions of high stress, we focus on program features that relate most directly to helping at-risk children from the perspective of the literature on resilience: attachment relationships with emotionally significant adults (teachers); structure and control (program design); coping and self-esteem (developmental curriculum).

Caregiving, Learning, and Support:
Attachment Relationships

In the school-based intervention we have proposed, we stress the importance of close, mutually reinforcing, and growth-enhancing relationships between adults and children. We believe that all children, especially children at risk, learn and are able to control their behavior in the context of constructive relationships with emotionally significant adults in a school setting that is educationally enriching and developmentally appropriate. We further believe that these opportunities for children flourish in settings where interpersonal relationships among program adults and parents are positive—where collegiality, teamwork, and collaborative problem solving and decision making result in an esprit de corps that speaks to a sense of shared ownership and commitment to program goals. The pivotal role of adults as the mediators of development in normal caregiving and learning is underscored in these comments:

> Children learn to control the gamut of dysfunc-
> tional impulses and actions, [and] they learn how

to function in a personally and socially acceptable way by responding to and modeling their
own behavior on that of just and important
authority figures. The failure to understand this
and to respond accordingly is the root of many
control problems in schools [Comer, 1980, p. 70].

Although ultimately the motivation to learn
comes from within, learning is initially a process
of identification with emotionally important
people—parents and teachers—that occurs in a
supportive climate. . . . They don't have their
effect through the specific skills they transmit
alone, but through their values, climate, quality
of relationships. Especially in the early years, the
content is almost, *almost,* incidental. Children
learn by internalizing the attitudes, values, and
ways of meaningful others. And then, whatever
content you expose children to, they learn it
[Comer, 1980; in Schorr and Schorr, 1988, p. 234].

At the deepest level, particularly for the youngest children, these interpersonal processes are "curriculum." *They
also constitute the basis of "mental health."* From a pedagogi-
cal perspective, these are the kinds of interactions between
adults and children that mediate the development of higher-
order mental functions—what might be called "assisted performance" interactions (Tharp and Gallimore, 1988, p. 20).
Likewise, from a clinical perspective, we can see the basis for
effective intervention in a complex interpersonal process built
on relationship, trust, and respect (Wood and Long, 1991).
Axline (1969, p. 140) comments: "The most important single
factor in establishing sound mental health is the relationship
that is built up between the teacher and his or her pupils.
This is as true in the kindergarten as it is in the high
school. . . . It is the permissiveness to be themselves, the
understanding, the acceptance, the recognition of feelings,
the clarification of what they think and feel that helps chil-

dren retain their self-respect; . . . the possibilities for growth and change are forthcoming as they . . . develop insight. It is the prerequisite for desirable growth."

Rutter (1979) found that one strong relationship with a close family member—not necessarily the primary caregiver—served as a protective factor for children in times of deprivation, stress, or disadvantage. He further hypothesized that a close relationship with someone outside the immediate family, such as a teacher, also would have a protective effect. We find corroboration for Rutter's hypothesis in studies documenting the significance of important adults in buffering the type and depth of a child's trauma under extreme conditions, such as war (Chapter Three), and in Werner and Smith's (1982) study of the children of Kauai, where a favorite teacher was among the "most frequently encountered positive role models" (Werner, 1990, p. 110) for the resilient children studied (Hyman, Zelikoff, and Clarke, 1987).

A favorite teacher appears to function for resilient children in one or more capacities: as an instructor of academic skills, as a confidant, and as a positive role model for identification (Wallerstein and Kelly, 1980; Werner, 1990). In their research on children of divorce, Wallerstein and Kelly (1980) provide a number of examples of the ways in which children under stress were supported by their close relationship with a friendly teacher at school:

> Preschool and kindergarten children climbed into the laps of teachers to receive nurturance and solace. These youngsters stayed close to the teacher, checking often to receive assurance that they and their work were approved. The comfort that the teacher provided was important to those who sought it because it temporarily reduced anxiety and brought a small measure of security [p. 278].

> [Teachers at all levels] talked of children increasingly seeking them out, needing more atten-

tion. . . . As one second grade teacher said . . .
"These are the kids that are waiting by the gate
when I come to school in the morning" [p. 270].

One child sought out the teacher to talk, especially to talk of her anger at her mother for not
taking her side in anything. This child also made
friends with sensitive male teachers and utilized
a creative writing class to express her angry feelings about her father and his girlfriends [p. 275].

For the children in Ramon's program, the assignment
of a primary caregiver supports the development of a strong
relationship with a caring adult. Such a relationship is a
basic requirement for educational or clinical intervention,
since it provides opportunities for meaningful communication in situations that hold personal significance (Wood and
Long, 1991, p. 5; Tharp and Gallimore, 1988, p. 93). If ongoing opportunities for meaningful, personally significant communication and discourse with children do not exist, the
potential for positive cognitive and affective change declines
significantly. The small-group setting and attachment teacher
arrangements in Ramon's program substantially increase
the probability that positive cognitive and affective growth
will be achieved.

Ramon's strong relationship with his teacher allows
him to trust in her ability to comfort him and to respond to
his overtures for help. This is the teacher who knows that his
favorite toy is the red fire truck, that he likes his juice best
when it is in the red glass, and that he doesn't like raisins.
This is the teacher who knows that he needs a reminder to
stop playing in time to unbuckle his belt so that he doesn't
have an accident, and that a quick hug starts his day best, but
no conversation. This is the teacher who knows that he
begins to need extra help around 4 o'clock to manage the end
of a long day without problems, perhaps anticipating a difficult night at home. This is also the teacher who can say:
"You look very upset about our visitors today, Ramon. I won-

der if you are still thinking about your trip to Puerto Rico.
You are safe here at school. No one is going to hurt you. I
will take care of you."

And then, later in the day, in response to Ramon's
mounting anxiety that is expressing itself in increasingly
aggressive behavior (related to the problems at home elicited
by the morning visitors), she can say with warmth but firmness: "Ramon, I think you are still upset by the visitors this
morning. You are safe here, and I will take care of you, but
you cannot take Rashid's blocks." She takes his hand—with
warmth but firmness—and says, "Why don't you come with
me, and we'll pick out the story we're going to read." Because
of her close relationship with him, Ramon can accept his
teacher's respectful limitations on his behavior, just as he is
able to accept comfort from her. (See Chapter Nine for other
details in the plan developed for Ramon.) On a better day,
this is the same teacher who will share in his delight as he
masters a particularly difficult puzzle, rewarding his competence, promoting his self-esteem (Werner, 1990).

In this regard, we note with particular interest Rutter's
(1979) hypothesis that the "protective effect" of a relationship may depend on the quality and strength of the relationship rather than the specific person with whom the relationship happens to be formed. Programs that support the
establishment of strong relationships between a teacher and
child enhance the probability of "protective effects" for these
children. Werner (1990, p. 112) underscores the importance of
this role: "Research on resilient children has shown repeatedly that if a parent is incapacitated or unavailable, other
significant people in a young child's life can play an enabling
role, whether they are grandparents, older siblings, family
day-care providers, or nursery school teachers. In many situations, it may make better sense to strengthen such available
informal ties to kin and community than to introduce additional layers of bureaucracy into the delivery of services, and
it might be less costly as well."

A personal understanding of the profound significance
of important "teachers" in our lives—of those pivotal indi-

viduals who have nurtured, shepherded, and insisted on personal growth—lies behind the heartwarming, frustrating, and engrossing portrayals found, most recently, in Samuel Freedman's narration of Jessica Siegel's struggles in a Lower East Side high school in New York (*Small Victories*, 1990); in Tracy Kidder's story of Christine Zajac's fifth-grade classroom in Holyoke, Massachusetts (*Among School Children*, 1989); in Quincy Howe Jr.'s personal account of his work with adolescents in residential treatment (*Under Running Laughter: Notes from a Renegade Classroom*, 1991); and in Patsy Walker's story (Chapter Six).

Structure and Control: An Environment That "Holds"

In virtually every discussion of resilient children, we see emerging the importance of structure and control—the need for order and predictability in a safe, disciplined, but not rigid environment. High-risk children seem to benefit from this structure as an environmental factor that operates at many levels to enhance resilience in the family and school childrearing environment. In this regard, structure has both physical and psychological dimensions. Most important, it concerns the personal interactions, discussed in the preceding section, that structure the social context of caregiving and learning at the level of the individual and the overall organization (for example, responsiveness, attunement, nurturing, and warmth; expectations, limits, rules, and responsibilities). "Structure" also concerns arrangements in the external environment, such as those that relate to the use of space, time, materials, and the availability of staff.

   Wallerstein and Kelly (1980) suggest that school provided structure for the children in their study at a time when the predominant structure of their lives was disintegrating. For some children, the mere act of going to school each day and performing certain regular tasks gave a sense of support. For other children, schoolwork provided structure by channeling energies and encouraging sublimation in the service of coping. Rutter (1979, p. 65) also concludes that "a degree of structure and control . . . seems more important in conditions of severe deprivation, chaos, and uncertainty." And, in reference to the overall school environment, Comer argues that you "can't learn in chaos." That is, an organized and well-managed environment, grounded in sound principles of child development, is needed to offset the less developed social, emotional, cognitive, and linguistic skills that children bring to school from their neighborhoods and homes (cited in Schorr and Schorr, 1988, pp. 232–233).

In settings organized to ensure this structure, children like Ramon experience a greater sense of control over their otherwise unpredictable lives. This sense of control enhances coping, self-esteem, and resilience even when there is little reason to expect outside therapeutic intervention that ultimately ameliorates the family child-rearing environment. At Ramon's day-care center, children develop an inner feeling of security and trust about their surroundings and the people who care for them through a program design that provides:

1. Consistent assignment and scheduling of staff, so that one adult is clearly designated as the "primary caregiver" or "attachment teacher" for each subgroup of six to seven children.
2. A consistent "substitute attachment teacher" and "substitute subgroup."
3. Consistent and unvarying placement of children in small groups ("subgroups").
4. Consistent subgroup space, including regularly assigned places at the table, at circle, and at story time, as well as the consistent placement of cots at nap and personalized use of cubbies or lockers.
5. Consistent scheduling of all components of the daily program (see the section headed "Transitions and Change," below).
6. Programming that reflects and anticipates the preschool child's normal developmental concerns with attachment and separation (see the section headed "Transitions and Change," below).

The well-ordered, predictable, physically and psychologically "safe" environment that results from these arrangements frees the child to focus on other needs and supports the development of competence. The child experiences this environment as follows: "I know where to go here; I know what to do here; I know what happens next; I know who will take care of me when I need help." The small-group experience with one adult within a structure that keeps expectations, numbers of people, and exposure to stimulations within manageable proportions says to the child: "You are safe here. I will take care of you. You can play [do your schoolwork]."

Children struggling with traumatic events are helped by an environment that can "take over" when coping abilities are diminished by stress. When the classroom setting is not structured to provide this support, children may not be able to rise to the potential of their own inherent strengths. The parallels with the family environment seem obvious. Repeatedly, we have seen children like Ramon improve when the classroom setting has been arranged to reflect the principles listed above. In one setting, the child disintegrates; as the classroom environment improves, the same child begins to come under control—even when the teacher(s) may be very inexperienced.

Year after year, the well-designed, developmentally appropriate, child-responsive classroom also produces fewer children for referral from the same population of families— even when the most difficult children are regularly assigned to such a classroom. Rutter, Maughan, Mortimore, and Ouston (1979) allude to a similar phenomenon, indicating that the more productive school environments they studied can exist independently of the characteristics of the population at enrollment. In other words, the "good" schools were not good because they started with "better" children. As we shall see later in this chapter, this structure also serves to overcome some of the negative consequences of less trained teachers and staff turnover—the results of low salaries and inadequate funding (Abt Associates, 1987). This structure also appears to maximize significantly the talents and efforts of very compe-

tent teachers—and, correspondingly, the protective effects for
children. Good schools for high-risk children are "strong" in
the sense that they overcome characteristics of the child rather
than just mirror them (Garbarino and Asp, 1981).

Coping and Self-Esteem:
A Developmental Approach to Curriculum

A developmental approach to curriculum can be used to support a child's self-righting tendencies, inherent strengths, and
potential for resilience—coping abilities that translate into
self-esteem. Such an approach acts in two ways. It supports
the child's current functioning, thereby fostering growth; and
it provides opportunities to rework earlier stages of development. With this ego support, the child experiences satisfaction and competence in mastering the daily challenges
presented by life (Williamson and Zeitlin, forthcoming).

In addition, a program designed with sufficient flexibility and sensitivity to adapt to individual needs ensures that
a child can shift between higher and lower states of functioning. These opportunities help the child develop coping skills
without losing self-esteem. Children "achieve better integrated
personalities and gain strength through repeating inade-
quately mastered tasks or missed experiences . . . [which
enables them] to move up the developmental ladder" (Virginia Frank Child Development Center, 1974). In this regard,
we note that young children develop resilience not when
stress and adversity are completely removed from their lives
but, rather, when they "encounter graduated challenges that
enhance their competence and confidence" (Werner, 1990,
p. 112).

Accordingly, in a developmental approach to curriculum, the teacher adapts the expected program of activities to
meet the particular needs of that group of children, and of
individuals within that group. The combined benefits of a
small-group experience with one adult and a daily program
of manageable activities, tailored to Ramon's varying experiences at home, support the development of resilience. On the

"good days," children can move ahead with new lessons that demand close attention, or they can engage in complex activities requiring new skills or group problem solving—for example, new puzzles, more difficult games requiring turn-taking and sharing, finger painting, or story dramatization. The addition of more complex props in the doll house or block area, and reading more involved stories are possible. Through their important relationship with the children, the teachers pull them to higher levels of achievement—facilitating and appreciating the development of initiative, new skills, competence, internalized controls, and the ability to cooperate (Virginia Frank Child Development Center, 1974).

On days when one child or a number of children in the group are having difficulties—after a long weekend at home, perhaps—the teacher may substitute the simpler (that is, already mastered) activities of an earlier developmental phase. The teacher may also offer opportunities for more disciplined self-expression through the arts—a chance to "escape" from current realities through the use of a wide range of art materials and many opportunities for dramatic play. The arts and dramatic play provide important opportunities to substitute a socially approved goal for a drive whose normal channel of expression or normal goal is blocked (that is, "sublimation"). For school-age children, similar experiences are achieved through reading, writing, hobbies, or games. The use of dramatic play and the arts—an important component of any developmental approach to curriculum for preschool and early primary children—will be discussed in more detail as a therapeutic intervention in Chapter Ten.

During these periods when children regress to earlier developmental levels, complex activities that require close teacher supervision (for example, finger painting or cooking) are replaced by activities that allow the teacher to be available, physically and psychologically, to the children who need her or him. Activities that are soothing and individualized (for example, *individual* play in water or sand or with pegboards) replace sharing activities (such as group murals or board games). Books are selected for their ability to create feelings of warmth and being taken care of (for example, *Little Fur Family* or *Goodnight Moon*).

In this role, the teacher gives nurturance and support, manages stimulation (people and events), anticipates needs, and provides relaxation and comfort (Virginia Frank Child Development Center, 1974). Clear expectations, firm but gentle limits, and reduced but interesting choices are offered. In managing exposure to stimulation and setting protective and realistic limits; providing comfort, support, approval, and acceptance; and rewarding genuine accomplishments, the teacher and program of selected activities are effective in nurturing the building blocks of self-esteem.

Transitions and Change

As we noted in Chapter Seven, children like Ramon are particularly vulnerable or sensitive to the effects of change. Accordingly, considerable attention is paid to all aspects of the program that involve transitions or change in expected routines. Concerns about separation from primary caregivers and changes in the caregiving environment represent a normal developmental challenge for all preschool children. These situations revive in children their earliest experiences of caregiving and attachment to a primary caregiver. When children can depend on the availability and responsiveness of primary caregivers to meet their most basic physical and psychological needs, "basic trust" is the result (Erikson, 1950). For children like Ramon, anxiety about abandonment (separation issues), evoked by change and transition in the daily program, is frequently heightened because of deficits in the early nurturing environment—for example, the lack of physical and psychological safety in their own home. When not anticipated, these changes often result in anxiety, panic, or flight behaviors.

Consistency, predictability, and attention to transitions, therefore, are significant concerns for staff in planning the daily program. The following routine occurrences, which are typical in the day-to-day operations of any child-care program, are considered from this point of view: staff absences or terminations, a new teacher, the presence of a new child in the group, the number of new children in a group, the arrival and pick-up of children, visitors (including parents, consultants, health providers, photographers, and the media), changes in scheduling, changes in routines, new activities, movement from one activity to another, parties, holidays and celebrations, changes in room arrangement or other changes in the use of space (for example, a group using a different bathroom), and group contagion effects that may be the result of heightened stimulation (for example, a police siren out on the street or a water pistol that emerges from someone's pocket).

Activities away from the center (for example, walking trips or field trips) are of particular concern, since large open spaces—whether indoors or outside—may present special problems for these children. In Ramon's program, change, transition, and stimulation are carefully evaluated from the perspective of their potentially disruptive effects on children who are especially vulnerable. A wide variety of individual plans can be made to enhance a child's coping skills and sense of control in these situations.

In Ramon's classroom, certain stresses affect all the children: the effects of low income, single parenthood, poor health and housing conditions, and the exposure to community violence. In addition, at least four of the children face significant problems or are evidencing developmental harm: four-year-old Jamilla, who killed her brother's pet bird, plucking out its feathers one by one and stomping on it because it "made too much noise"; four-year-old Karen, whose mother is dying of cancer; four-year-old Ronald, who was seen pulling the baby doll's legs apart, kissing the vaginal area, and then, repeatedly, banging the doll's head against the wall; and five-year-old Daniel, whose father is in prison for murder.

Young as these children are, 25 percent of the children in the class have had seriously traumatic experiences. This figure does not include as-yet undisclosed trauma in the lives of other children in the group. In these programs, it is not unusual to have three or four cases per classroom at any one time. If this classroom were not designed to be responsive to children's needs, and structured to shore up a child's faltering ability to cope on the "bad days," the inevitable regressed behavior would tend to destroy the classroom as a functioning social unit. In Ramon's classroom, however, these children are given some relief from their distress through a consistent, well-structured program that supports a close relationship with an emotionally important adult in a small-group setting; these arrangements further enhance the potential for self-esteem and coping through a developmental approach to curriculum.

Special Services and Consultation

In each of the cases mentioned above, the center's social worker and director, the education director and social work supervisor from the central office, and the program consultant, who has a background in mental health, work together with the classroom staff as a unified team to discuss and develop plans for each child. These plans include work in the classroom and with the family. In cases such as Jamilla's, for example, even if serious emotional disturbance is diagnosed, an attempt is made to serve the family as long as the center can manage the child and the child is able to benefit from the program's services. This is a particularly important concern because there may be no other placement available for this child. If the family refuses to seek help for the child after an appropriate psychological evaluation has been made, a subsequent determination to report neglect might have to be considered. The combined significance of the center's supervisory process and the availability of outside consultation is discussed in the following section and in Chapter Nine.

Relationship, Structure, Coping, and Self-Esteem: A Parallel Experience for Staff

In addition to the benefits for children, a program that emphasizes clearly defined staff roles, a consistently implemented supervisory process, and well-developed procedures for the regular staffing of children provides a parallel experience for staff. The opportunity to discuss individual children's needs, to raise problems, and to explore classroom issues in supervisory sessions socializes new teachers into the program "ethos" and provides a developmental framework in which ongoing training can take place. These ideas and processes are reinforced at team meetings and in weekly staffings.

As we shall see in Chapter Nine, the emphasis on staffing children, teacher supervision, and consultation also serves to contain other emotional conflicts that may emerge in teachers as a result of their work with difficult children. These arrangements—which provide systematic outlets for expression, clarification, or reframing issues—are particularly helpful to teachers who have little training and experience in this work.

These training and supervisory processes provide the interpersonal and programmatic support that assists new teachers as they learn, enhances the ongoing development of long-term staff, and ensures the continuity of program philosophy and its implementation in daily operations. New teachers are hired on the basis of their philosophical compatibility with the overall program design, their enthusiasm about its "vision"; and changes in program and curriculum are explored in the context of the supervisory process. These procedures further ensure program continuity and protect children and the remaining staff from the upheavals of continual programmatic shifts resulting from staff turnover. Both children and adults develop a sense of belonging and ownership that is supported by these interpersonal processes and a program design that guide participation in the program.

The School as Social Organization

The principles described in Chapter Six, emphasizing the significance of context and individual as a combined unit for intervention, find their expression in the child-care center we have described. These comments by Tharp and Gallimore

(1988, p. 113) speak to our understanding and experience of this issue: "A major lesson learned is this: Teaching transactions in the classroom are organically related to organizational transactions throughout the school administrative and authority lines. . . . *The dialectic between the teaching/learning interactions and their organizational context must be appreciated,* or else the theoretical principles and operational admonitions . . . will be deceptive. . . . For teaching excellence to survive, it must be supported systemically" (italics added).

Effective organization, however, is not a random assembly of operations. Instead, the operations are driven by a set of principles and values: the "invisible hand of the ecoculture" (Tharp and Gallimore, p. 73) or the "ethos." The "operations performed in the service of the goal are not random; they are distributed according to the personnel mix and given shape by the goal itself" (p. 73). Rutter and his colleagues (Rutter, Maughan, Mortimore, and Ouston, 1979) use the term *ethos* to refer to the accepted set of norms—values, attitudes, behaviors, formal and informal "rules,"—that result in an "institutional effect" (p. 179). "Ethos" here is a *gestalt,* whose combined symbolic, physical, and psychological meaning has properties that cannot be derived from its parts (see Comer, 1980, "climate"; Redl, 1966, "milieu").

In their study comparing the children from the middle-class environment of the Isle of Wight and those in three disadvantaged boroughs of inner-city London, Rutter and his colleagues (1979) found that children's development was influenced by the overall social organization of the school itself and that some schools were able to exert a positive and beneficial influence on pupils' progress and to protect them from difficulties (for example, dropping out, delinquency). These effects existed independently of the characteristics of the population at intake (enrollment). Children were more likely to show good behavior and good scholastic attainments if they attended some schools than if they attended others.

In an attempt to understand these effects, Rutter and his colleagues went on to examine specific features of the schools. Their results indicated that the different outcomes of different schools were systematically related to their characteristics as social institutions, all of which were "open to modification" by the staff rather than "fixed by external constraints" (p. 179). They also found that the overall effect of these various social factors was considerably greater than any single factor in isolation. They therefore postulated an "institutional effect."

In their review of the "effective schools" literature, Schorr and Schorr (1988) also underscore the significance of cumulative, interactive effects and the need to consider the total school climate. Their analysis supports the conclusion reached by Rutter and his colleagues: that "the overall school environment has a powerful impact on student outcomes . . . [and that] the full impact of schools on children might be missed by looking only at discrete elements rather than the whole school environment" (p. 226). Comer (1980) speaks to this issue as follows: "People aren't educated in pieces, and kids don't learn in pieces. . . . That's why it's essential to address the entire social system of the school because of the way many variables interact and because attitudes, morale, and hope all affect school performance" (quoted in Schorr and Schorr, 1988, p. 235).

It is in both these senses, then, in the details and the overall institutional effect, that we speak of an overarching structure or ethos that intends to be nurturing, developmentally appropriate, and educationally enriching and that functions as a protective factor for children. Indeed, at its best, it is also therapeutic and healing (that is, it promotes mental health). In this regard, caregiving, learning, and mental health combine as a single process that is both "vehicle and destination" (Tharp and Gallimore, 1988, p. 73) to support the development of resilience in children like Ramon.

Although a *particular* program, philosophy, or "prescription" cannot be shown to have a simple and direct relationship to desired outcomes, our experience and the research literature on "effective schools" and "resilient children" (Hyman, Zelikoff, and Clarke, 1987; Milgram, 1983; Freud and Burlingham, 1943; Wallerstein and Kelly, 1980; Werner, 1990; Hetherington,

Cox, and Cox, 1982; Tharp and Gallimore, 1988; Wood and
Long, 1991; Abt Associates, 1987; Schweinhart, Koshel, and
Bridgman, 1987; Snow, 1983) indicate that quality programs
for at-risk children have the following features:

1. Adults serving as the most significant mediators of a
    child's affective and cognitive development.
2. Strong, constructive relationships with the family.
3. Sufficient staff who are trained in early childhood educa-
    tion, temperamentally suited to work with young chil-
    dren, and responsive to their needs.
4. Small group size.
5. A program of developmentally appropriate activities re-
    sponsive to individual needs.
6. Support services, consultation, and supervision.
7. Effective administration.
8. A unifying programmatic philosophy.

     A positive school climate that meets these guidelines is
synonymous with the "mental health" environment we envision. We believe that most students will try and are able to
learn in a school setting such as we describe—one in which
instruction, discipline, social activities, and relationships at
the school are coordinated to provide a secure school environment in which children are encouraged to exercise self-
discipline and are also provided with opportunities to enhance their self-esteem (Comer, 1980; see Schorr and Schorr,
1988, p. 227, for a more detailed discussion of similar characteristics that apply to secondary schools).
     We further believe that the vast majority of poor chil-
dren, even poor children from chaotic families, are not psychologically ill and can perform adequately in school,
provided the school climate is positive. For these children, a
positive school climate is even more important than it is for
children who bring fewer liabilities with them to school.
Moreover, only after the school climate becomes positive is it
possible to identify students with emotional or developmental
problems that require referral for individual treatment.

For those children whose problems are beyond the scope of the classroom or school intervention, a special plan of services can be developed, which may include referral to an outside agency. Referral to an outside resource, however, assumes a collaborative effort for the delivery of appropriate services and the development of special plans for the child in the school setting, whenever possible.

Years of observing adapted versions of this program design convinces us that problems such as Ramon's can often be managed in a well-designed classroom in a program with the support services we have described. The far-reaching potential inherent in a well-designed program is so strong that it has important diagnostic implications. Indeed, one of the first steps in determining the depth of the child's problems is to determine to what extent the classroom or school environment is contributing to or failing to relieve the problem. Comer (1980) is emphatic on this point: "The most basic problem in education today is the assumption that if the kid doesn't learn, it's the kid's fault. The school doesn't take the responsibility" (cited in Schorr and Schorr, 1988, p. 237). From this perspective, it is schools, not children, who fail: "I would argue that for the vast majority of kids, structuring the environment to facilitate learning and development is going to do more than trying to change the kid (p. 235). . . . What I've tried to do here in New Haven is to shape the system, the school, so that it becomes the advocate and support for the kid, a believer in the kid in the same way that my parents were" (p. 232).

Our personal experience and the research on resilience and effective schools repeatedly confirm the importance of this supportive, holding environment for children and staff—an environment based on respect and trust. But the factors we have posited as crucial to the development of resilience in at-risk children will not be effective without the theoretical grounding (in child development, human relationships, and instructional theory), administrative competence, strong interpersonal skills, and emotional commitment of leadership behind them.

While we have concentrated on organizational structures and principles that undergird the caregiving and learning context of the school, we close this discussion by returning full circle to the significance of relationships with important authority figures. Dr. Kriftcher is the principal of Seward Park, a beleaguered inner-city school on New York's Lower East Side, portrayed in Samuel Freedman's book *Small Victories* (1990). Through Freedman's eyes, we glimpse the significance of Dr. Kriftcher's role as he interacts with students, teachers, parents, and the community, setting the standards for protection, caregiving, and learning in this school that will become the hallmark of its "ethos."

The lessons of three male role models in his youth have served Dr. Kriftcher well in his relationships with students. He is an ongoing, "overt" physical presence in their lives. His daily schedule begins with "hall walking" throughout the building, during which he engages personally with many students: "Every single encounter, no matter how mundane, carries the seeds of confrontation. . . . Every interchange requires Dr. Kriftcher to project resolve, respect, and a trace of threat. . . . [He has found that to survive in this community] a male must exude strength and will, must suggest that he is capable of meeting a physical challenge without ever inviting one." Dr. Kriftcher addresses "wayward students with polite words and sardonic tones . . . [standing] only inches from such students, his arms folded and his back arched, near enough to see anger flicker across their faces." And yet "a punch has never flown . . . in Dr. Kriftcher's twenty-eight-year career" (pp. 361–362).

In an environment plagued by violence and savage brutality on the streets, Freedman comments: "What intrigued me was how little of that violence ever infiltrated Seward Park. The school does not have armed guards, or metal detectors; it does not search bags and lockers. It could not summarily dismiss students. Seward Park's approach began with its principal . . . whose instruments of discipline were not bat and bullhorn" but personal authority and interpersonal relationships (p. 362).

This is a principal who knows that "discipline [does] not replace learning; it only [makes] it possible . . . [and that] to invoke discipline without offering education in return [makes] a school nothing but a penal colony" (p. 364). This is a principal who vacates his office for ninety minutes a day in the spring, so that screening interviews for prospective scholarship recipients can be held, a man who believes that the principal of an inner-city school "cannot afford to be timid and reactive . . . that he must be an advocate [for his students]" (p. 361). This is a man who delegates responsibility and shares credit, a man who respects and values the efforts of his staff. He is a principal who seeks out parents, attends all school functions, and shops in the neighborhood.

"The one area in which he assumes more direct control," Freedman tells us, "the area that he considers the foundation of a credible school, is in ensuring its safety" (p. 361). Dr. Kriftcher works cooperatively with local police and neighborhood store owners. His "watchful eyes" ensure that empty parking places in front of the school are filled by staff cars—leaving fewer opportunities for drug dealers and gang members to gain access to the school. This is a principal who sets a standard for his school that says, "This is not 'Out There.' This is 'In Here' "—a man who says that a "neighborhood school must be a welcoming refuge, what he calls a "mother with a light on in the kitchen," and that it must also be "a fortress defended against barbarism" (Freedman, 1990, pp. 360-363). The young adults, families, and the staff at this school, no matter the odds, have a better chance under such leadership, commitment, direction, and vision.

Conclusion

In this chapter, we have tried to describe the ways in which schools—*with support from a caring society*—can act to safeguard the well-being of children in institutions where caregiving, learning, and mental health are institutionalized as values to create a unifying "ethos"—a "socially integrating sense of purpose" (Schorr and Schorr, 1988, p. 227)—that

supports normal growth and development and acts as a therapeutic intervention or protective factor for children at risk.
These are programs that nurture and support staff in their
dual role as caregivers and teachers and that welcome, engage,
and hold out an open hand to as many parents as are able to
take it.

9

Helping Teachers
Help Children

As we have seen in earlier chapters, children and youth caught up in war and other forms of social crisis need sympathetic adults—parents and professionals—to help them deal with the trauma that can result from exposure to chronic danger. These adults can help create a new, positive reality that can withstand the "natural" conclusions a potentially traumatized child or youth is likely to draw about self-worth, about the reliability of adults and their institutions, and about safe approaches to adopt toward the world. Accordingly, any effort to deal with the problems of children living in multirisk communities—communities where violence and danger have become a fact of life—must include a program to inform and support professionals who work with these children: educators, administrators, social workers, and health-care providers. Such a program must help teachers and staff deal with the intense feelings and thoughts they have about violence, loss, and the grieving process. Unless they can come to terms with these personal and professional concerns in a way that fortifies and sustains them, these very crucial adults will have neither the knowledge nor the confidence necessary for them to be available to the children and parents who need their help.

Teachers' Experiences in the Classroom

In our meetings with teachers of Head Start and after-school programs, the teachers often ask questions such as these: "What am I to say when a child comes to the center and says

that on his way to school he saw a man 'thrown in the garbage' [dumpster]—and adds, in a terrified whisper, that there
was 'blood coming out all over his head'?" Or "How am I to
respond when a child tells me, 'My uncle said he killed those
police'?"

They ask us what they should do when a child draws a
picture of his cousin in a grave, or when the children play
funeral in the block corner, or when they build a coffin. They
ask whether they should allow the children to play "shooting
up" (drugs, not guns), or "robbing," or "rolling joints," or
"drinking beer."

They wonder what to say when the children report that
"Ronny," a program child and friend, was "taken away last
night for bad things" or when a woman, wounded from gunfire, is dragged off the sidewalk and into the building by
program staff as the children are returning from the library.
They wonder what to tell the children about the new bullet
hole in the door of the school where they enter and leave
every day. They wonder what to say to the children about the
men they saw carrying Uzis on the walk to the library, knowing that some of these children's family members are involved
in the gangs. They wonder whether they should go to the
library anymore. They wonder whether they are safe.

We heard similar accounts in the elementary school training sessions in three different housing project communities:

> A kindergarten teacher in one school said: "I don't know
> what to do or if I should do anything. I know that this child
> saw his mother beaten to death about a month ago. Little by
> little, he seems to be withdrawing. He doesn't say anything
> anymore, and he used to be so bright and good at his work.
> I can see him going downhill. What can I do? Should I say
> anything to him? This happens to a lot of our children.
> Should we talk about it? How can we talk to just one child!
> This is happening to every child! What will happen if we
> start talking to each child?"

> In another school, a first-grade teacher told us: "A child told
> me this awful thing yesterday, and I checked and found out
> that it was true. I said something to her. Was that right?

What should I say now? Please just tell me if what I did was OK. I know you're coming back later, but I have to know now. It's just awful. It's just awful . . . what happened to that little girl. I have to say something more. What should I say? Was that all right to say to her?"

In another neighborhood, a teacher reported that one of her eight-year-old girls approached her hesitantly and whispered: "I don't like him to touch me. I don't want to touch him. Do I have to do that?" The teacher, angry, frustrated, and feeling helpless, said to us: "Why does your training only address the children exposed to community violence? This is violence too, and it's happening to a lot of children! How can I help these girls? They are only eight and nine years old."

At a school on the West Side, another teacher told us about a little boy in her first-grade class, the son of a psychologically disturbed woman. This shy, worried child is being scapegoated by the other children because the family moved into the same Chicago Housing Authority (CHA) apartment where a "bloody" murder took place. In the community lore, this apartment is "tainted." ("The blood is still on the walls," according to local rumor.) No one had lived there since the murder, until this family moved in. ("That woman, she's crazy. No one in their right mind would move in there!") The teacher feels at a loss to combat both the community and classroom scapegoating of this child.

In every school, the outbreak of the war with Iraq became an issue. Both the tragedy and the irony of the teachers' plight were all the more pronounced because the lesson plans so carefully prepared in honor of Martin Luther King Day—*developed with particular reference to nonviolence*—coincided with the beginning of the war. The staff felt confused, angry, and frustrated in their attempts to address, *simultaneously,* issues of nonviolence and the war. Can anyone fail to empathize with a teacher who is trying to help the children in her class make sense of these issues? In one housing project community, against a backdrop of ongoing violence, these events occurred within the space of several weeks:

- A gang shoot-out requiring evacuation to the inner corridors of the school.
- The outbreak of a war with around-the-clock television coverage that portrayed shooting scenes not unlike the gang shoot-outs taking place in the community.
- Martin Luther King Day, celebrating the message of civil rights and nonviolence.

Shortly thereafter, one CHA resident in this same neighborhood reported that she saw a white Cadillac *in broad daylight,* in full view of anyone passing by, pull up in front of one of the more notorious gang-controlled buildings. The driver got out, opened the trunk of the car, and handed one weapon after another to the young men who had been waiting inside the building to receive them. Several weeks later, we received this note from a teacher in the same neighborhood who had participated in the training:

> Our school situation has worsened. We have had more gang-related activity than "usual" for this time of year. We have had one more incident involving shooting (no one hit) this time as school dismissed. I am not the only teacher who senses yet more problem[s] around the corner. Gang conflict entered the school this time, though guns did not. [This school] is especially vulnerable with [CHA] buildings so very close on three sides, in a highly troublesome gang area. I'm not sure how much more . . . you can do for us. Whatever could be [done] would be welcomed.

These stories speak for themselves. They highlight the salient concerns of teachers; raise major philosophical, theoretical, and methodological questions; and suggest content areas rarely covered in traditional teacher education programs. These are the stories and issues that will shape the training programs designed to prepare preschool teachers, primary school teachers, and administrators to respond to the concerns brought into the classroom by children living in dangerous areas of the city.

Areas That Training Programs Need to Emphasize

Teachers need preparation in the following areas: child development theory and practice, the developmental consequences of risk, protective factors and resilience, the development of mental health skills, emotional availability, and the role of affect in helping relationships. Because much of this information is broadly available in the general literature or has been referenced in earlier chapters, we will discuss only those issues that raise particularly thorny questions for training and implementation.

Child Development Theory and Practice

The implementation of a school-based model of intervention assumes that teachers have a working knowledge of child development theory that views the developing child in the context of family, culture, and community. It also assumes that teachers are competent in the application of these principles—in short, that the notion of "developmental appropriateness" is fundamental to their understanding of children and program design.

Developmental Consequences of Risk

When we speak about the need for a "more comprehensive and deeper understanding of the psychological development of children" (Wallerstein and Kelly, 1980, p. 266), we are especially concerned that teachers comprehend the nature and meaning of "risk," the potential for developmental harm that results from exposure to temporary or prolonged stress and trauma, and the changes in behavior that suggest the presence of an underlying problem.

We stress this topic as an area for concentration because

teachers have not usually been adequately prepared for the level of problems facing many children in today's classrooms (see Wallerstein and Kelly, 1980, chap. 15, for discussion). Moreover, the profound and troublesome "shift in the burden of caregiving—of nurturing, protecting, socializing, and caring for others—in American society" (Halpern, 1990b, p. 265) suggests that schools, inevitably, will bear the burden of these problems (Wood and Long, 1991). It is more crucial than ever before, therefore, for teachers to understand the relationship between exposure to chronic, cumulative risk and the resulting psychological, physical, and behavioral effects that may impinge on the mental health and academic success of disadvantaged children and, correspondingly, to develop more effective intervention strategies and skills to help these troubled children.

Accordingly, teachers and staff must understand the concept of "regression"—the particular behaviors, defense mechanisms, and coping strategies that are a response to stress ("loss" of primary caregivers or other emotionally significant individuals through death, divorce, family disruption, or substance abuse; physical harm or abuse, sexual abuse, neglect, substance abuse; and so forth). They must also be able to recognize the fluctuating patterns of these effects over time and be sensitive to children's shifting needs as they revisit (or, rework) earlier issues from the perspective of a new developmental stage or challenge.

For teachers who are working with children exposed to chronic violence, two specialized topics are particularly relevant: post-traumatic stress disorder (PTSD) and children's understanding of and reaction to death.

PTSD and "Psychological First Aid." In their paper "Psychological First Aid and Treatment Approach to Children Exposed to Community Violence: Research Implications," Pynoos and Nader (1988) present an overview of children's responses to community violence, early intervention, and treatment approaches following a violent event. They discuss post-traumatic stress, the grieving process in children, loss of significant relationships, and experience with previous trauma. The intervention strategies they propose are described from a developmental perspective and include discussions of approaches for the classroom, the family, the individual, and the group.

We recommend the use of this material as a springboard for designing training programs; however, it must be adapted to the particular circumstances of children and communities exposed to chronic violence. Interventions developed in response to single-event situations are not always appropriate in communities where exposure to traumatic events are routine. Such strategies are quickly dismissed by teachers and school administrators, who understand that sending out letters, for example, or calling school meetings on the occasion of every "traumatic event" simply begs the issue. The need to develop interventions that respond to the particular needs of these communities is critical. We further recommend that this information be presented in a format similar to the one described below, where the presentation of didactic material is skillfully interwoven or combined with the opportunity to process feelings. (Parental consent must be obtained when interventions exceed what would be considered usual or expected educational services or teaching practices. Such clinical interventions should not be undertaken unless the consultant has access to supervision or is otherwise credentialed or licensed to undertake them.)

Children's Understanding of Death. These sessions should be designed to help teachers understand children's reactions to death from a developmental perspective, while offering support to teachers as they explore their own feelings about death.

We conducted two pilot studies to provide this information and support to Head Start and public school primary teachers who work in housing project communities. The "New Mourning" program, developed in 1987 at Evanston Hospital in Evanston, Illinois, was presented in four to six sessions, at program locations in the community. The format of the "New Mourning" training program was adapted to address the needs of teachers and classrooms in communities where the exposure to chronic violence is a norm—a fact of everyday life—as opposed to those situations in a school or community where such an event has disrupted the usual order of business (for example, the Laurie Dann shootings at the Hubbard Woods School, referred to in Chapter Four).

Based on the premise that early intervention facilitates the normal grieving process, the program is designed to provide adults with the appropriate skills to offer children help and support as soon as possible after a death has touched their lives. The program further assumes that, in order to be successful in this effort, adults must explore and become comfortable with their own feelings surrounding dying and death. This approach to intervention, therefore, recognizes children's habits of identifying with adults' ways of handling grief and clarifies that issue for participants in the course of training.

We attribute the success of these sessions to the following factors: the high level of interest in the topic; the presenter's ability to draw upon adult feelings and experiences as a springboard for discussion and to contrast their feelings and reactions with those of children at different developmental levels; the presenter's sensitivity to racial, cultural, and socioeconomic differences as they emerged in the training sessions; the presenter's ability to support individuals when the material elicited painful memories, modeling the "emotional and behavioral availability" that is the desired goal of these efforts; and, finally, the presenter's credentials and expertise as a school social worker in both public and preschool settings, so that he was able to address teachers' questions and discuss interventions, *specifically,* from the perspective of these school settings. These observations were confirmed in follow-up discussions with teachers and a final evaluation. In later sessions, teachers described their use of this material with the children. This example is illustrative:

> On Monday morning, three children came in mentioning incidents about death. [Three deaths had occurred in the lives of these preschool children: a low-birthweight, premature baby sister

died at birth; a father of a friend died of cancer; and an uncle was killed in a fight.] If I hadn't been to those workshops, I would never have dared say anything to them. We had such a good discussion even though it was very sad. I was so surprised and proud of myself. I would never have done this before. The children seemed so much better after we talked. They were all very serious, but it was OK. We talked for about 15 minutes. Everyone [the three children] was involved, and they listened to each other. It was one of the best talks we have ever had. I was very pleased.

Good Grief: Helping Groups of Children When a Friend Dies (Fox, 1988) is an excellent monograph providing information on children's understanding of and reaction to death, including specific and valuable recommendations for the handling of this issue by teachers and schools (see also Pynoos and Nader, 1988).

Protective Factors and Resilience

Although they may develop symptoms of stress from ongoing exposure to community and domestic violence, loss of possessions, separation from loved ones, and personal devaluation in their daily lives, many of these children still can cope and achieve if they are provided with a school experience that is sensitive to them and their burdens. In Chapter Eight, we discussed three "protective factors" in the school setting: attachment relationships, structure and control, and a developmental approach to curriculum that supports coping and self-esteem. Within the framework of developmental appropriateness, training should address the corresponding interpersonal, programmatic, and curricular practices that contribute to the development of resilience in children and help teachers assess the factors that interfere with or facilitate the capacity of these children to develop and learn in the school setting (see Comer, 1980, chap. 7). The role of play and art (discussed later in this chapter and in Chapter Ten) should receive special emphasis for its significance as a developmentally appropriate, autotherapeutic intervention of particular value for children at risk.

Mental Health Skills

Professionals who work with these children also should acquire new skills in the area of mental health—skills that are grounded in the interpersonal relationship and ongoing interactions between adult and child (student). This relationship, based on trust and respect, is characterized by understanding and acceptance, friendliness and warmth. It is the most significant component in "helping" (Axline, 1969).

Teachers also must acquire skills that help a child recognize feelings, clarify issues, correct distortions, solve problems, and decide on alternative solutions. Such skills enable teachers to create an environment that promotes growth, self-respect, and self-regulation. (See Axline, 1969, for nondirective therapy approaches; see Wood and Long, 1991, for "life space intervention" techniques based on the work of Redl and Wineman, 1951, 1952; Redl, 1966; see Petrillo and Sanger, 1972, for play therapy techniques in hospitals.)

Emotional Availability and the Role of Affect in Helping Relationships

Teacher education or in-service training programs that do not explore the role of affect in a helping relationship will leave teachers with little more than "information," rather than a deeper appreciation of the very difficult nature of the task and personal resources for applying these newly acquired skills and knowledge in practice. If our overall goal is to help teachers serve as role models who are emotionally accessible, cognitively competent to understand the child's experience, and behaviorally available to the child, we must find ways to support the teachers and help them explore their intense feelings about these issues before those teachers can, in turn, be a source of support and help to the children. This observation relates to the process of training itself as well as to the development of ongoing procedures in school settings that are integral to program implementation.

Domains of Silence

As we attempt to deal with whole communities of children whose already overburdened lives may now also include the potential for impaired development, physical damage, and emotional trauma resulting from exposure to community violence, we are catapulted headlong into the murky waters of maintaining psychological distance or objectivity as we become immersed in the complex, chaotic, and destructive circumstances of their lives. The daily experiences of working in these communities arouse deep emotions, often reviving unconscious feelings that may prevent us from helping and supporting children even when we are sincere in our desire to do so (Musick and Stott, 1990). Halpern's term *domains of silence* (cited in Musick and Stott, 1990, p. 658) has been used to describe the reluctance of adults who are not clinically trained to address such "loaded" topics as sexuality, domestic or community violence, death, child abuse, family disruption, or substance abuse. These are the "domains of silence" that may significantly inhibit any effort to establish a helping relationship with a child and his or her family.

"Emotional and behavioral availability" is not easily attained. If we allow ourselves to become involved in the personal and communal experiences of ongoing, untimely, and unnatural loss—the loss of family members and friends through violent death, or the loss that results from the pervasive threat of physical and psychological trauma—we are engaged, almost immediately, at a psychologically disturbing level. These are stories of violation and the abrogation of fundamental life expectations. They are stories about personal and collective guilt—shared alike by victims, witnesses, and bystanders—a circumstance not unlike the "conspiracy of silence" that Danieli (1985, p. 298) addresses in her discussion of Holocaust survivors. They are stories that are bound to resonate in us as they arouse deeper feelings related to the loss of emotionally important relationships, the loss of life and threat to body integrity, the loss of homes and property— the loss of a secure base (van der Kolk, 1990).

It does not take much introspection to imagine that each of us who will be involved with these children, their families, and their communities will confront head-on a most basic human motivation: the natural and insistent desire to protect ourselves from unpleasant feelings and conflicts that threaten a sense of inner balance and the psychological integrity necessary to continue to function effectively. These feelings may result from deeper, unresolved conflicts (for example, personal experiences of loss) or from the impact of current situations (for example, fear of personal safety). Frequently, these situations are concerned with violence, abandonment, withdrawal of support, or similar areas that affect people deeply. The feelings may or may not be unconscious, and may not be irrational (Wallach, 1991).

When strong feelings or emotions overpower the ego and dominate behavior, individuals defend themselves against being hurt or overwhelmed by these feelings. The defenses against strong affects can take many forms. They can result in the service provider's denying their existence. They can result in an unwillingness to share these feelings with others, particularly people perceived as outsiders. They can lead to taking an opposite stance (Wallach, 1991).

It is precisely these feelings that are at the heart of any preservice or in-service training that purports to help adult caregivers help children cope with the negative experiences of their daily lives. In addition, the added complexities of working in community-based settings, as we shall see, vastly complicate an already difficult area for intervention.

To illustrate further the difficulty of helping teachers and staff achieve a position of psychological objectivity in these communities, we offer three examples that underscore the complexity of work in community-based settings. Taken together, these examples paint a vivid picture of the emotional wellsprings that are tapped when we ask the staff who work in these programs to "see and hear" the wider range of mental health concerns that children bring to school each day. While these experiences are less prevalent in public school settings, we believe that a similar situation may occur whenever staff have had experiences in their background similar to those of the children and families with whom they are working.

The Central Experience of Loss

In the pilot studies mentioned earlier, we developed a composite profile of all participating Head Start staff in three different communities. A review of this material demonstrates the need for *extreme sensitivity* and respect in training efforts that deal with the conditions of life in housing project communities—conditions that touch intimately on the experiences of staff, children, and families who work and participate in these programs:

- Sixty-seven percent of the staff are or have been community residents. Their children attend or have attended the Head Start program. They are "the parents" in the program. Many of their children will live out their lives in this community; some of those children have children. They are "the community residents" exposed to "chronic violence."

- Teenage pregnancy, violent death, use of illegal substances, imprisonment of acquaintances and family members, gang involvement, incest, family disruption, single parenthood, truancy, illiteracy, school dropouts, juvenile detention in institutional settings, mental illness, rape, poor health care, inadequate housing, limited access to economic opportunity, and infant mortality are added to minority status and characterize the ongoing "risk factors" present in the lives of program staff.

- For some members of the staff, violence per se is not intimately woven into the daily fabric of their personal lives,
  but other experiences of loss are: adolescent children who
  are having difficulty in school, early and unexpected
  death or illness of close family members because of poor
  health care, teenage pregnancy, depression, suicide, injury,
  alcoholism, and permanent unemployment by a spouse
  or other close family member.

- AIDS is perhaps the only major social tragedy that was
  not reported among the staff in these programs (1989).

     In community-based training programs such as these, the
experience of loss—in every possible dimension—is often central
to existence. Under such conditions, the difficulty of achieving
psychological objectivity that would result in emotional availability to the children is well understood. To the extent that similar experiences exist for staff working with children in less
extreme communities, they will also bear directly on training
initiatives designed to deal with the exposure to chronic violence
and death. Accordingly, it is with *forethought and respect that we
approach and plan for such training—particularly when it is
designed to explore and become comfortable with personal feelings
about death and dying and community violence.*
     We do not have a similar profile for the staff in public
schools. However, in training sessions conducted in the public
schools, 18 percent of the total number of participants said that
they had had experiences similar to those of the children they
were working with. Of related interest, 100 percent of the Head
Start and public school participants indicated substantial and
increasing concern for their safety as a result of working in the
community. Concern for personal safety can prevent them from
establishing an effective helping relationship with children
exposed to chronic violence (Eth and Pynoos, 1985).

Responses of Staff to Community Violence

In the Head Start training sessions, when death was discussed
as the inevitable outcome of life—a fact of life—it was ap-

proached with less apparent conflict. When the subject of death became attached to "community violence" and "loss," there was a noticeable shift in group reactions, especially among community-resident staff. To acknowledge the reality of community violence was to acknowledge something about the "kind of place I live" and "the place I raise my children." The emotionally charged response of one of the staff to our inquiry about how you could use this material to help children seemed to voice the feelings of this group. D. began by saying that she "did have one problem with this stuff." She wondered why it was that "everyone always had to point out the bad things," since, in her opinion, "the child wouldn't be thinking these things if someone didn't put them in his head." She wondered why "people have to remind him how unhappy he is," asking him "if he is sad when he saw blood coming out of the hole [in his father's head]." "Of course, he's sad! [voice rising] Who wouldn't be sad! [outrage] But why do you have to remind him!" Her comments became more heated as she went on. Then she pushed her chair back from the table emphatically and concluded: "this just makes him know it every day!"

On the basis of a well-established relationship with this teacher, we asked her if we could discuss this strong reaction to the training. We tried to affirm her feelings of violation, indicating that she was correct in believing that people should not callously invade a child's private world unbidden if the child had not shown a desire or pressing need to be helped. We also said that it was really a problem knowing how to help children with these issues and asked her to reflect on the staff's earlier descriptions of "relief" at being able to express their feelings and having those feelings affirmed. Did she think that the children might also experience some of this relief—if the child had given some indication that he needed to talk about it?

There was a momentary opening up at this suggestion, but it was so fleeting as to have not existed. The subject could not be approached again. It was very apparent that D. had given voice to the pent-up reactions of this group of community-resident staff, all of whom have children and even grandchildren living there. She spoke to their anger, their sense of having been violated, and their feelings of helplessness. Her voice betrayed their unambiguous opinion about the "people who come in . . . always suggesting" to a child "how bad it must be to live here." Above all, her response captures the emotional pain and powerful need for self-protection in the face of such challenges. To the extent that these responses represent the community as a whole, training must be sensitive to that pain and to the defenses that this material elicits. Trainers and consultants must also be sensitive to the "labeling" ("community violence," "children in danger," "urban war zone") that may be the inherent, although unintended, by-product of the discussion, and to the perceived sense of disrespect, of "dining out" on their misery (Warren, 1977).

Such emotions were far less evident in the responses of staff who did not live in the community. If the goal of such training or supervision is to help teachers become emotionally available to children, ongoing support for staff who share these feelings will be necessary before they are able to respond more accurately to the child's affective signals or acknowledge the "loaded" content of play episodes, drawings, or stories. Program administrators, consultants, and trainers—along with parents and staff who live in the community—will need to develop responses and strategies that support children but are also consistent with the cultural norms and values of these families.

In situations of chronic violence, outcomes are still undetermined. Accordingly, a different problem emerges for staff. To "see" or "hear" these problems also requires a decision to act or fail to act in the child's interests. Frequently, the issue of reporting child abuse or neglect or raising questions about parenting skills and the home environment may be the consequence of "seeing" or "hearing." Where there is substantial, *ongoing* supervisory support to help staff manage these issues, they are enabled to see themselves in an appropriate helping role as advocates for the child, separate from but professionally allied to the community. *Where this supportive supervision is lacking, the costs of seeing and hearing the child may be too great.*

The following story illustrates the conflicts that can arise for staff if they "choose" to "hear" material presented by a child. During free play, the following story was dictated by one of the children:

Rashid: When I was in bed, I saw a monster in my bed. He ate me up.

Teacher: And then what happened?

Rashid: He threw me out the bed, and my daddy got up and threw him out the window.

When we reviewed the children's stories later on, a possible meaning behind Rashid's story began to unfold—one that had deeper significance than the expected, age-appropriate "monster" story of the preschool child. Emotionally displaced at a safe distance in "his story," Rashid may have been telling us something about his perception of the death of his baby brother, who had fallen out of a fourth-floor window a year ago. By itself, of course, this story only suggests the possibility of Rashid's preoccupation with his brother's death; in and of itself, it does not tell us anything about the actual circumstances of that death. That he continued to be preoccupied by it, however, may also be inferred from his later behavior. Rashid was one of the first children to initiate "funeral" play in the block corner after he discovered a long, black "dress-up" robe, which he wore to play "preacher," presiding over the funeral service.

Rashid's mother is a young, physically handicapped woman who has made significant gains with the help of the program. For over two years, she attended the program on a daily basis and was greatly helped to develop new parenting, social, and educational skills. Today she is enrolled in a GED program and has a part-time job.

If, indeed, the meaning of this story had been "heard"

in the classroom, it is not likely that the staff would have brought it to anyone's attention. Given their desire to support Rashid and his mother, who eventually became "success" stories at the center, perhaps fearing that the police would be called, knowing that the family was already involved with child protective services, undergirded by a latent fear of the man involved, the staff members probably would not have *publicly acknowledged* "hearing" the meaning of Rashid's story.

In some cases, problems such as this one are further complicated for community-resident staff because, as "mandated reporters," they may be faced with the possibility of "reporting" a *neighbor or friend.* To add to the difficulty, in many Head Start classrooms, it is not uncommon for one member of the teaching team to be a community resident whereas the other member is not. Under such circumstances, where the complexity of professional and personal relationships and community issues confounds almost every issue, "hearing" and "seeing" may become highly selective. These are the topics avoided at staff meetings, the areas for intervention detoured—the "domains of silence"—that interfere with effective helping relationships.

An In-Service Approach to Training, Program Implementation, and Support

As we have seen, it is particularly important to help staff come to terms with the strong emotions and difficult conflicts that emerge—or are silenced—in their work with children in these communities. Without this understanding, the application of new information and new skills will remain stillborn. For most teachers who have not been trained and supervised in this kind of work, the material is simply too difficult and raises too many conflictual issues for them to venture forth in this uncharted territory as if they were tackling a new approach to learning math.

Our interest in a school-based intervention for children who live in multiproblem communities leads us to focus on the process and mechanisms for achieving these goals in the school setting. Our experience working with hundreds of teachers in day-care and Head Start programs further suggests that *training is most effective when it is integrally related to program implementation and is grounded in the interpersonal, interpsychological processes that structure growth and change* (staffing children, consultation, supervision, team conferences). "Tacked-on," nonspecific, system-wide approaches are less responsive to the most urgent needs of staff and are frequently "tolerated or endured rather than beneficially exploited" (Comer, 1980, p. 266).

In Chapters Seven and Eight, we described the benefits of a supervisory process that includes individual supervision, team planning, consultation, and weekly staffing conferences with the center director, social worker, and classroom teaching team to provide an ongoing forum for addressing the special problems that emerge for children and staff in these settings. We also indicated that the most effective intervention for helping at-risk children function successfully *in the classroom* is the availability of ongoing consultation to the center as a complement to the center's supervisory process. And, finally, we indicated that these combined program features provide the basic mechanism for ensuring ongoing professional development and support for staff. At Ramon's center, for example, all of the issues raised in this chapter can be handled through these mechanisms.

The explicit purpose of the consultation is the identification, assessment, and early intervention with children at risk for developmental harm. The consultation is provided by an outside agency specializing in mental health services to young children and their families. The consultation process is integral to the service delivery system of the overall program and complements its supervisory process. Both agencies share a similar theoretical and philosophical approach to practice.

The program consultant, a specialist in early childhood education with a strong background in mental health, works with the classroom team and supervisory staff to develop feasible treatment interventions. These plans include referral to an outside agency, when necessary, but emphasize helping children manage successfully in the classroom and work with families at the center.

During team meetings, the consultant helps teachers determine the nature of the problem and identify appropriate responses. In the course of this work, teachers develop a broader understanding of the child development principles involved; explore their own feelings, attitudes, and values; and begin to build an increasing repertoire of appropriate verbal and programmatic responses to classroom problems. A teacher's professional growth emerges through the interpersonal interactions with supervisory staff, consultants, and peers in ongoing dialogue about the problems of children in the classroom.

The consultation process begins with the goal of establishing strong working alliances, based on trust, and then proceeds developmentally, in relation to the team's increasing ability and desire to enlarge their effectiveness in expanding arenas of professional expertise. While the process is guided and structured *through* the relationship with the consultant, it is based on mutual identification of problems, collaboration, problem solving, and consensus building.

In the early stages of this process, teachers are given concrete assistance in managing their daily work lives. In high-risk settings, for example, they may receive help with the problems they face in their attempts to respond to the behaviors and verbalizations that children bring to the classroom. This approach tends to minimize anxiety and offers emotional support through affirming the feelings they reveal and demonstrating empathy about their discomfort (Wallach, 1991). Only after there is a well-established relationship between the consultant, trainer, or supervisory staff and the classroom teacher or team, based on many positive experiences, can the next steps be taken: engaging teachers more directly in discussions of inner psychological processes that underlie their efforts to cope with violence, fear, and trauma (Wallach, 1991). This latter stage may not be reached until the second year of consultation and then only if a consistent, well-established relationship, based on trust and respect, exists between the consultant and classroom team.

If an outside consultant is not available, the principles of this model can be applied to other supervisory or in-service training arrangements. A social worker, counselor, program director, curriculum specialist, or education director with combined expertise in child development, developmentally appropriate practice (curriculum), and mental health could act in the capacity of consultant to help teachers identify, assess, and make plans that facilitate a child's successful coping in the classroom. Like the consultant model described above, this process is most effective when it is based on the establishment of strong working alliances and compatible approaches to practice; when it is consistently available and related to program implementation; and when it is based on a process model that emphasizes relationship building and collaborative problem solving.

As we saw in Chapter Eight, these initiatives are most successful when they are "guaranteed" through the ongoing support of leadership and integrated into the organizational and administrative functions of the school (see also Comer, 1980, chap. 7, "The Mental Health Program"). If such support is not forthcoming, informal peer support networks should at least be established. These networks can provide a regular mechanism for discussing problems, seeking solutions, and providing mutual support.

Helping Teachers Understand Children's Play

In Chapter Ten, we will explore the role of play in the lives of at-risk children and emphasize its therapeutic value—as a natural phenomenon that the child uses "to make up for defeats, sufferings, and frustrations" (Erikson, 1940, p. 561; cited in Petrillo and Sanger, 1972, p. 99). As a coping strategy that leads to learning, the opportunity to play is a pivotal component of developmentally appropriate practice for preschool and early primary children and provides an added tool in the repertoire of interventions for children like Ramon.

However, because children make abundant use of the opportunity to play out their concerns and fears, many teachers now struggle with their own concerns about the content of play that surfaces—content involving coffins and funerals, "shooting up" and "robbing," "pimps" and "gang-bangers" with "big gold." Recognizing that teachers feel troubled and uncertain about how to react when children begin to play out the more negative dimensions of their lives, a consultant will try to help them become more "emotionally available" to the children. (For purposes of this discussion, we shall use the terms *consultant* or *consultation* with the understanding that this role could be played by a trainer or supervisor provided the other criteria for the process we have described are met.)

In a team meeting with the consultant, the matter of "funeral" or "gun" play or "shooting up" may come up for discussion in any number of ways: as a problem with an individual child, or for the group, or for the team or one member of the team, or as a problem from parents. We have grouped the issues into these categories, but in reality the concerns they represent weave in and out of the discussion over a period of many weeks. The consultant begins with whatever seems most important to the staff at the time.

Let us suppose that the team asks the consultant to "look at what is happening in the doll house corner during free play, because there is a lot of shooting and gun play," and they are not sure whether that is "OK," especially for Ramon. As requested, the consultant observes the classroom in the morning, making sure that she follows up on any of the children or issues from prior meetings. At naptime, the center director, social worker, and classroom team meet with the consultant. The consultant shares her thoughts on what she observed and begins to explore the teachers' concerns. Over a period of weeks, the questions around which these discussions are focused begin to structure or frame the team's understanding of the significant issues for consideration.

These are the questions that are gradually internalized by the teachers as they begin to see their classrooms through the consultant's eyes.

Effect of Play on the Group

The consultant begins by exploring the "quality" of the play episodes she has been asked to observe, comparing her thoughts and impressions with those of the teachers. Her goal is to direct their attention to the overall "feel" of the play for the group and to begin to grapple with the idea of "constructiveness." Are children able to use the play constructively—to reduce fears and anxiety, clarify meanings, and gain insight that leads to learning? In this process, terms that reflect theoretical concepts (for example, "psychological safety," "constructive," "group contagion," "inventive," "repetitive") and word meanings open to relative interpretations (for example, "wild," "safe," "too intense," "anxious") are discussed, challenged, and explored. These questions are typical:

> How does the classroom feel when the children are involved in this play? What is the noise level? Is the play constructive and busy? Is it wild? Is it safe? Is it overstimulating? Is it too intense? Does the excitement keep escalating? Do the children look anxious? Are the group contagion effects within constructive bounds? Do children look as though they are enjoying themselves?
>
> Do the children bring new things into the play? Is the play inventive? Can the children or play be redirected? How long has this kind of play been going on? When did it start? Do the children repeat the same play every day? Does it look like something on TV? Do the same children engage in this play all the time? Is there something happening in the school or community, at home, on TV that is causing the children to play in this

way at this time? How can we change the props
or the play equipment to make these play experiences work better? (In situations where play
opportunities are too limited, the task will be to
explore how to enhance these opportunities for
the children.)

Effect of Play on Individual Children

A parallel area of consideration is the effect of the play on
individual children who are particularly vulnerable—Ramon,
for example; or the child who saw his mother beaten up; or
the child who is being scapegoated for living in the "bloody
apartment"; or Piya, whose family was robbed at gun point;
or Rashid, who is preoccupied with funeral play. Again, the
consultant begins with questions about the quality and feel
of the play episodes for the individual child. What are the
effects of this kind of play on this child? Is the child's ego
overwhelmed by flooding emotions, or is he able to use the
play to reduce his fears and anxieties? The child's developmental history and experience in the center are reviewed, and
changes in behavior that may be a reaction to temporary or
chronic stress are explored in contrast to the child's normal
pattern of functioning.

Throughout this process, the consultant is attempting to
ascertain how this particular set of circumstances, including
staff interactions and programmatic considerations, can be used
to support the child's mastery of a traumatizing event—whether
the team should limit, redirect, change, or expand the opportunity for gun play, for example, through their relationship with
this child. Is the child's subgroup teacher able to facilitate these
experiences? Or is this a new teacher who has not yet established
a close relationship with the child in question? Is the "substitute" subgroup teacher a better choice for intervention with
this child? Does she have the necessary background, understanding, skills, and the "emotional availability" that would
allow a more sophisticated intervention? The following questions frame the discussion of a new plan for Ramon:

Is this gun play something new for Ramon, or is he doing what he always does when this happens? Is he the one who is getting the other children involved in the gun play now? Every day? When? Which other children are involved? All the time? Can they handle the play? Is anyone getting hurt? What happens to him when he starts to fall apart?

Do you think that the plan that we set up last time will work this time? Have you [the social worker] had a chance to speak to his mom yet? Is there anything new happening at home? How about Ramon's dad? Will his mother agree to go along with the same plan again? Can she arrange to pick him up for the next few weeks instead of letting his older brother come for him?

If I recall, this means that Ramon may have a hard time for the next several weeks. Does Mary [a new assistant teacher who is not Ramon's sub-group teacher] know the history and what her role is in the plan when Marsha [Ramon's sub-group teacher, with whom he is very close] leaves at 4 o'clock? Is there anything that has been scheduled for the classroom—trips? parties?— that is going to be a problem for him? Are there any new children coming into the group? Any staff changes? Should we set up a special plan for "circle," or wait until we see how he does?

How are you feeling about having to go through this again with him? This is the third time, isn't it? Marsha [Ramon's subgroup teacher], you look like you've just about had it with this. I know it's Ramon's family that upsets you. What are we going to do to help you get through these next few weeks? Maybe we'd better spend some time

talking about it? In fact, it looks like you're all
pretty tired of this!

Effect of Play on Teachers

As a matter of routine, the consultant explores the teachers'
attitudes, beliefs, and feelings about every problem that is
raised. When the consultation is well established as a safe
forum to risk sharing deeper concerns, teachers begin to use
this opportunity more openly. In the examples, cited below,
we observe, once again, the intense feelings and conflicts elicited by the children's play.

> *"Gun" Play.* I know it is important for the chil-
> dren to be able to play, but how much do I allow?
> When do I stop it? How do I stop it? How do I
> let some of the children play this way, but not
> others? Can I do that? Is it fair to stop one child
> from playing when all the others get to play? We
> have to stop this shooting and killing!

> *"Funeral" Play.* Is it OK to stop it if I am uncom-
> fortable with it? I don't know why it bothers me
> so much? I know it's important. No one is get-
> ting hurt. It isn't wild or crazy. They look like
> they're playing "house." But I get goose bumps
> every time I see them put the sheet over the cof-
> fin. I keep trying to get them to play something
> else. What would the parents say if they came in
> and saw the children playing funeral? What
> would I say to them?

> *"Shooting Up."* I don't care what you say about
> how important it is for children to play, I just
> can't let them play "shooting up." None of the
> parents want this; we [team] don't want it. It's
> crazy! It just makes me want to cry every time I
> see it." My own brother died last year.

Through her strong relationship with staff, the consultant begins to explore these feelings and conflicts, one step at a time, perhaps over many, many months. From the perspective of intervention, at each of these points along the way, the consultant must decide: Is this an area for limiting, redirecting, or expanding the parameters of this particular kind of play, in this classroom, at this time, with these children, for this team, or for this teacher, for this group of parents, in this community? How can we make the necessary adjustments? What is the next step? If discussion of these issues (for example, violence, "gun" play, "shooting up") would benefit from a larger forum, a decision can also be made to provide a series of workshops or convene discussion groups for this purpose. At some point, parents might be invited to participate or form their own groups to discuss these issues. And finally, as in the last example, teachers who may be struggling with very difficult problems in their own lives should be offered support—perhaps by counseling services in the community if they are desired.

Conclusion

In this chapter, we have described some of the underlying conflicts that emerge for staff in their efforts to help children cope with the harsh realities (Warren, 1977) of their lives. We have noted the intense emotions and the lack of psychological objectivity that may result in a "failure to notice, understand . . . or help a [child] because of . . . unrecognized feelings" (Musick and Stott, 1990, p. 659). When teachers repress or deny painful feelings that have emerged in their role as teachers and caregivers, "domains of silence" may, and often do, prevail.

We know that the concerns of teachers are real. The sense of frustration, the anger, the feeling of helplessness evoked by the following words echoed through the halls in every school we entered: "How can we do anything? Every child has these problems. It's not just once in a while; it's every day. If we deal with these issues, we won't ever get to teaching! We would do nothing else but talk to the children. It's never going to change. . . . Maybe we should just go on trying to ignore it? But it's getting worse. The children are more aggressive. It never used to be this bad. They used to run in and tell us what happened at night. Sometimes now, they don't even bother anymore."

Teachers need help, and they cannot take on these problems alone. Through the collaboration, expertise, and support of an experienced consultant or supervisor, little by little, one step at a time, the floodgates can be opened that will result in help to children without overwhelming the teacher or classroom in this process.

But we must also help teachers regain confidence in their enormous potential to effect change in children's lives: to remember that no matter how often it seems like a "losing battle," they are the role models and confidants whose influence will be remembered when, like Patsy Walker, children and young adults look for other answers; that it is only through strong relationships with emotionally important adults that children can mobilize their own inherent strengths and self-righting capabilities.

When a consultant is not available, we need to help teachers develop other formal and informal support networks within their school to help them cope with the ongoing stresses of this environment, so that they, too, do not succumb to the numbing and desensitization that can be the outcome of work in these communities. As teachers are given emotional support and resources that enable them to respond to the newer problems of the children in their care, they begin to feel their sense of effectiveness return. As they become more receptive to children's overtures for help and more sure of their own abilities to effect change, *children begin to experience their teachers' growth as their own enhanced capacity to cope successfully in the classroom.*

It seems helpful here to reflect on Warren's comments regarding our responsibility to children as child-care professionals. She reminds us that if we are "charged with helping children develop to their fullest possible potential . . . [then]

we are also charged . . . to help them when development comes to a screaming halt . . . when their lives are laid waste by catastrophic events" (Warren, 1977, p. 23). She goes on to say: "It is also true that you cannot really make the unbearable manageable or the inexplicable understandable. But in your stance of being ready, willing, and able to help, the child can find at least temporary peace and support for his efforts to cope. If little children have a 'right' to a safe and joyous childhood, they also have a right to scream out their rage and fear and to be heard and supported when their safety and joy are breached" (Warren, 1977, p. 24).

10

The Healing Role
of Play and Art

For most children, healing childhood trauma depends on the strength of adult-child relationships. Few children can do the job on their own: the challenges are too great, their resources too few. Teachers of children who live in the urban war zone must be prepared to hear the children tell their stories in and on their own terms, *no matter how upsetting those terms are for the teacher*. This acceptance of the child's reality is the starting point for the healing process. "It is the permissiveness to be themselves, the understanding, the acceptance, the recognition of feelings, the clarification of what they think and feel that helps children retain their self-respect; and the possibilities of growth and change are forthcoming as they all develop insight" (Axline, 1969).

Coping strategies are important to survival in a chronically dangerous environment. Adults devise practical safety measures to help children function in communities where the possibility of danger is ever present. Children are instructed early in these measures, so that any five-year-old living in a public housing development in Chicago is prepared to "take cover" under the protection of the playground slide if he or she hears gunfire.

When violence is experienced in a community-based school setting, these strategies "kick in." At one preschool center in Chicago, children were observed at group story time when gunshots from outside were heard. The children immediately got up from the rug on which they sat, proceeded to the coat lockers, and put on their coats. They stood silently waiting for their mothers (or other caretakers). This was not a first-time or single-event occurrence. The children know the rules. They understand that when there are shootings, mothers come to the center to take the children home, where they will remain safely together (Dubrow and Garbarino, 1989).

Children as young as three years old can describe traumatic events in detail and are likely to recall exactly what they witnessed during these events (Terr, 1990). However, when children are exposed to repeated trauma, they begin to prepare mentally for the next assault. They expect future trauma and, thus, develop psychological defenses to protect themselves. Denial and numbing are common defense mechanisms employed by children and adults who live in dangerous environments.

The children kidnapped at Chowchilla, California, created "omens" to rationalize the event. The children mentally searched the events prior to the kidnapping, in an attempt to discover a reason for the occurrence. They attributed their "bad luck" to something they did or to some omission in their actions: a fight with a brother or a failure to finish homework (Terr, 1983).

While young children express their fears openly by crying and clinging, older children are often directed culturally, through adult advice and peer pressure, away from these open expressions, and begin to employ coping mechanisms. Survival in a dangerous environment depends on maintaining an outward show of strength in the face of danger. One child reported to us, "If you let them [gang members] know you're afraid, if you cry, you're beat." Thus, adult directives, peer pressure, and the chronicity of violence in the environment converge to influence how children cope with trauma. Generalized fears, avoidance, denial, and numbing are the result. Psychological trauma does not disappear when defenses are engaged; it becomes more deeply buried. Thus, coping mechanisms employed by children to deal with the stress of danger in the environment often mask the presence of their concerns (Terr, 1990).

As we saw in Chapters Three and Four, young children have little or no control over the violence in their environment. Lack of control results in a chronic assault to children's self-esteem, feelings of safety, and level of trust, which ultimately leads to increased vulnerability. What children *can* control is their account of experience, and they sometimes seek to do so in ways that seem desperate to the observer.

Play and art activities encourage children to express themselves and to form and communicate an account that can be the starting point for a healing dialogue with an understanding adult. These activities enable the child to give voice to a traumatic experience without the prerequisite of cognitive understanding, verbal capability, or overt cultural permission. The therapeutic use of play and art can help children reinstate their sense of inner control, reestablish self-worth and self-esteem, and develop relationships of trust. Thus, we see it as central to any programmatic efforts to help children overcome the trauma that comes of living with community violence.

Children Who Play and Children Who Cannot

In every war zone that we visited, we observed children playing. Children invent play activities no matter how impoverished the environment. They experiment, solve problems, and interact with their peers. They abandon the harsh realities of real life for a playful counterpart reality.

One of the most inventive toys in evidence among the children of Mozambique was the *carlinio* (little car), a toy made out of silver wire with soda-can wheels. Children roll automobile tires down the street, and they create dress-up clothes from leaves, cardboard boxes, and sticks. Palestinian children play in natural sandpiles in the streets of the Old City of Jerusalem. In Cambodia, children play fisherman along the Mekong River, using small pieces of discarded paper to make fishnets. They catch tiny minnows and put them in containers filled with water. Children who live in Chicago's inner-city neighborhoods play trampoline on discarded mattresses, jump rope

with a rope made from pieces of found string, and have sword fights with sticks. Children in war zones are still children.

Along the way, we also met children who were too injured to play. In Mozambique, we met many malnourished children who could not lift the weight of their own heads. One child could not focus his eyes after he suffered a serious head wound inflicted by a Renamo machete (see Chapter Two). We also remember the Palestinian child who did not come out to play. She had stayed close to the safety of her room ever since a soldier's bullet made her blind. These are seriously injured children. But it is their psychological rather than their physical injuries that do the most damage to their capacity to play. This is a general truth not confined to these extreme situations.

The Role of Play in Development

Children seek to understand external reality in play. It is a process that has no assigned or expected product. Children cannot fail when they engage in free play. Thus, there is freedom to explore, invent, and test a full range of possibilities (Sylva, Bruner, and Genova, 1976). Children living under the emotional constraints of a war zone have a special need for this freedom.

Children develop physical, social, and logico-mathematical knowledge in play (Piaget, 1936; Kamii and DeVries, 1977). They find out how things work (Garvey, 1977). For example, block building shows them something about the principles of physics. Their knowledge of weight, balance, and inclines grows as towers and roads are erected. Ball play helps them understand force, speed, and angles (Kamii and DeVries, 1978). Group games and activities allow children to develop ideas about cooperation, conflict resolution, and consideration of different points of view. A game of tag or "Candy Land" presents children with a rich opportunity to explore these ideas (Kamii and DeVries, 1980).

In play, children experiment with the nature of number, or logico-mathematical knowledge. They observe the

properties of objects and construct ideas about the relationships of objects. This knowledge develops through the process
of revising existing concepts and adding new ones through
assimilation and accommodation. Children at play are con-
stantly at work, adding new observations to the existing relationships they have established. When faced with ideas that
do not fit into what they already know, children must adjust
the existing framework to accommodate the new information
(Piaget, 1936; Kamii, 1982).

Playful experimentation increases children's repertoire
of questions and responses (Sutton-Smith, 1971). As options
develop, so do choices. Flexibility experienced in play encourages children to solve problems, to dismantle ideas and recon-
struct them (Bruner, 1976). We know that an adequate level
of cognitive competence can help a child formulate a resilient
response to stress (see Chapter One). Children living in a war
zone need every skill and concept they can acquire to handle
what lies before and around them.

Theoretical Perspectives on Play as Therapy

In counterpart to adult concentration, children's play is a
state of withdrawal. It is the activity that allows children to
leave reality, with all its functional and external demands,
and explore the affect attached to events that occur in their
lives (Winnicott, 1971). The ability to play is a key element in
psychotherapy. Winnicott (1971) describes psychotherapy with
children as a twentieth-century phenomenon designed to
allow two people, patient and therapist, to communicate
through play. Communication in a therapeutic setting includes listening to and reflecting on the child's feelings and
concerns. Trust is built on the adult's respect for the child's
ability to develop inner control. Insight gained in this process
gives children the necessary tools to initiate problem solving
(Axline, 1969). Thus, play is self-healing and self-cure (Winnicott, 1971; Erikson, 1950).

When adults are exposed to traumatic events, they work
to resolve their feelings by talking about the event repeatedly.

This makes them feel better (Erikson, 1950). "Repetition compulsion," the need to repeat in some form the experiences that we have not assimilated, is a hallmark of Freud's psychoanalytic theory—and it is fundamental to the process of coping with trauma.

Adult dreams were of particular interest to Freud (1926), who believed that in dreams the human ego is driven to conquer experiences that have not yet been assimilated. For example, Vietnam War combat veterans reexperience events that occurred during military service in their dreams; they report dreaming themes of death, guilt, fear, and loss (Lifton, 1973). Children, particularly very young children, take a somewhat different approach. Play is a reflection of their inner world. In play, there is "fulfillment of the child's needs, his incentives to act, and his affective aspirations" (Vygotsky, 1976).

Across cultures, children play some common themes: nurturing, family relationships, and roles of people. The themes represent children's human and physical environment (Feitelson, 1977). These themes are played in the context of a child's real environment and affective life. When reality or affect changes, so does play. Significant events and children's feelings about themselves and other people affect the themes and tones of the play.

"Play is the royal road to the child's conscious and unconscious inner world. If we want to understand his inner world and help him with it, we must learn to walk this road" (Bettelheim, 1987, p. 35). Play is the activity that allows young children to repeat experiences and to understand them more completely. In play, children can express ideas for which they have no words.

An eight-year-old girl in Chicago was observed playing the role of mother in the dramatic-play area of the afterschool program. According to her teachers, this was one of her favorite activities. But something was added to the play following a traumatic event in the child's life (see Chapter Four). Her mother was shot in the neck and seriously wounded when she was caught in the cross fire of gang warfare. The mother was unable to speak for five months, and doctors placed a device in her throat to help her breathe. A plastic tube protruded from the device, and the mother wore a cover over it.

After the event, the child searched the classroom for a tissue or a piece of cloth to place on her neck. She said this was a bandage. Then she proceeded to play the mother role as she always had, making toast for the other children and taking care of the house.

How does it feel to be shot in the throat? How does it feel to have a bandage on your neck? How does it feel to be unable to talk? How does it feel to go on with everyday life after serious physical and psychological injury? This child searched for answers to her questions in her play. Play gave her an opportunity to try out alternative answers. As we shall see, however, play is not fool-proof for children. They may need help in making the most of it when faced with the tough questions posed by life in the war zone.

Playing Out Reality in a Dangerous Environment

Children are able to deal with complex psychological difficulties through play (Bettelheim, 1987). They seek to integrate the experience of pain, fear, and loss. They wrestle with concepts of good and evil. There is a long history of children playing some version of what today we call "cops and robbers." The triumph of good over evil, of heroes protecting innocent victims, is another common theme of children's play (Bettelheim, 1987). In classrooms in the United States today, fantasy toys like the Ninja Turtles are used by children as vehicles to explore these issues.

Children who live in dangerous environments play the dangerous environment. In Mozambique, children who have been captured by the bandits (Renamo) play their experience of being kidnapped. They demonstrate in their play the treatment they received at the hands of their captors (Save the Children, 1989). In the West Bank, Palestinian kindergarten children play soldiers arresting people. They play Intifada (the popular Palestinian uprising) complete with soldiers, demonstrators throwing stones and chanting, military jeeps, and ambulance drivers administering emergency assistance to the wounded victims.

In Chicago, children as young as three years old play shooting up drugs and strutting like "gangbangers." School-age children take turns being victims, mourners, and preachers as they act out the common occurrence of funerals resulting from gang warfare.

In play, children can move from passivity to activity (Freud, 1926). The child can take control of an event by playing different roles and altering the outcomes of events. For example, following a visit to the dentist, a child may be observed playing dentist at school. In his play, the child can decide to be the dentist, performing painful dental procedures on the teddy bear "patient." The play allows the child to reverse roles and be in control of the experience. Furthermore, even if the child does not reverse roles, as the child who decided to play the wounded mother did, she is in control because she *chooses* to play.

In symbolic play, children bridge the gap between reality and fantasy. Freud (1926) observed a young child who experienced separation anxiety when his mother left him. The child played with a spool tied to the end of a string. He threw the object away and retrieved it repeatedly. In play, therefore, the child was able to control both the leaving and the coming back. When we are open to such symbolism, we can recognize and appreciate it in the play of children—even those not as creatively inventive as Freud's little patient. Children cannot stop kidnappers from capturing them. They cannot stop adults from engaging in armed conflict. And they cannot stop gang members from shooting their mothers. But in play, they can have the control they lack "in reality."

Facilitating Play in the Classroom Environment

School programs for young children can offer a rich physical environment, an environment that encourages them to represent their experiences and to engage in complex play individually and in groups. Young children need a school curriculum that lends itself to children playing throughout the course of a day (Paley, 1990).

A well-designed classroom for young children will contain building blocks, a water table, and a dramatic-play area. Time will be scheduled for storytelling and writing, game playing, and music. Outdoor play and gym time are part of the daily routine. The adult-child ratio is low—perhaps eight children to one adult. This low ratio is crucial for effective work with children at risk, as we saw in Chapters Seven and Eight.

Finding the space to play in traditional kindergarten and primary school classrooms is more difficult, as we learned in our teacher-training sessions in the Chicago public schools. Opportunities for play depend on the individual school, classroom, staff, and community. For example, some teachers keep a bag of toys in their classroom, which they offer to children on special occasions. Others define play as a frill or a luxury or a waste of time, rather than the necessity it is for children, particularly for children with unresolved trauma. In so doing, they are thwarting what may be necessary for children to move forward on their most important agendas. Dealing with trauma is no luxury; it is the most basic of necessities.

If the spontaneous dramatic play of a few children is not disruptive to the entire class, some teachers report that they allow the children to pursue the activity. One teacher said that she let the children play a skipping game in the school hallway, much to the dismay of the principal.

For some elementary school children, there is no time allocated for play. Funding for music and art classes was cut in many of the nation's public schools in 1980. Athletic programs also have been reduced, so that funds can be allocated to the academic curriculum. But even if funds for athletic programs were reinstated, children who attend school in a dangerous neighborhood would still find many obstacles in the path of play. The neighborhood outside the school is too dangerous. One principal reported to us that he canceled recess for all 1,100 children in his inner-city primary school. There had been numerous shooting incidents while the children played outside, and staff concurred: "It wasn't safe to have recess." With no outlet for free-time group discussion, conversations in the lunchroom became boisterous. Talking at lunch was therefore canceled. Teachers cannot help children understand the world and themselves in relation to the world when communication comes to a screeching halt. The ironies of life in the urban war zone are often painful. The children who most need a play-oriented curriculum are least likely to get it.

The therapeutic use of play and art is both an attitude and a method. It is based on a genuine and mutual exchange, as is any good relationship (Alexander, 1976). As we saw in Chapters Seven and Eight, the relationship between teacher and child must be one of trust, and it must be reliable (Erikson, 1950). The classroom atmosphere needs to convey acceptance and respect for the children's play. Play represents children's innermost thoughts and feelings, and teachers must be willing to accept all of them—even when children bring the war zone into the classroom.

Many of the rules and curriculum decisions made by schools in an effort to control children are actually self-defeating. More time to talk, more time to explore their potential in all the domains of intelligence, will expand children's opportunities for self-understanding and actualization (Gardner, 1983). It will also improve children's behavior. This is no frill for children of the war zone. It is a matter of basic psychic survival.

Traumatized children engage in dramatic-play activities at older ages than do their nontraumatized counterparts (Terr, 1990). Where play and the appropriate materials are not a part of the daily classroom curriculum, teachers can develop a mobile or temporary playroom. For example, a large Chicago-based hospital with no room for a permanent playroom developed a collection of toys with therapeutic value that fit inside a suitcase. So arranged, the equipment was mobile and could be easily stored. The collection includes family figures, cars and trucks, block sets, paper and crayons, clay, and puppets. A suitcase can be developed for specific groups of children in educational settings. The materials can be used in a scheduled time slot or spontaneously as needed (Cassell, 1976).

A variety of writing and storytelling techniques can increase children's opportunities to develop language and expressive skills. Gardner's "Bag of Words" game is a technique that can be used with individual children or in a group. The teacher collects objects and places them in a bag. A child is asked to remove an object from the bag and tell a story about it. For older children, a bag of word cards can be used. The teacher can encourage children to discuss particular topics by choosing the objects or words for the bag. Her objective is to facilitate children's expression of their inner feelings and concerns, and to explore the affective nature of events that occur in their lives (Gardner, 1975).

The "Squiggle Game" was developed as a collaborative game between therapist and child, but it can also be used by teachers (Winnicott, 1971). The teacher makes a squiggle mark on a piece of paper and gives it to a child. The child is asked to make a picture from the squiggle. Upon completion, the teacher asks the child to tell a story about the drawing. From the child's story, the teacher learns the theme of the child's thoughts and can identify affect attached to the story. Using the child's lead, the teacher asks the child to draw a squiggle, which the teacher completes. In the story that the teacher tells, she can offer alternative outcomes to the child's story in an effort to help the child understand concerns and feelings.

The Role of Art in Development

Like children's play, children's art is a spontaneous and deeply rooted activity. Their drawings represent the mental pictures and perceptions they have of the world. Virtually all the children we have met around the world enjoy drawing pictures once given the opportunity. In countries where they do not have access to paper and crayons, they use their fingers or a stick to scribble in the earth or snow (Kellogg, 1969).

Across cultures, children's artwork progresses through developmental sequences (Kellogg, 1969). As soon as children are able to hold the writing tools, they begin to scribble. Research indicates that scribbling is a precursor to early literacy tasks (McLane and McNamee, 1990), such as representational drawings and printing. Progressively, children's drawings express perceptions of their personal and material environment (DiLeo, 1973). The first human representations are circles. The head is the point of interest for infants and preschool-age children, because of its association with eating, talking, seeing, hearing, and smiling. Children then progress to drawing the trunk and then complete body parts (DiLeo, 1973; Kellogg, 1969). Their favorite subjects are people, animals, and houses.

The Goodenough Draw-a-Person test is a tool used to evaluate children's mental age by their drawings of human figures. The Goodenough approach was standardized with 7,000 children in the United States and correlates significantly with standard intelligence tests (DiLeo, 1973). Children's family drawings also have been used as diagnostic aids; the size, position, and inclusion or exclusion of individual family members provide clues to children's feelings about themselves in relation to others (Burns and Kaufman, 1972).

Drawings reflect the historical moment and children's reality. For example, racial segregation was clearly a theme among black and white schoolchildren in the North in the 1960s (Coles, 1968), just as apartheid is the predominant theme of South African black children's drawings (The Open School, 1987). Children who live in the war zones of the world depict the elements of armed conflict in their drawings (Garbarino, Kostelny, and Dubrow, 1991; Vornberger, 1986). Following the start of the Gulf War, children in a Chicago elementary school drew pictures of the 1991 air attacks on Iraq. Missiles, grenades, helicopters, fighter planes, and dead men with bloody faces were depicted in graphic detail.

Along with their drawings of real events, children draw fantasies. For example, during World War II, the children confined to the Terezin concentration camp in Czechoslovakia "drew the things that adults also saw . . . endless queues, funeral carts, and executions, and the things that adults don't see: princesses, wizards, witches, and insects with human faces" (Volavkova, 1944). Similarly, when Palestinian children, who have known no other environment than a barren refugee camp in the West Bank, drew pictures, they add the flowers and butterflies they rarely encounter.

Children's Drawings as Expressions of Their Fears

We have collected children's drawings from all over the world. We ask them to "draw a picture of where you live, a picture of yourself, a picture of your family." We have used these drawings as a technique to elicit children's feelings and concerns in one-to-one situations and in group settings (an orphanage in Mozambique, an after-school program in Chicago, individual family homes on the West Bank).

We have said that children draw reality as well as fantasy. But the line between fantasy and reality for young children is flexible. That flexibility may enable children to use play for emotional release (Freud, 1926), but it may also cloud their perception of danger in the environment.

Adults understand that there are no monsters under the bed or in the closet at night, but children may not. Adults know that frightening television and movie characters are portrayed by actors, but children may not. Adults know that bombs aimed at Iraq will not hit them, but children may not understand this. Children often share their concerns about these fears. However, keeping real and imagined fears in perspective in a dangerous inner-city neighborhood is a complex task.

Nightmare on Elm Street *and Arresting Gangbangers*

When asked to draw a picture of where he lives, Dennis, a seven-year-old boy who lives in a public housing development

in Chicago, completed a series of four drawings. The first
drawing was of his high-rise apartment building. He pointed
out that he lives on the fourth floor, and he proceeded to
identify each window as a family member's bedroom: "This
is where my brother sleeps, and this is where my mother
sleeps."

Dennis's Drawing: High-Rise Apartment Building.

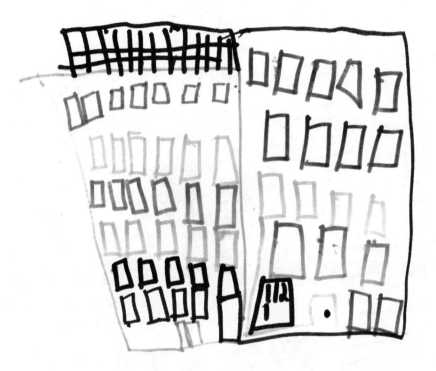

The second drawing was of Freddie Krueger, the fic-
tional character in a series of horror movies called *Nightmare
on Elm Street*. Dennis's drawing depicts Freddie with the characteristic razor blade fingers with blood on them. Freddie's
hands are outstretched wide. Dennis said, "Freddie gets in my
dreams. I have to grow claws to protect myself from Freddie."
He continued, "Even if you put Freddie in the oven and burn
him, he can come back and be alive."

Dennis's Drawing: Freddie Krueger.

Night mar on am
Street

Fredi's bake

4

1 Night mar on am
street

The third drawing was of Godzilla and the Swamp Monster. Dennis said, "Godzilla is very old, he is fifty-two years old."

Dennis's Drawing: Godzilla and the Swamp Monster.

Finally, Dennis drew a picture of two gangbangers being arrested and handcuffed by a policeman. He said, "one gangbanger has a bottle, and the other one has a bat." The gangbangers' hats are pointed in opposite directions, denoting rival gang affiliation. There is a second policeman waiting nearby in a squad car.

Dennis's Drawing: Policeman Arresting Gang Members.

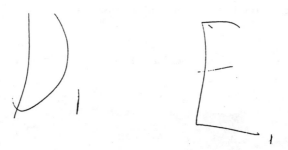

Freddie Krueger is a frightening character for many of the children we have interviewed. For the children who live in the Cabrini Green public housing development, the fact that Freddie lives on Elm Street is particularly stressful. There is an "Elm Street" running through the apartment complex, and community residents report that there is indeed a safe and a dangerous side to the street.

We are not able to calculate the number of children who have witnessed people carrying real knives in their neighborhoods. In fact, parents and teachers have reported that there are gang members who openly carry weapons, including guns, while walking through the housing development.

Dennis expressed themes of crime and punishment in the "arresting" picture. He seemed to believe that the police have some control and power over the "gangbangers" who commit the crimes. He was formulating ideas about morality, justice, and safety. There is a possibility that he will draw on this knowledge when developing future alliances.

When children are forming ideas about internal control, it is important to respond to their attempts to wrestle with these ideas. Their feelings of internal versus external control of their lives affect their self-esteem. In their drawings, they give the adult a door to open. The door leads to conversations about experiences; in these conversations, the adult can help the children find meanings that enable them to cope.

Dennis's drawings were completed as part of a group drawing project at an after-school program. The four pictures emerged over a period of an hour. In them, this child's complex ideas unfolded for the supportive adult. The material would not have been as rich if the task had been limited to a ten-minute "art period."

Additionally, we note that the child practiced his writing skills: "Night mar on am streat. Fredis bake." He also practiced his verbal skills in the art of communication and storytelling.

The Kidnapper and the Car Gun

There had been several attempted kidnappings near nine-year-old Matt's public elementary school. He drew a picture of a

Matt's Drawing: Car with Girl Being Kidnapped.

Matt's Drawing: "Car Gun."

man driving a blue car with a girl in the back seat. Matt said that the girl was being kidnapped from the school. He drew a second picture—this one showing a large car with what appears to be a missile launcher on the back. He called this invention "a car gun." He said, "The man in the car snatches children. He gives them ice cream and drives them to the south side of Chicago. I'm afraid." Matt pointed to his picture and said, "The car gun would shoot the kidnapper car. I wish he would try to take my little sister. I'd kill him."

Conclusion

When Elizabeth drew the picture of the "guy shooting my mom" (see Chapter Four), she divided the paper into quadrants and numbered the images: "the Sunday afternoon family barbecue, guy shooting my mom, me and my sisters running by houses, and me and my sisters at the park." This school-age child has been chased by gangbangers wielding baseball bats, and she has heard gunfights in the neighborhood.

Most of the research and clinical practice underlying our understanding of post-traumatic stress disorder in children address the acute traumatic event. But how do we help children who experience horror not as an event that disrupts the normal flow of life but as something that is constant— children for whom there is no "post"-trauma period but, instead, chronic traumatic stress disorder? Children like Elizabeth face the emotional challenge of not simply "getting over" a horrible experience but living it. They must find a way to make sense of a world in which horrible experiences become part of the fabric of life.

Teachers can help children who live in dangerous environments cope with traumatic events and complex feelings and concerns; they can be powerful psychic healers. The freedom of expression that is inherent in children's playful activity and in their art needs the adult's approval, permission, assurance, and support. Of course, teachers themselves will need guidance, support, and supervision to do this important job. Ensuring that guidance, support, and supervision will require institutional commitment from school boards, super-intendents, and principals. We hope they see the need for that commitment. How can we help them see their way clear to making and following through on that commitment? That is the topic of our next chapter.

11

Giving the Most
to Those Who Need It

Throughout this book we have confronted the tension—we hope it is a creative tension—between acknowledging the terrible threats to development posed by community violence and affirming the capacity of children to recover. On the one hand, we recognize that community violence is traumatizing for children. On the other, we assert that traumatized children are not doomed. Werner (1990, p. 111) suggests a framework for conceptualizing this tension.

> As long as the balance between stressful life events and protective factors is favorable, successful adaptation is possible. However, when stressful life events outweigh the protective factors, even the most resilient child can develop problems. Intervention may thus be conceived as an attempt to shift the balance from vulnerability to resilience, either by decreasing exposure to risk factors and stressful life events, or by increasing the number of available protective factors (e.g., competencies and sources of support) in the lives of children.

As Lenore Terr (1990), Robert Pynoos (1988), Bessell van der Kolk (1987), Carl Bell (1991), and others make powerfully clear, children are changed by trauma. And some of those changes are not readily apparent to the casual eye of the outside observer or even to the eye of the involved parent or teacher who wants—often wants desperately—to believe that the traumatized child is "OK."

This well-intentioned conspiracy is one in which children may themselves participate. They too want everything to be "OK." And often they don't want to alarm their parents and their teachers. They too want it to be over. We understand that. And yet we know that it isn't over until it has been thoroughly "processed" by the child, with the guidance and assistance of others.

So we know that while everyone involved in trauma wants it to be over, it will not be over until we acknowledge that healing and recovery require active measures, measures that may seem to "reopen wounds." In this case, recovery comes from actively confronting the trauma and its consequences.

Four Themes Revisited

In Chapter Two, we mentioned four themes that had emerged from our interviews with children in war zones:

- Resilience among children.
- The challenge to adult caregivers.
- Alternative conceptions of revenge.
- Ideology as a motivator.

Each has found an important place in our thinking about children coping with community violence.

Resilience and Its Limits

Children are resilient, but their resilience is not unlimited. Moreover, resilience is not some ineffable, magical property. We can account for it in psychological and social terms. Children with more resources—psychological and social—are more resilient. But the children of the urban war zone are loaded down with risk factors and denuded of protective factors. They are poor. They often come from families lacking positive role models—families often headed by single women whose own personal struggle saps their strength. They are often minorities who have suffered a history of discrimination. They tend to go to rigid and uninspiring schools. They are often plagued by health problems attributable to prenatal conditions, inadequate health care, and unhealthy life-styles. As we saw in Chapter One, developmental damage precipitates when risk accumulates. For poor inner-city children, community violence is often "the last straw."

What can we do? We can mount a coordinated campaign to prevent the accumulation of risk *and* to enhance the social and psychological resources that underlie coping and resilience. More specifically, to reduce community violence, we must stimulate and support efforts to reclaim the community. Citizen action groups are an essential element of such a strategy of neighborhood revitalization (Unger and Wandersman, 1985). In some areas, it may be necessary to provide police "peacekeeping forces"—modeled after United Nations peacekeepers—who combine the capacity to oppose criminals with an active campaign of dispute mediation, preventive presence, and socially supportive services. The areas targeted for such peacekeeping forces would also be designated "prevention zones" for the delivery of key human services, such as job training, health care, child care, and parent education (Garbarino and Kostelny, 1992b).

This community strategy would offer twofold promise for the children of inner-city war zones. It would reduce the pressure on these children by reducing the accumulation of risk factors. And it would strengthen the hand of adults who are in a position to serve as supportive resources for children.

The Challenge to Adult Caregivers

Community violence threatens children not just directly but indirectly, through its effects on adult caregivers. The adults are often themselves traumatized. Their experiences with violence and emotional deprivation reduce their capacity to meet the needs of the children they care for. The harsh realities of their individual situations reduce their capacity for providing the nonviolent nurturance their children need so desperately. And all too many adults in the urban war zone are sources of the domestic violence that compounds the problem of community violence.

One goal of peacekeeping forces in urban war zones would be to encourage adults to act responsibly as neighbors and citizens. Once these adults feel secure, they will be more psychologically available to participate in and lead citizen councils designed to rebuild the social structure (and in some cases the physical environment) of the community (just as people rebuild any war zone after peace comes).

This process also will strengthen the role of these adults in their direct relationships with children. Feeling secure and activated, they will be more able to form the secure attachments and supportive relationships that children need if they are to overcome risk (Lösel and Bliesener, 1990). Thus, a process of positive feedback will replace the negative and vicious cycles that prevail today in inner-city neighborhoods afflicted with community violence.

Alternative Conceptions of Revenge

One of the most important domains of concern we have discovered is the domain of moral development, particularly as it is played out in alternative conceptions of revenge. All too often, this is a neglected dimension in efforts to understand and ameliorate the problem of community violence. In war zones around the world, we have seen children helped to find a way through the moral minefield of negative revenge to a positive moral consciousness in which being a good person becomes a child's revenge. We see precious little of this in the urban war zone. Helping teachers and parents take on the task of cultivating positive revenge should be one of the highest priorities for the professional community, indeed for the entire prosocial community.

But all this will not be easy. It will require a conscious and deliberate commitment to the "moral socialization" of children in inner-city communities. Neither the rigid and narrowly academic curriculum of most inner-city schools nor the simplistic preaching of authoritarian religious institutions will be sufficient. What is needed is a democratic milieu that helps the child "process" risk, make sense of it in the largest possible scheme of things (Lösel and Bliesener, 1990). This processing is more than inculcating rote answers. It requires dialogue and the largeness of spirit we often define as "humanistic."

Ideology as a Motivator

The urban war zone is often "meaningless," in the sense that the struggles are simply for raw power, survival, and advantage. The lack of meaning deprives adults, youth, and to some degree children of a resource that other war zones have revealed to be powerful. Ideology can motivate organized and prosocial behavior. Of course, it can also be a source of destructive fanaticism. Are America's urban war zones better off for being nonideological? We doubt it. Without something to believe in beyond self, there can be little basis for community as anything other than geographical coincidence.

Is there an appropriate ideological foundation for inner-city communities? Given their predominant racial and ethnic makeup—mainly African-American and Hispanic—we might look to an ideology of collective identity and development for the answer. Some professionals in the field (perhaps most notably Carl Bell, an African-American psychiatrist working on the Chicago's South Side) have adopted such an approach. Black Muslims pursue a similar course (strong racial identity, pride in African heritage, a critique of mainstream society and its racist underpinnings). Bell has focused on "black on black" violence and its relation to racism.

Strong support for Bell's analyses comes from Gilligan's (1991a) penetrating exploration of shame as a causal factor for violence (both individual and collective). How does one counter shame? The destructive response is to use violence as an affirmation of power (and thus existence). The constructive answer is to re-create self and identity in positive terms—perhaps invoking collective action to restructure the conditions of life that breed shame: to replace poverty with the meeting of basic needs and to replace racism and bigotry with reconciliation.

School-Based Interventions and Community Mobilization

The principal hope for children traumatized in large numbers because of community violence lies in a renewed understanding of the role of the school as a caregiving environment and a center for community organization. Schools (day-care centers, preschools, after-school programs) can be powerful protective factors in the lives of children at risk; they are the key to the problem of helping children cope with their experiences resulting from exposure to community violence. They also can be catalysts for mobilizing adult resources. That is, they have the potential to serve as a focal point for community mobilization and ideological coherence.

Fulfilling this potential will require several innovations. First, "peacekeeping" forces must create a secure reality in the community. Without this security, people will not readily take the risk involved in participating—the risk of going out at night to meetings, the risk of standing up and speaking out in a situation where hostile forces may punish such behavior.

Once "peace" is restored, the next task is to persuade parents that the school is an ally in the optimal development of their children. The third task is to provide a curriculum that fosters ethnic pride and group identity.

To actualize these programming possibilities, we must assert that developmentally oriented, structured, and responsive schools are the birthright of every child—but are especially important for the children of the urban war zone. One of the pernicious ironies of our society is that those who need the most generally receive the least. When a lone killer entered an affluent suburban school north of Chicago and shot five children (one fatally), the community was flooded with resources, keenly motivated to help heal the psychic wounds of children who witnessed this terror; in the inner city, where traumatic experiences with violence are routine, there is little to offer the children. The suburban school mobilized "state of the art" psychological support. The run-down, overburdened inner-city school is locked into a rigid curriculum that makes it difficult to meet the special psychological agenda imposed by trauma. The suburban school has been flexible and responsive in gearing its curriculum to the needs of traumatized children. But administrators in inner-city schools have told us that there is no room in the art class for children to draw about their experiences, because the official art curriculum mandates jack-o'-lanterns in October, turkeys in November, Santa Claus in December, snowmen in January, and so on through the rest of the year.

Despite the current pall that looms over the system of public education in this country, any adult who has had a reasonably constructive school experience—in spite of its warts and flaws—should understand the force for good that the school can be. Over and over again, one hears testimonials to the healing power of a master teacher, an insightful counselor, a caring principal. Schools are the one system operating in the lives of all children. They are an essential part of the social environment of families and communities. Schools are critical in promoting resilience and coping. But helping the school systems in the urban war zones is no easy task.

We would like to see this intervention as a complement to an elaborate program of individualized, therapeutic interventions directed to the remediation of these problems *and* community mobilization involving "peacekeeping" and "prevention zones." But the scale of the problem and the commitments our society is prepared to make for inner-city poor children make other therapeutic options and social-change approaches totally unrealistic if they are not school-based. Given the numbers of children now involved and the resources likely to be made available, we must acknowledge the schools as more than a complementary force. They are likely to be the only alternative in the short run (however much we envision a broader program of social reform in the long run); and, though limited, school-based approaches can even create positive momentum upon which other efforts can build (Comer, 1980).

Traditional individual or family interventions must be conserved as precious adjunct services. They must be reserved for the cases that are so severe or aggravated that they are beyond the environmental interventions we have described. Prevention is always the foremost goal. Where prevention fails, a "general practitioner" should intervene. The specialist should be saved for the most difficult cases, where such expertise becomes cost-effective.

We believe in the school-based interventions we have described. But we recognize that our belief is as much clinical faith as anything else, since data from the research literature that would prove the case and undergird these claims are limited. Several landmark studies clearly establish a benchmark for this work and suggest the direction for future research. (On the role of the schools in providing "psychological first aid," see Pynoos and Nader, 1988, and van der Kolk, 1987. On the role of the schools in "disadvantaged" communities, see Rutter, Maughan, Mortimore, and Ouston, 1979; Comer, 1980; and Schweinhart and Weikart, 1983.) Nonetheless, there is a lengthy research agenda implicit in our efforts to date. We need a wide range of studies designed to evaluate the validity of our hypotheses, beliefs, and assumptions.

But our colleagues join us in asserting that schools can be effective in ameliorating conditions for disadvantaged children and that some schools are better than others. These studies notwithstanding, while the growing body of literature on resilient children systematically indicates that "schools" are a significant factor in supporting resilience (Werner, 1990), the existing data do not provide sufficient detail on which to base operational guidelines that would transfer reliably over a wide range of ages and programs, particularly with regard to the significant but elusive concept of school "ethos" discussed in Chapters Eight and Nine.

In Conclusion: A Path for Ramon

In presenting the case of Ramon, in Chapters Seven and Eight, we hoped to stimulate interest in a reexamination of the role of the school or caregiving environment as a "mental health" intervention. For those practitioners and theoreticians, teachers, administrators, clinicians, social workers, and providers of social services and health care—especially in the field of early childhood education—who have long experienced or hypothesized the successes of such interventions, this offering will seem prosaic indeed. On the other hand, we must confront the results of a decade of enervating funding cuts to child services. As a society, we have systematically drained the energy, expertise, and commitment that would otherwise have predicted more widespread recognition of both the actual successes and the unrealized potential inherent in such models. As the cumulative quality of early childhood education slips, risk accumulates.

For Ramon and his family, and for many thousands like them, there is little immediate hope that things will change. Ramon's life at home in a cramped, chaotic, violent household finds its parallel on the streets where he plays. Neither offers safety nor sanctuary. He has no place to grow except in school. This is his life. This is our responsibility. The fact that Ramon's behavior gives some evidence of resilience and the ability to rebalance—no matter how tenuous—speaks in part to the "healing magic" of the well-structured, developmentally supportive environment where he is cared for eight or nine hours every day, five days a week.

The program at his day-care center supports his need to have some control in his otherwise chaotic life, and provides him with a daily respite in which learning and growth may continue on some approximation of a normal developmental timetable. Can anyone fail to appreciate the significance of such an environment for this child? Bettelheim (1974) reminds us that if an environment can harm, an environment can also promote healing. That is the meaning we intended by sharing Ramon's story. The help offered by this program may be all the help that children like Ramon are going to get. Although he is just a young child, in a very real sense the buck stops here for Ramon. We help him now, or chances are we lose him.

Next year Ramon will go to public school. Who will help him there? Will the structure of the program support his needs? Will he feel safe enough to grow and learn there? Will the program be appropriate for his age? Will a consistent, committed, well-trained, caring teacher "hear" him and understand the gun behavior?

In Ramon's case, there was nothing else to see. His behavior was not troublesome. He was not aggressively "acting out" his harrowing fears and anxiety. He was quietly using his hand as a gun in a behavior that—except for its compulsivity—was probably not going to trouble anyone. Probably no one would even notice this behavior, particularly if other children's problems were more demanding. His checking out of visitors or strangers could also have gone unnoticed—unless you cared and had the energy to see, had the skills to deal with his overtures, and had support services available to help you struggle with a good plan for this child. If his problem did go unnoticed, left to "fester" as the years went by before he became an adolescent, his wound might later be revealed in serious delinquent or self-destructive behavior.

In considering the role of the school and caregiving environment as an external source of support for children at risk, we should remember its "garden variety" nature. The programs we know and endorse are community-based, publicly funded programs. They are "normal" programs, *not* "demonstration" programs. They were not developed in rarefied laboratory school settings. Nor do they rely on such impressive measures as entire teams of psychologists and educational specialists infusing the setting with their expertise. They require adequate funding but not the extraordinary funding that "demonstration" projects might require. Although they do not require luxury or genius to work, they *do* require competence, integrity, *and* institutional commitment.

From an administrative perspective, these programs require staff who are educated in child development and temperamentally suited to work with young children. That is the absolute minimum. Such staff must be paid fair wages, and they must work in well-managed programs and schools that meet the guidelines for developmentally appropriate practice, such as the guidelines produced by the National Association for the Education of Young Children (Bredekamp, 1987). Provision for a well-developed program of special services such as we describe is crucial. All this may not seem like much, but it is the exception rather than the rule in the urban war zone.

Programs like these act out of a sense of purpose and have a strong sense of identity—a unifying programmatic philosophy, a "socially integrating purpose" (Schorr and Schorr, 1988) that is evident in their daily interactions with children and families. They know what they are about, and they set themselves to achieving those goals. The programs we describe are competently administered by well-managed agencies and well-trained administrators who have a strong educational background and experience in early childhood education. Everyone—staff and clients alike—has a sense of being cared for and respected.

Impressive as these minimal requirements may sound given current funding levels, they are not unreasonable or heroic expectations for any child-care setting or public school system, not in an affluent society such as ours. These are the responsible, high-quality child-care settings that were envisioned as the norm at an earlier time, when belief in their potential for disadvantaged children reigned supreme and resonated in well-articulated goals for program design. We needed them then; we desperately need them now.

Today these programs, and all programs similar to them, are threatened. They suffer from ongoing turnover of staff and the corresponding depletion of expertise resulting from the relentless erosion of funding that has not even kept pace with inflation. Increasingly, these programs provide service to a deeply troubled population trying to survive the effects of deteriorating economic conditions and shifting polit-ical priorities (Garbarino, 1992). We are in danger of losing an entire generation of inner-city children.

Children of the urban war zone cannot tolerate inferior programming. Risk accumulates. We must search for every opportunity to enhance resilience, promote coping, and pre-vent risk. Neighborhood mobilization and psychologically ori-ented schooling *must* be the foundation for our nation's response to children in danger.

REFERENCES

Abt Associates. *Preliminary Findings and Their Implications: National Day Care Study.* Cambridge, Mass.: Abt Associates, 1987.

Aldrich, R. "The Influence of Man-Built Environments on Children and Youth." In W. Michelson, B. Levine, and E. Michelson (eds.), *The Child in the City.* Toronto: University of Toronto Press, 1979.

Alexander, E. "School Centered Play Therapy." In C. Schaefer (ed.), *Therapeutic Use of Child's Play.* New York: Jason Aronson, 1976.

Allodi, F. "The Psychiatric Effects in Children and Families of Victims of Political Persecution and Torture." *Danish Medical Bulletin,* 1980, *27,* 229–332.

American Psychiatric Association. *Diagnostic and Statistical Manual of Mental Disorders.* (3rd ed. rev.) Washington, D.C.: American Psychiatric Association, 1987.

Anthony, E., and Cohler, B. (eds.). *The Invulnerable Child.* New York: Guilford Press, 1987.

Axline, V. *Play Therapy.* New York: Ballantine Books, 1969. (Originally published 1947.)

Baker, S., O'Neill, B., and Karpf, R. *The Injury Fact Book.* Lexington, Mass.: Lexington Books, 1984.

Bandura, A. *Aggression: A Social Learning Analysis.* Englewood Cliffs, N.J.: Prentice-Hall, 1973.

Bass, M., Kravath, R., and Glass, L. "Death-Scene Investigations in Sudden Infant Death." *New England Journal of Medicine,* 1986, *315,* 100–128.

Bell, C. "Traumatic Stress and Children in Danger." *Journal of Health Care for the Poor and Underserved,* Sept. 1991, *2*(1), 175–188.

Belle, D. *Lives in Stress: Women and Depression.* Newbury Park, Calif.: Sage, 1982.

Bennett, S. N. "Recent Research on Teaching: A Dream, a Belief and a Model." *British Journal of Educational Psychology,* 1978, *48,* 127–147.

Bernstein, B. "Education Cannot Compensate for Society." *New Society,* 1970, *387,* 344–347.

Bettelheim, B. "Individual and Mass Behavior in Extreme Situations." *Journal of Abnormal and Social Psychology,* 1943, *38,* 417–452.

Bettelheim, B. *A Home for the Heart.* New York: Knopf, 1974.

Bettelheim, B. "The Importance of Play." *Atlantic Monthly,* March 1987, p. 35.

Bilu, Y. Cited in "What the Arabs Dream" in *The Yellow Wind* by Grossman, D., New York: Farrar, Straus and Giroux, 1988.

Blau, R. "Child in Wrong Place at Wrong Time Is Blinded." *Chicago Tribune,* April 6, 1990, sec. 2, p. 1.

Blau, R. "Gang Violence Defies Any Easy Answers." *Chicago Tribune,* June 10, 1990, sec. 1, p. 5.

Bloch, D., Silber, E., and Perry, S. "Some Factors in the Emotional Reaction of Children to Disaster." *American Journal of Psychiatry,* 1956, *113,* 416–422.

Bowlby, J. *Attachment and Loss.* Vol. 2. New York: Basic Books, 1973.

Bowlby, J., *Attachment and Loss.* Vol. 3. New York: Basic Books, 1980.

Bowlby, J. "Violence in the Family as a Disorder of the Attachment and Caregiving Systems." *American Journal of Psychoanalysis,* 1984, *44,* 9–27.

Bredekamp, S. *Developmentally Appropriate Practice in Early Childhood Programs Serving Children from Birth Through Age 8.* Washington, D.C.: National Association for the Education of Young Children, 1987.

Bronfenbrenner, U. *The Ecology of Human Development: Experiments by Nature and Design.* Cambridge, Mass.: Harvard University Press, 1979.

Bronfenbrenner, U. "Ecology of the Family as a Context for Human Development Research Perspectives." *Developmental Psychology*, 1986, *22*, 723–742.

Bronfenbrenner, U., Moen, P., and Garbarino, J. "Families and Communities." In R. Parke (ed.), *Review of Child Development Research*. Vol. 7. Chicago: University of Chicago Press, 1984.

Bruner, J. "Nature and Uses of Immaturity." In J. Bruner, A. Jolly, and K. Sylva (eds.), *Play: Its Role in Development and Evolution*. New York: Basic Books, 1976.

Bryce, J., Walker, N., Ghorayeb, F., and Kanj, M. "Life Experiences, Response Styles and Mental Health Among Mothers and Children in Beirut, Lebanon." *Social Science and Medicine*, 1989, *28*(7), 685–695.

Burns, R., and Kaufman, S. *Actions, Styles, and Symbols in Kinetic Family Drawings*. New York: Brunner/Mazel, 1972.

Caplan, G., and Killilea, M. (eds.). *Support Systems and Mutual Help*. New York: Grune & Stratton, 1976.

Caseso, J., and Blau, R. "Fear Lives in CHA's Taylor Homes." *Chicago Tribune*, June 18, 1989, sec. 1, p. 16.

Cassell, S. "The Suitcase Playroom." In C. Schaefer (ed.), *Therapeutic Use of Child's Play*. New York: Jason Aronson, 1976.

Chilton, R. "Twenty Years of Homicide and Robbery in Chicago: The Impact of the City's Changing Racial and Age Composition." *Journal of Quantitative Criminology*, 1987, *3*(3), 195–214.

Chollet, D. *Uninsured in the US: The Non-Elderly Population Without Health Insurance*. Washington, D.C.: Employee Benefit Research Institute, 1987.

Christrup, J. "Sharks on the Line." *Greenpeace Magazine*, Jan.–Feb. 1991, pp. 17–19.

Cobb, S. "Social Support as a Moderator of Life Stress." *Psychosomatic Medicine*, 1976, *38*, 300–314.

Coles, R. *Children of Crisis: A Study of Courage and Fear*. New York: Dell, 1964.

Coles, R. "Northern School Children Under Segregation." *Psychiatry: Journal for the Study of Interpersonal Process*, February 1968, *31*(1), 1–15.

Coles, R. *The Political Life of Children.* Boston: Houghton Mifflin, 1986.

Collins, A., and Pancoast, D. *Natural Helping Networks: A Strategy for Prevention.* Washington, D.C.: National Association of Social Workers, 1976.

Comer, J. P. *School Power.* New York: Free Press, 1980.

Cottle, T. J. *Black Children, White Dreams.* Boston: Houghton Mifflin, 1974.

Cottle, T. J. *Children's Secrets.* New York: Anchor Press/Doubleday, 1980.

Cutting, P. *Children of the Siege.* London: Heinemann, 1988.

Danieli, Y. "The Treatment and Prevention of Long-Term Effects and Intergenerational Transmission of Victimization: A Lesson from Holocaust Survivors and Their Children." In C. R. Figley (ed.), *Trauma and Its Wake.* New York: Brunner/Mazel, 1985.

Danieli, Y. "Treating Survivors and Children of Survivors of the Nazi Holocaust." In F. Ochberg (ed.), *Post-Traumatic Therapy and Victims of Violence.* New York: Brunner/Mazel, 1988.

Davidson, J., and Smith, R. "Traumatic Experiences in Psychiatric Outpatients." *Journal of Traumatic Stress Studies,* July 1990, *3*(3), 459–475.

Davis, A., and Dollard, J. *Children of Bondage: The Personality Development of Negro Youth in the Urban South.* Washington, D.C.: American Council on Education, 1940.

de Lone, R. *Small Futures: Children, Inequality, and the Limits of Liberal Reform.* Orlando, Fla.: Harcourt Brace Jovanovich, 1979.

DiLeo, J. *Children's Drawings as Diagnostic Aids.* New York: Brunner/Mazel, 1973.

DiLeo, J. *Child Development: Analysis and Synthesis.* New York: Brunner/Mazel, 1977.

Dubrow, N. F., and Garbarino, J. "Living in the War Zone: Mothers and Young Children in a Public Housing Development." *Child Welfare,* Jan.–Feb. 1989, *68*(1), 3–20.

Dunst, C. J., and Trivette, C. M. "Assessment of Social Support in Early Intervention Programs." In S. J. Meisels and

J. P. Shonkoff (eds.), *Handbook of Early Childhood Education.* Cambridge, England: Cambridge University Press, 1990.

Dyson, J. "Family Violence and Its Effect on Children's Academic Underachievement and Behavior Problems in School." *Journal of the National Medical Association,* 1989, *82*(1), 17–22.

Egeland, B., and Farber, E. "Infant–Mother Attachment: Factors Related to Its Development and Changes Over Time." *Child Development,* 1984, *55*, 753–771.

Egginton, J. *Day of Fury: The Story of the Tragic Killings That Forever Changed the Village of Winnetka.* New York: Morrow, 1991.

Eitenger, L. "The Concentration Camp Syndrome and Its Late Sequelae." In J. Dimsdale (ed.), *Survivors, Victims, and Perpetrators: Essays on the Nazi Holocaust.* New York: Hemisphere, 1980.

Erikson, E. H. "Studies in the Interpretation of Play." *Genetic Psychology Monographs,* 1940, *22*, p. 561.

Erikson, E. H. *Childhood and Society.* New York: Norton, 1950.

Escalona, S. "Babies at Double Hazard: Early Development of Infants at Biologic and Social Risk." *Pediatrics,* 1982, *70*, 670–676.

Eth, S., and Pynoos, R. (eds.). *Post-Traumatic Stress Disorder in Children.* Washington, D.C.: American Psychiatric Press, 1985.

Feitelson, D. "Cross-Cultural Studies of Representational Play." In B. Tizard and D. Harvey (eds.), *The Biology of Play.* London: Heinemann, 1977.

Fields, R. "Terrorized into Terrorist: Sequelae of PTSD in Young Victims." Paper presented at the meeting of the Society for Traumatic Stress Studies, New York, Oct. 25, 1987.

Figley, C. (ed.). *Trauma and Its Wake.* New York: Brunner/ Mazel, 1985.

Fish-Murray, C. "Memories of Trauma: Place and Path." Keynote presentation, NAIM Foundation Conference on Children and Trauma, Washington, D.C., Oct. 10, 1990.

Fish-Murray, C., Koby, E., and van der Kolk, B. "Evolving Ideas: The Effect of Abuse on Children's Thought." In B. van der Kolk (ed.), *Psychological Trauma*. Washington, D.C.: American Psychiatric Press, 1987.

Fortune Magazine. "A Bigger Role for Parents." Spring, 1990, pp. 25–26.

Fox, S. S. *Good Grief: Helping Groups of Children When a Friend Dies*. Boston: New England Association for the Education of Young Children, 1988.

Fraser, M. *Children in Conflict*. Middlesex, England: Penguin, 1974.

Freedman, S. G. *Small Victories: The Real World of a Teacher, Her Studies, and Their High School*. New York: HarperCollins, 1990.

Freud, A., and Burlingham, D. *War and Children*. New York: Ernest Willard, 1943.

Freud, S. *Beyond the Pleasure Principle*. New York: Norton, 1961. (Originally published 1926.)

Garbarino, J. "Preventing Childhood Injury: Developmental and Mental Health Issues." *American Journal of Orthopsychiatry*, 1988, *58*(1), 25–45.

Garbarino, J. "Early Intervention in Cognitive Development as a Strategy for Reducing Poverty." In *Giving Children a Chance*. Washington, D.C.: Center for National Policy Press, 1989a.

Garbarino, J. *A Note on Children and Youth in Dangerous Environments: The Palestinian Situation as a Case Study*. Chicago: Erikson Institute, 1989b.

Garbarino, J. "The Experience of Children in Kuwait: Occupation, War, and Liberation." *Child, Youth, and Family Services Quarterly*, 1991, *14*(2), 2–3.

Garbarino, J., and Asp, E. *Successful Schools and Competent Students*. Lexington, Mass.: Lexington Books, 1981.

Garbarino, J., Guttmann, E., and Seeley, J. W. *The Psychologically Battered Child: Strategies for Identification, Assessment, and Intervention*. San Francisco: Jossey-Bass, 1986.

Garbarino, J., and Kostelny, K. "Child Maltreatment as a Community Problem." *Child Abuse and Neglect*, 1992a.

Garbarino, J., and Kostelny, K. "Neighborhood and Community Influences on Parenting." In T. Luster and L. Okagaki (eds.), *Parenting: An Ecological Perspective.* Hillside, N.J.: Erlbaum, 1992b.

Garbarino, J., Kostelny, K., and Dubrow, N. *No Place to Be a Child: Growing Up in a War Zone.* Lexington, Mass.: Lexington Books, 1991.

Garbarino, J., Stott, F. M., and the Faculty of the Erikson Institute. *What Children Can Tell Us: Eliciting, Interpreting, and Evaluating Information from Children.* San Francisco: Jossey-Bass, 1989.

Garbarino, J., and Associates. *Children and Families in the Social Environment.* (2nd ed.) Hawthorne, N.Y.: Aldine, 1992.

Gardner, G. "Aggression and Violence: The Enemies of Precision Learning in Children." *American Journal of Psychiatry,* 1971, *128*(4), 445–450.

Gardner, H. *Frames of Mind: The Theory of Multiple Intelligences.* New York: Basic Books, 1983.

Gardner, R. *Psychotherapeutic Approaches to the Resistant Child.* New York: Jason Aronson, 1975.

Garmezy, N. "Children Under Stress: Perspectives on Antecedents and Correlates of Vulnerability and Resistance to Psychopathology." In A. Rabin, J. Aronoff, A. Barclay, and R. Zucker (eds.), *Further Explorations in Personality.* New York: Wiley-Interscience, 1981.

Garmezy, N., and Rutter, M. (eds.). *Stress, Coping, and Development in Children.* New York: McGraw-Hill, 1983.

Garvey, C. *Play.* Cambridge, Mass.: Harvard University Press, 1977.

Gelles, R., and Lancaster, J. *Child Abuse and Neglect: Biosocial Dimensions.* Hawthorne, N.Y.: Aldine, 1987.

Gelles, R., and Straus, M. *Intimate Violence.* New York: Simon & Schuster, 1988.

Gil, T., and others. "Cognitive Functioning in Post-Traumatic Stress Disorder." *Journal of Traumatic Stress Studies,* 1990, *3*(1), 29–45.

Gilligan, C. *In a Different Voice.* Cambridge, Mass.: Harvard University Press, 1982.

Gilligan, J. "Shame and Humiliation: The Emotions of Individual and Collective Violence." Paper presented at the 1991 Erikson Lectures, Carpenter Center, Harvard University, Cambridge, Mass., May 23, 1991a.

Gilligan, J. "Violence, Myth and Tragedy: Dead Souls and the Psychopathology of Violence." Paper presented at the 1991 Erikson Lectures, Carpenter Center, Harvard University, Cambridge, Mass., May 21, 1991b.

Goleman, D. "Terror's Children: Mending Mental Wounds." *New York Times,* Sept. 2, 1986, p. B15.

Goodnow, J. J. "The Socialization of Cognition: What's Involved." Paper presented at conference on Culture and Human Development, Chicago, 1987.

Grossman, D. "Report from Israel: The Yellow Rain." *New Yorker,* Feb. 8 and Feb. 15, 1988, pp. 41ff. and 58ff.

Grubb, W. N., and Lazerson, M. *Broken Promises: How Americans Fail Their Children.* New York: Basic Books, 1982.

Halpern, R. "Community Based Support for High Risk Young Families." *Social Policy,* Summer 1986, pp. 17–18.

Halpern, R. "Community-Based Early Intervention." In S. J. Meisels and J. P. Shonkoff (eds.), *Handbook of Early Childhood Education.* Cambridge, England: Cambridge University Press, 1990a.

Halpern, R. "Fragile Families, Fragile Solutions." *Social Service Review,* December 1990b, pp. 637–648.

Halpern, R. "Poverty and Early Childhood Parenting: Toward a Framework for Intervention." *American Journal of Orthopsychiatry,* 1990c, *60*(1), 6–18.

Hetherington, E. M., Cox, M., and Cox, R. "Effects of Divorce on Parents and Children." In M. Lamb (ed.), *Non-Traditional Families.* Hillsdale, N.J.: Erlbaum, 1982.

Horowitz, M. *Stress Response Syndromes.* New York: Jason Aronson, 1976.

Howe, Q., Jr. *Under Running Laughter: Notes from a Renegade Classroom.* New York: Free Press, 1991.

Hyman, I. A., Zelikoff, W., and Clarke, J. "Understanding PTSD in Children: A Study of Educator-Induced Trauma." Paper presented at the annual meeting of the American Psychological Association, New York, Sept. 1, 1987.

Janis, I. *Air War and Emotional Stress.* New York: McGraw-Hill, 1951.

Jeffers, C. *Living Poor: A Participant Observer Study of Priorities and Choices.* Ann Arbor, Mich.: Ann Arbor Publishers, 1967.

Jensen, A. R. "How Much Can We Boost IQ and Scholastic Achievement?" *Harvard Educational Review,* 1969, *39,* 1–123.

Kagan, J. "Stress, Coping, and Development in the Opening Years of Life." In N. Garmezy and M. Rutter (eds.), *Stress, Coping, and Development in Children.* New York: McGraw-Hill, 1983.

Kamerman, S., and Kahn, A. *Mothers Alone: Strategies for a Time of Change.* Dover, Mass.: Auburn House, 1988.

Kamii, C. *Number in Preschool and Kindergarten.* Washington, D.C.: National Association for the Education of Young Children, 1982.

Kamii, C., and DeVries, R. "Piaget for Early Education." In M. Day and R. Parker (eds.), *The Preschool in Action.* (2nd ed.) Needham Heights, Mass.: Allyn & Bacon, 1977.

Kamii, C., and DeVries, R. *Physical Knowledge in Preschool Education: Implications of Piaget's Theory.* Englewood Cliffs, N.J.: Prentice-Hall, 1978.

Kamii, C., and DeVries, R. *Group Games in Early Education: Implications of Piaget's Theory.* Washington, D.C.: National Association for the Education of Young Children, 1980.

Kellam, S. *Mental Health and Going to School: The Woodlawn Program of Assessment, Early Intervention and Evaluation.* Chicago: University of Chicago Press, 1975.

Kellogg, R. *Analyzing Children's Art.* Palo Alto, Calif.: Mayfield, 1969.

Kidder, T. *Among School Children.* Boston: Houghton Mifflin, 1989.

Kinzie, J., and others. "The Psychiatric Effects of Massive Trauma on Cambodian Children." *Journal of the American Academy of Child Psychiatry,* 1986, *25,* 370–376.

Kotlowitz, A. *There Are No Children Here.* New York: Doubleday, 1991.

Kotulak, R. "Study Finds Inner-City Kids Live with Violence." *Chicago Tribune,* Sept. 28, 1990, pp. 1, 16.

Kozol, J. *Rachel and Her Children: Homeless Families in America.* New York: Crown, 1988.

Krystal, H. (ed.). *Massive Psychic Trauma.* Madison, Conn.: International Universities Press, 1968.

Langmeir, L., and Matejcek, Z. *Psychological Deprivation in Childhood.* New York: Halsted Press, 1963.

Lifton, J. *Death in Life: Survivors of Hiroshima.* New York: Simon & Schuster, 1967.

Lifton, J. *Home from the War.* New York: Simon & Schuster, 1973.

Lösel, F., and Bliesener, T. "Resilience in Adolescence: A Study on the Generalizability of Protective Factors." In K. Hurrelmann and F. Lösel (eds.), *Health Hazards in Adolescence.* New York: Walter de Gruyter, 1990.

Lyons, H. "Psychiatric Sequelae of the Belfast Riots." *British Journal of Psychiatry,* 1971, *118*(544), 265–273.

McCallin, M. "The Impact of Traumatic Events on the Psychological Well-Being of Mozambican Refugee Women and Children." Geneva, Switzerland: International Catholic Child Bureau, 1989.

McGrath, E., Keita, G., Strickland, B., and Russo, N. *Women and Depression: Risk Factors and Treatment Issues.* Washington, D.C.: American Psychological Association, 1990.

Macksoud, M., Dyregrov, A., and Raudain, M. "Traumatic War Experiences and Their Effects on Children." *International Handbook of Traumatic Stress Syndrome.* New York: Plenum Press, in press.

McLane, J., and McNamee, G. *Early Literacy.* Cambridge, Mass.: Harvard University Press, 1990.

Margolis, L., and Runyan, C. "Accidental Policy: An Analysis of the Problem of Unintended Injuries of Childhood." *American Journal of Orthopsychiatry,* 1983, *53*, 629–644.

Marin, C. *Grief's Children.* WMAQ TV Documentary (Chicago), June 21, 1989.

Masten, A., and Garmezy, N. "Risk, Vulnerability and Protective Factors in Developmental Psychopathology." In B. B. Lahey and A. E. Kazdin (eds.), *Advances in Clinical Child Psychology.* Vol. 8. New York: Plenum, 1985.

Meers, D. R. "Psychoanalytic Research and Intellectual Functioning of Ghetto-Reared Black Children." In R. Eissler, A. Freud, M. Kris, and A. Solnit (eds.), *Psychoanalytic Study of the Child*, 1973, *28*, pp. 395–417.

Milgram, N. A. "War-Related Stress in Israeli Children and Youth." In N. Garmezy and M. Rutter (eds.), *Stress, Coping, and Development in Children*. New York: McGraw-Hill, 1983.

Montana, C. "West Side Boy, 9, Injured in Gunfire." *Chicago Tribune*, May 23, 1988, sec. 2, p. 3.

Morgenthau, T. "Children of the Underclass." *Newsweek*, Sept. 11, 1989, pp. 16–32.

Moriarty, A. E. "John, a Boy Who Acquired Resilience." In E. Anthony and B. Cohler (eds.), *The Invulnerable Child*. New York: Guilford Press, 1987.

Murphy, L., and Moriarty, A. *Vulnerability, Coping and Growth: From Infancy to Adolescence*. New Haven, Conn.: Yale University Press, 1976.

Musick, J. S. "Psychological and Developmental Dimensions of Adolescent Pregnancy and Parenting: An Interventionist's Perspective." Paper prepared for the Rockefeller Foundation, New York, Dec. 1987.

Musick, J. S., and Stott, F. "Paraprofessionals, Parenting, and Child Development: Understanding the Problems and Seeking Solutions." In S. J. Meisels and J. P. Shonkoff (eds.), *Handbook of Early Childhood Education*. Cambridge, England: Cambridge University Press, 1990.

Musick, J. S., and others. "Maternal Factors Related to Vulnerability and Resiliency in Young Children at Risk." In E. Anthony and B. Cohler (eds.), *The Invulnerable Child*. New York: Guilford Press, 1987.

National Association of Housing Redevelopment Officials. *The Many Faces of Public Housing*. Washington, D.C.: National Association of Housing Redevelopment Officials, 1989.

National Committee for Prevention of Child Abuse. "Public Attitudes and Actions Regarding Child Abuse and Its Prevention: The Results of a Louis Harris Public Opinion Poll." Chicago, 1987.

Newman, C. "Children of Disaster: Clinical Observations at Buffalo Creek." *American Journal of Psychiatry*, 1976, *133*, 306–312.

Ochberg, F. (ed.). *Post-Traumatic Therapy and Victims of Violence*. New York: Brunner/Mazel, 1988.

Ogbu, J. "A Cultural Ecology of Competence Among Inner-City Blacks." In M.B. Spencer and others (eds.), *Beginnings: The Social and Affective Development of Black Children*. Hillsdale, N.J.: Erlbaum, 1985.

The Open School. *Two Dogs and Freedom: Black Children of South Africa Speak Out*. New York: Rosset, 1987.

Orbach, I. *Children Who Don't Want to Live: Understanding and Treating the Suicidal Child*. San Francisco: Jossey-Bass, 1988.

Osofsky, J., and others. "Chronic Community Violence: What Is Happening to Our Children?" Unpublished paper, 1991.

Page, C. "In Henry Horner or Winnetka, Nobody Gets Used to Killing." *Chicago Tribune*, May 25, 1988, sec. 1, p. 21.

Paley, V. *Bad Guys Don't Have Birthdays: Fantasy Play at Four*. Chicago: University of Chicago Press, 1988.

Paley, V. *The Boy Who Would Be a Helicopter*. Cambridge, Mass.: Harvard University Press, 1990.

Peck, E. C., Jr. "The Traits of True Invulnerability and Post-traumatic Stress in Psychoanalyzed Men of Action." In E. Anthony and B. Cohler (eds.), *The Invulnerable Child*. New York: Guilford Press, 1987.

Peterson, C., Luborsky, L., and Seligman, L. "Attributions and Depressive Mood Shifts: A Case Study Using the Symptom-Context Method." *Journal of Abnormal Psychology*, 1983, *92*, 96–103.

Petrillo, M., and Sanger, S. *Emotional Care of Hospitalized Children: An Environmental Approach*. Philadelphia: Lippincott, 1972.

Piaget, J. *The Origins of Intelligence*. New York: Norton, 1963. (Originally published 1936.)

Pines, R. "Why Do Israelis Burn Out? The Role of the Intifada." Paper presented at the International Conference on Psychological Stress and Adjustment, Tel Aviv, Israel, Jan. 1989.

Punamaki, R. "Psychological Stress Responses of Palestinian Mothers and Their Children in Conditions of Military Occupation and Political Violence." *Quarterly Newsletter of the Laboratory of Comparative Human Cognition,* April 1987, *9*(2), 76–84.

Pynoos, R., and Eth, S. "Children Traumatized by Witnessing Personal Violence: Homicide, Rape or Suicide Behavior." In S. Eth and R. Pynoos (eds.), *Posttraumatic Stress Disorder in Children.* Washington, D.C.: American Psychiatric Press, 1985.

Pynoos, R., and Nader, K. "Psychological First Aid and Treatment Approach to Children Exposed to Community Violence: Research Implications." *Journal of Traumatic Stress Studies,* 1988, *1*(4), 445–473.

Raspberry, W. "New York Kids See Violence Every Day of Their Lives." *Athens Daily News,* May 23, 1989, p. 4a.

Reardon, P. "CHA Violent Crimes Up 9% for Year." *Chicago Tribune,* June 22, 1988, sec. 1, p. 1.

Redl, F. *When We Deal with Children.* New York: Free Press, 1966.

Redl, F., and Wineman, D. *Children Who Hate.* New York: Free Press, 1951.

Redl, F., and Wineman, D. *Controls From Within.* New York: Free Press, 1952.

Ressler, E., Boothby, N., and Steinbock, D. *Unaccompanied Children: Care and Protection in Wars, Natural Disasters, and Refugee Movements.* New York: Oxford University Press, 1988.

Rosenblatt, R. *Children of War.* New York: Doubleday, 1983.

Rutter, M. "Protective Factors in Children's Responses to Stress and Disadvantage." In M. W. Kent and J. E. Rolf (eds.), *Primary Prevention of Psychopathology.* Vol. 3. Hanover, N.H.: University Press of New England, 1979.

Rutter, M. "Prevention of Children's Psychosocial Disorders: Myths and Substance." *Pediatrics,* 1982, *70*, 883–894.

Rutter, M. "Continuities and Discontinuities from Infancy." In J. Osofsky (ed.), *Handbook of Infant Development.* New York: Wiley, 1987.

Rutter, M., Maughan, B., Mortimore, P., and Ouston, J. *Fifteen Thousand Hours: Secondary Schools and Their Effects on Children.* Cambridge, Mass.: Harvard University Press, 1979.

Sameroff, A. J., and Fiese, B. H. "Transactional Regulation and Early Intervention." In S. J. Meisels and J. P. Shonkoff (eds.), *Handbook of Early Childhood Education.* Cambridge, England: Cambridge University Press, 1990.

Sameroff, A., Seifer, R., Barocas, R., Zax, M., and Greenspan, S. "Intelligence Quotient Scores of 4-Year-Old Children: Social-Environmental Risk Factors." *Pediatrics,* 1987, *79,* 343–350.

Save the Children. *Children of Mozambique.* Documentary. Westport, Conn.: Save the Children US, 1989.

Scheinfeld, D. "Family Relationships and School Achievement Among Boys of Lower-Income Urban Black Families." *American Journal of Orthopsychiatry,* 1983, *53*(1), 127–143.

Schorr, L., and Schorr, D. *Within Our Reach: Breaking the Cycle of Disadvantage.* New York: Doubleday, 1988.

Schweinhart, L. J., Koshel, J. J., and Bridgman, A. "Policy Options for Preschool Programs." *Phi Delta Kappan,* 1987, *68,* 524–530.

Schweinhart, L. J., and Weikart, D. P. "The Effects of the Perry Preschool Program on Youths Through Age 15." In *As the Twig Is Bent . . . Lasting Effects of Preschool Programs.* Hillsdale, N.J.: Erlbaum, 1983.

Secretary's Task Force on Black and Minority Health. "Report of the Secretary's Task Force on Black and Minority Health, Vol. 1. Executive Summary." Washington, D.C.: U.S. Department of Health and Human Services, 1985.

Seligman, M. *Helplessness: On Depression, Development, and Death.* New York: W. H. Freeman, 1975.

Sheehan, N. *A Bright Shining Lie: John Paul Vann and America in Vietnam.* New York: Random House, 1988.

Sheppard, N. "Chicago Project Dwellers Live Under Siege." *New York Times.* Aug. 6, 1980, p. A14.

Sherman, L. *New York Times,* Aug. 12, 1990, sec. 4, p. 5.

Shipler, D. *Arab and Jew: Wounded Spirits in a Promised Land.* New York: Viking Penguin, 1985.

Silverstein, B., and Krate, R. *Children of the Dark Ghetto.* New York: Praeger, 1975.

Smith, Z. "Whites in Survey Back Equality, Keep Stereotypes." *Chicago Sun Times,* Jan. 9, 1991, sec. 1, p. 7.

Snow, C. "As the Twig Is Bent: A Review of Research on the Consequences of Day Care with Implications for Caregiving." Paper presented at the annual conference of the National Association for the Education of Young Children, Atlanta, Nov. 1983.

Society for Traumatic Stress Studies. *The Initial Report of the Presidential Task Force on Curriculum, Education, and Training.* Dubuque, Iowa: Kendall-Hunt, 1990.

Solnit, A. *Working with Disadvantaged Parents and Their Children.* New Haven, Conn.: Yale University Press, 1983.

Sternberg, R. *Beyond IQ: A Triarchic Theory of Human Intelligence.* Cambridge, England: Cambridge University Press, 1985.

Sutton-Smith, B. "The Role of Play in Cognitive Development." In R. Herron and B. Sutton-Smith (eds.), *Child's Play.* New York: Wiley, 1971.

Sylva, K., Bruner, J., and Genova, P. "The Role of Play in the Problem-Solving of Children 3-5 Years Old." In J. Bruner, K. Sylva, and A. Jolly (eds.), *Play: Its Role in Development and Evolution.* New York: Basic Books, 1976.

Terr, L. "Children of Chowchilla: A Study of Psychic Trauma." *Psychoanalytic Study of the Child,* 1979, *34,* 547–623.

Terr, L. "Forbidden Games: Post-Traumatic Child's Play." *Journal of the American Academy of Child Psychiatry,* 1981, *20,* 741–760.

Terr, L. "Chowchilla Revisited: The Effects of Psychic Trauma Four Years After a School-Bus Kidnapping." *American Journal of Psychiatry,* 1983, *140,* 1543–1550.

Terr, L. "Psychic Trauma in Children and Adolescents." *Psychiatric Clinics of North America,* 1985, *8*(4), 815–835.

Terr, L. *Too Scared to Cry.* New York: HarperCollins, 1990.

Terry, D. "In Harlem, Death In an Old and Busy Neighborhood." *New York Times,* May 6, 1990, p. 18.

Tharp, R. G., and Gallimore, R. *Rousing Minds to Life: Teaching, Learning, and Schooling in Social Context.* Cambridge, England: Cambridge University Press, 1988.

Uehara, E., Chalmers, D., Jenkins, E., and Shakoor, B. "African-American Youth Encounters with Violence: Results from the Community Mental Health Council Violence Screening Project." *Journal of Black Studies,* forthcoming.

Unger, D., and Wandersman, L. "The Importance of Neighbors: The Social, Cognitive, and Affective Components of Neighboring." *American Journal of Community Psychology,* 1985, *13*(2), 139–169.

UNICEF. "Children on the Front Line. The Impact of Apartheid, Destabilization and Warfare on Children in Southern and South Africa." New York: UNICEF, 1989.

United Nations and the World Bank. World Conference on Education for All, Jomtein, Thailand, March 5, 1990.

van der Kolk, B. A. *Psychological Trauma.* Washington, D.C.: American Psychiatric Press, 1987.

van der Kolk, B. A. "Traumatic Stress and Children in Danger." Paper presented at the Erikson Institute/Wingspread Conference on Children in Danger: Coping with the Consequences, Johnson Foundation, Racine, Wis., May 1990.

Virginia Frank Child Development Center. "A Developmental Approach to Families with Young Children: Applications and Implications." Paper presented at the annual conference of the Chicago Association for the Education of Young Children, Chicago, 1974.

Volavkova, H. *I Never Saw Another Butterfly: Children's Drawings and Poems from Terezin Concentration Camp, 1942–1944.* New York: McGraw-Hill, 1944.

Vornberger, W. *Fire from the Sky: Salvadoran Children's Drawings.* New York: Writers and Readers Publishing Cooperative, 1986.

Vygotsky, L. "Play and Its Role in the Mental Development of the Child." In J. Bruner, A. Jolly, and K. Sylva (eds.), *Play: Its Role in Development and Evolution.* New York: Basic Books, 1976.

Vygotsky, L. *Thought and Language*. Cambridge, Mass.: MIT Press, 1986.

Wacquant, L., and Wilson, W. "The Cost of Racial and Class Exclusion in the Inner City." *Annals of the American Academy of Political and Social Science*, 1989, *501*, 8–25.

Waelder, R. "Psychoanalytic Theory of Play." In C. Schaefer (ed.), *Therapeutic Use of Child's Play*. New York: Jason Aronson, 1976.

Wallach, L. B. Unpublished notes. Chicago: Erikson Institute, 1991.

Wallerstein, J. S., and Kelly, J. B. *Surviving the Breakup: How Children and Parents Cope with Divorce*. New York: Basic Books, 1980.

Warren, R. M. *Caring: Supporting Children's Growth*. Washington, D.C.: National Association of Young Children, 1977.

Webster's New World Dictionary of the American Language. Cleveland: World Publishing, 1968.

Werner, E. E. "Children of the Garden Island." *Scientific American*, April 1989, pp. 106–111.

Werner, E. E. "Protective Factors and Individual Resilience." In S. J. Meisels and J. P. Shonkoff (eds.), *Handbook of Early Childhood Education*. Cambridge, England: Cambridge University Press, 1990.

Werner, E. E., Bierman, J. S., and French, F. E. *The Children of Kauai: A Longitudinal Study from the Prenatal Period to Age Ten*. Honolulu: University of Hawaii Press, 1971a.

Werner, E. E., Bierman, J. S., and French, F. E. *Kauai's Children Come of Age*. Honolulu: University of Hawaii Press, 1971b.

Werner, E. E., and Smith, R. S. *Vulnerable but Invincible: A Longitudinal Study of Resilient Children and Youth*. New York: McGraw-Hill, 1982.

Williamson, G. G., and Zeitlin, S. "Assessment of Coping and Temperament: Contributions to Adaptive Functioning." In B. Gibbs and D. Teti (eds.), *Interdisciplinary Assessment of Infants: A Guide for Early Intervention Professionals*. Baltimore: Paul Brookes, forthcoming.

Wilson, W. J. *The Truly Disadvantaged: The Inner City, the Underclass, and Public Policy.* Chicago: University of Chicago Press, 1987.

Wilson, W. J. "Foreword." In L. Schorr and D. Schorr, *Within Our Reach: Breaking the Cycle of Disadvantage.* New York: Doubleday, 1988a.

Wilson, J. "Understanding the Viet Nam Veteran." In F. Ochberg (ed.), *Post-Traumatic Therapy and Victims of Violence.* New York: Brunner/Mazel, 1988b.

Wiltz, T., and Johnson, S. "Once Safe Havens, Schools Now in Line of Fire." *Chicago Tribune,* Sept. 26, 1991, sec. 1, p. 19.

Winnicott, D. *Playing and Reality.* New York: Basic Books, 1971.

Wood, M. M. *Developmental Therapy: A Textbook for Teachers as Therapists for Emotionally Disturbed Young Children.* Baltimore: University Park Press, 1975.

Wood, M. M., and Long, N. J. *Life Space Intervention: Talking with Children and Youth in Crisis.* Austin, Tex.: ProEd, 1991.

Zigler, E. F. "Foreword." In S. J. Meisels and J. P. Shonkoff (eds.), *Handbook of Early Childhood Education.* Cambridge, England: Cambridge University Press, 1990.

Zinsmeister, K. "Growing Up Scared." *Atlantic Monthly,* June 1990, pp. 49–66.

Ziv, A., and Israel, R. "Effects of Bombardment on the Manifest Anxiety Level of Children Living in Kibbutzim." *Journal of Consulting and Clinical Psychology,* 1973, *40,* 287–291.

INDEX

253